Resorting to Romance

A SWEET SINGLE-MOM, FAKE-DATING ROMCOM

SAVANNAH SCOTT

Connect with Savannah Scott

You can connect with Savannah at her website
www.SavannahScottBooks.com

You can also follow Savannah on Amazon.

For free books and first notice of new releases, sign up for
Savannah's Romcom Readers email at https://www.
subscribepage.com/savannahscottromcom/

For Jon
Because you endure bed and breakfasts for me
and so much more.

~

For everyone who thinks
they can see all the way down the road ahead.
Life is full of surprises.
Some of them will actually sweep you off your feet.
Don't miss them.
They may be standing right in front of you.

Every so often you can hear
the future whisper a promise,
if only you listen.

～

"Oh what a tangled web we weave ...
when first we practice to deceive."
Sir Walter Scott said it.
But oh, that untangling ... and what can come from it.
Maybe even a delightfully delicious romance.

～

A GENTLE HEADS UP FOR YOU, MY READERS ...

I love writing romcom.

The way I write this genre is very personal to me. I write characters who feel very, very real to me. Real people face real problems. You do. I do. We all do. My characters do.

In this story, *Resorting to Romance*, you will read about: Divorce (not on page), child abandonment (not on page), parental reconciliation with child (on page), and death of parents (character backstory).

If you find any other content in this story you think would warrant a content warning, please feel free to reach out to tell me.

Possible Spoiler (this paragraph only):
Resorting to Romance is partly a story of how one woman handles re-integrating an estranged parent into her child's life. It is a work of fiction and only represents how *SHE* would handle this. This story is not a prescription as to how other families might or should handle similar situations.

And now, I hope you enjoy this sweet, heartfelt, beautiful love story ... and the humor and tenderness I sprinkled within these pages to make you laugh, smile, and maybe even tear up a time or two.

Happy Reading!
~ Savannah

ONE

Kai

*I'd like to think that I've got determination,
and I'm fiercely protective of the people I love.*
~ Andrew Lincoln

"And now it's my honor and pleasure to welcome the two people we're all here to support and cheer for, our island's own: Kalaine Kapule and Bodhi Merrick. Give it up for these two!"

From his spot on the stage, Cameron gestures his hand toward our table as my sister and my best friend stand, scooting their chairs out and locking eyes with one another before Bodhi puts his hand on my sister's back to escort her onto the platform.

We're seated at tables covered in white tablecloths. Twinkle lights sway overhead on strings between palm trees. Candles and tiki torches reflect in a soft glow over the surface of the pools around the edge of this back patio at Alicante Resort.

The crowd claps politely, and Ben, my employee at the watersports shack here at the resort, places his fingers in his mouth and whistles long and hard. Then, from his spot across the table from me, he shouts, "Let's hear it for the *it* couple of surfing!"

Our table erupts into laughter. I can't help but crack a smile.

Ben's outburst serves as a catalyst, and the crowd shifts from behavior matching our formal attire to howls and shouts far more fitting the true beach-surf community camouflaged beneath our tuxedos and gowns.

Bodhi takes the mic from Cameron. His hand remains on Kalaine's back. He catches my sister's eyes again and they share a private smile—one I've had to get used to over the years they've been dating, and especially now that they are engaged with a wedding mere months away.

"Thank you!" Bodhi shouts, which draws another wave of cheers from the crowd. "We're so grateful all of you came out tonight. It's pretty crazy seeing my best friend in anything but board shorts and a pair of flip-flops, unless he's going in for his weekly business meeting in the main building. So, for that alone, I thank you."

The crowd rewards Bodhi with a collective laugh. He smiles his trademark winsome smile in return. A few people at my table and the surrounding seats glance over at me in acknowledgment, so I spread my arms out to show off the fact that, yes, I'm wearing a tux.

"Mavs—Kalaine—and I will always hold Marbella close to our heart. This island is the place we made our way back to one another, and to surfing. So, as we go out, sponsored by Rip Curl and Roxy—I have to say that, so there you have it. If any of our sponsors are watching the live feed ... check."

The crowd laughs again. I suppress an eye roll. We've all been sponsored. When I was competing as a pro-surfer, I did the dance too. Bodhi and Kalaine are so big now, companies drool over the opportunity to have their names attached to these two. Still, there's the puppetry you have to engage in, letting sponsors pull the strings while you perform. We all have a love-hate relationship with the companies who help fund our passion and profession. I'm mostly glad to be out from under that pressure. Mostly.

"Anyway," Bodhi continues. "We've got a big trip ahead. We're going to Hawaii, and, yes, I'll be surfing Jaws. We both will. And then we're off to Nazare in Portugal to ride with some of the best. You can catch it all on ESPN and follow along on our YouTube channel for behind the scenes goofiness and a touch of reality."

My sister beams up at Bodhi while he speaks, her eyes never leaving him. As hard as it has been watching her re-enter their relationship, and then re-enter pro surfing, the bigger piece of me swells with pride and happiness. She's always going to be my baby sister. And that means I'll always watch out for her.

After a rundown of their itinerary, Bodhi hands the mic over to Kalaine, or Kala, as I usually call her.

A warm smile fills Kalaine's face. "Thank you all for being here. We're so grateful for your support. It's been good to be home between trips. Good to hang out with friends at C-Side, to surf the local break, to even give a few lessons. And to get back to being just me, you know? The girl who wakes up with wild hair, a dog in her bed, and no sense of direction until I've had my first cup of coffee."

The patio fills with soft laughter. It's a different flavor of response than the one Bodhi draws out with his charisma and strength. I feel my smile. It's one that won't easily recede. I'm tempted to shout, "That's my sister!" But I savor the moment privately instead, watching her take life by the horns and grab up all she deserves and more. I wish my parents could be here to share this send off. They're watching the live stream from their home in Hawaii, but it's not the same.

"And it's been sweet to get to spend time with Mila and Noah at Mila's place. Just sitting at the desk answering calls and making reservations."

Mila.

You know the feeling you get when you first taste hot cocoa, or bite into a warm pastry? That warmth and comfort? The flavors bursting on your tongue and drawing your attention to the sweetness of what's right in front of you? That sensation when your feet go from sand into the cool froth of the sea? The instant you step outside on a foggy morning and the fresh air hits your lungs, reminding you you're truly alive? For just the briefest moment, I feel all of that at the mere sound of Mila's name.

We're old friends. Well, I've only been on the island less than four years, but she was one of the first people I met—one of the first to make me consider the fact that Marbella could be my home, not just in location, but in a much deeper sense of the word. Mila has always made me feel like we've known one another forever. She's got this heart of hospitality that goes with her wherever she is, making everyone around her feel welcome and at ease.

My sister's been talking and my mind unintentionally wandered. I rein in my focus on what she's saying.

"... and don't get me wrong. I love my life as a pro surfer. It's like nothing else. My passion. My calling. Something I can't seem to pull myself away from, even if I wanted to—which, I don't. But I'm so glad to have Marbella as a place to call home, I can come here and just be me, not Kalaine Kapule, world-class surfer, but just Kala ..." Kalaine's eyes find mine in the crowd and she sends me a smile. "Sister to Kai. Or Mavs, as my fiancé calls me." She looks up at Bodhi and he leans in and kisses her temple. "Just another girl living on this island with all of you."

Someone claps. Ben shouts out, "We love you, Kalaine!" in his typical, very over-the-top way. His enthusiasm starts everyone clapping and hooting.

Kalaine blushes and grins, and then she hands the mic back to Bodhi.

He smiles at her and then at the crowd. "As you know, we're raising funds for The Shaka Foundation, helping animals in crisis. So, feel free to dig deep and support the charity of our choice—the charity my future wife started a few months ago that has already helped over a thousand animals in need. You're all aware

4

how much rescuing animals means to us. It's a cause close to our hearts."

A photo of the mutt who now lives with me full time fills the screen behind Kala and Bodhi. He's cute, I'll admit. And, now he's mostly mine since these two adopted him and then promptly rejoined the surf community, putting them off-island at least six months out of every year.

A few people in the crowd audibly sigh and a chorus of, "awww" goes up when Kalaine tells the story of how she and Bodhi snuck around to adopt Shaka. Snuck around *me*, to be clear.

When Kala and Bodhi wrap up their plea for financial donations to their charitable organization, Cameron jumps back on stage. "Thank you, Kalaine and Bodhi. We're looking forward to virtually following you on this next adventure. And I'm sure we're all going to help support The Shaka Foundation after that compelling story."

Cameron smiles one of his guest-services smiles. It's not the one he lets fly free around a bonfire. It's a curated smile, one that says he's here for you and whatever it is you might need from him.

"Drink up. Grab some of the desserts on the back buffet table, and be sure to stop by and chat with Kalaine and Bodhi before you leave. Thank you all for coming out."

Cameron places the mic back on its stand. The band to the side of the platform begins to play as Kala and Bodhi make their way back to our table.

A few hours later, the three of us sit around our living room. Suitcases and duffles line the wall next to the front door. Two surfboards in travel bags lean in the corner. Kalaine's on the couch next to Bodhi, and I'm in one of the side chairs. The dog, Shaka, is on Kala's lap. But he promptly jumps off and heads toward me for no apparent reason.

"He loves you!" Kala nearly coos.

"Yep. I'm a loveable guy," I deadpan.

The dog looks up at me with eyes that are meant to make me cave.

"Don't look at me like that," I tell him.

Bodhi and Kala crack up. The dog stands on his hind legs and places both paws on my knees. He locks eyes with me and tilts his head like he's trying to figure me out. That just draws more laughter out of my sister and my best friend.

"What do you think you want?" I stare back at the white and tan mutt as if he's actually going to answer me.

"He wants you," Kala says with the same voice she uses whenever she's trying to get her way with me.

"He's got me. I'll feed and water him while you're gone. And I'll let him poop in my yard, and I'll even pick that mess up for him."

My doggie babysitter to-do list sends my sister and Bodhi into a fit of laughter for some unknown reason.

"Oh my gosh!" Kala breathes out between cackles. "You'll water him? Like a houseplant?"

I shoot her a look.

"What about petting him? What about him sleeping with you?"

"No. The dog shouldn't even be in a bed. He's a dog."

"Kaaaaiii ..."

Kala draws out my name on the kind of whine that should make me irritated, but she knows it only makes me want to do whatever it takes to make her happy. It's not fair. Where she's concerned, I have buttons, and she knows just how to push them.

"I'll pet him. A couple times a day, even. But it's a big no to my bed. No one shares my bed. The end."

"Maybe that should change one day, huh, bro?" Bodhi unhelpfully suggests.

"Maybe you should get some sleep. You've got a long flight and big competitions lined up. You two need rest and fluids."

"Okay, Dad," Bodhi teases.

Kala just smiles up at him.

The dog hasn't given up. He's still got his paws on my legs. I shift so his paws hit the floor and then I stand. "Let's go kill some more grass, mutt." I head toward the back door to let the dog out to do his business. He's not even mine, but I've gotten into the habit of being the one to let him out at night since I'm the one who's here the most.

"Stop calling him that!" Kala laughs through her words. "You know you love him."

"If by love, you mean tolerate, I'm smitten. Fully head-over-heels."

I hear my sister tell Bodhi, "He loves him."

"Yeah. He does," Bodhi agrees.

Traitors. Dog-abandoning traitors. I chuckle to myself as the door falls shut behind me and the cool night air fills my lungs.

"Bruh!" Ben shouts from the back door of the watersports shack. "Did you see me catch that perfect left?"

"You're dripping water all over the floor." I raise an eyebrow at Ben, and he backs out the door, standing on the deck and smiling like a man without a care in the world.

Drops of water still roll off his hair, chest, and the wetsuit dangling at his hips after the surf session he and I had this morning. Only I called it early, paddled in, went home, showered, fed that dog who lives in my house, and came back here to open the shop, while Ben continued to catch some of the best waves we've had all season.

Kalaine and Bodhi left yesterday, and my house already feels strangely empty in the wake of their absence.

"But did you see the wave?" Ben's grin splits his face.

"Before I paddled in?"

"Yeah. It was my best wave yet since I moved to Marbella."

"I think I saw the one." I smile back at him.

"Dude. This is the life."

I nod. He's not wrong. We surf, teach watersports, live on a beautiful island with an exclusive resort as our backdrop. And when we want time off, we cover for one another because the employees out here may as well be family. This *is* the life. Somehow, I can't quite muster the enthusiasm Ben seems to easily tap into. He's the geyser on top of a natural spring of effervescent optimism. And I love him for it.

I'm more of a still waters run deep guy. No ripples. No waves. Steady, calm, reliable. I bat away the next word floating through my head: *boring.*

Kai, you are *boring.*

When did I become boring? I'm an ex pro surfer, a Hawaiian, a watersports instructor on an island most people would dream of calling home. I'm not boring.

I'm ... reliable, consistent, steady ...

Yeah. I think I might be boring.

"How'd everything go with Bodhi and Kalaine?"

Ben's question snaps me out of my self-flagellating spiral.

"Fine. Good. They left early. I borrowed a golf cart and hauled them and their luggage to the ferry before dawn yesterday."

"And now what?"

"They head to Hawaii. They're staying with my parents. One contest on Oahu. Then they surf Jaws. I think it's a little over a week on the islands and then they fly to Portugal for another week. Then they'll be back here."

"Yeah. Not them. I got all that when I talked to Bodhi. Now what for you, boss man?"

For *me?*

I just shrug.

"Dog sitting. Surf lessons. Enjoying some peace and quiet."

Ben shakes his head like I'm pathetic.

I lived that life—pro surfing with Bodhi and my sister. I actually made the circuit before the two of them. Eventually, we lived that life together, competing, traveling, training. Now I keep the home fires burning while they're off living the dream. I don't mind solitude. Sometimes I prefer it, actually.

Ben walks out to the outdoor shower to rinse off. When he's back and changed into his shorts and T-shirt, he approaches the counter where I'm sitting on a stool behind the cash register.

"You know what you need?"

"No. But I'm sure you're about to tell me."

He smirks. "You're lacking in female companionship, bro. It's as simple as that. You should just ask a girl out."

He looks at me and then his gaze shifts to a shelf of graphic surf T-shirts behind me. He walks over and starts re-folding the top few that were left askew by customers yesterday.

"Who?"

I shouldn't ask. Why am I asking Ben? I don't need to encourage him butting in on my love life—or lack of love life.

"Does it really matter? Just ask a girl out. Like, someone who works at Alicante. Or … Clarissa."

"Clarissa? As in C-Side Coffee Clarissa?"

"Yeah? Why? What's wrong with her?"

"Nothing. She's great. I like her a lot. Only, I think she could be old enough to have been my babysitter when we were younger."

"But you no longer need a sitter." Ben chuckles. "You're older now. Age is just a number after a while. Isn't that what they say?"

"A number that might mean I need to date someone who is less than ten years older than me."

"Okay. Fine. What about … Mila?"

He says the name so randomly—like he casually picked it out of a hat, like her name is just one among many.

There's nothing random or casual about Mila. And she's not someone I'm ever going to date. Between her job running her bed and breakfast on the North Shore, and her devotion to her son, Noah, she's off limits. We're friends. Good friends. But just friends. That's all we'll ever be. And I'm fine with that. A man could do way worse than having a friend like Mila.

9

Ben's facial expression says he's questioning the sanity of my acceptance of my place in her friend zone. Mila's beautiful. Actually, that word really doesn't begin to capture her. She's got chestnut brown hair that shimmers and falls down her back in soft waves. It's a color that would make you expect to gaze into warm brown eyes. But she's full of surprises. Mila's eyes are a stark contrast to her hair: a crystalline blue, nearly translucent, a lake in the tundra, rimmed in turquoise. Not cold, though. Nothing about Mila is cold. Her eyes are the thermal Blue Lagoon in Iceland, a place of warmth when everything around is stark and frigid. And there's so much more to her than her effortless beauty. She's bright, funny, and caring—the kind of woman a man might have overlooked in his twenties, but notices far more than he ought to in his thirties.

"Earth to Kai." Ben chuckles softly, as if he caught me withholding a secret.

"Yeah. No. Not Mila. She isn't ... that's not an option."

"I think she's definitely an option."

"Well, she's not."

"Okay, not Mila." Ben's ability to roll with the punches and remain buoyant should be bottled and mass marketed. "How about a night at Club Descanso? We could just go out dancing. Summer and me ... you. We could grab Cam and Riley ..."

And I could be the thirty-three-year-old fifth wheel.

"Just dancing with friends, and maybe a dance or two with someone attractive," Ben persists. "What do you say, Kai?"

I hear the word "Yes" come out of my mouth as if I'm not even the one saying it. Apparently, Ben's charm and capacity for persuasion doesn't end with his wife, Summer. If I'm honest, I could use a night out with friends, even if those friends will couple up, leaving me looking like a bicycle with only one tire.

"Great! I'll text Summer. We'll pull something together for tonight or tomorrow."

And just like that, it looks like I'm going out dancing.

TWO

Mila

Life is full of challenges and surprises,
and I've had my share.
~ John Daly

"Moooommmm! I'm hoooooommme!" Noah's voice echoes through the front room of the inn as the door slams shut behind him.

"In here," I shout at half the volume he just employed.

My son's face appears around the corner of the kitchen doorway. He shucks his super-hero backpack and plops it onto the floor.

"Inside voices, please," I remind Noah.

Not that it will do me any good. He's rambunctious, nearly seven years old, and he lives in the moment. He never did learn to whisper, maybe that skill will come with age.

"Okay. Is there guests here? I'm starved."

"It's *are*. *Are* there guests. And, yes. A couple checked in this morning and we have two other guests arriving tonight. And, starved, huh? That's pretty dire. Didn't you eat the lunch I sent you?"

"Yeah. But that was houuurs ago."

"Okay." I smile a private smile as I open the oven door. "Wash your hands and I'll get your snack. Do you have homework?"

"Nope. Just this All-About-Me thing. I have to take a picture of me too. And Mrs. Jensen said I can put just your name under parents."

I pull the baking sheet out of the oven.

"We can take a picture of you later today. Once Chloe arrives."

Noah pulls the step stool up to the sink and washes his hands while I place the snickerdoodles on a cooling rack.

"Snickerdoodles! My favorite!" As if I didn't know my son's favorite cookie.

Noah climbs onto one of the stools around the island.

"Mine too," my best friend, Chloe, says from the spot where she just appeared in the kitchen doorway.

"Hey, you. I wasn't expecting you 'til later."

"Well, I'm here. Maybe it's the cookies. They were calling to me."

"Believe it or not, I baked these for my guests."

"Am I your guest?" Noah asks, batting his lashes just the slightest. That boy.

"You are my favorite guest. And one of the hosts too, so no sneaking extras. Mkay?"

"Yes, Mom."

"Is that faucet dripping again?" Chloe asks, looking at my sink.

I give the knob a tug, hoping it's just that Noah didn't shut it all the way off. Sure enough, it's still dripping.

"Looks like it."

I had this kitchen renovated a number of years ago, right after I inherited the property. Back then, before Noah was born, I imagined running this bed and breakfast with the man who was my husband at the time, Brad.

But life had other plans. Or, Brad did.

I don't run this place alone, though. Far from it. My bestie, Chloe, cleans for me three afternoons a week. My three aunts all live on the island, and they're always chipping in somehow or another. I have a bookkeeper, Frank, and a few part-time employees. And there's Kai. He's become someone I lean on for repairs and upkeep, even though I probably shouldn't depend on him as much as I do. I trust him, though. And when it comes to home repairs, being able to count on someone not to cheat me or overcharge me, and to know what they are doing ... Well, that's Kai. For now, at least.

"Aunt Chloe!" Noah shouts as if she's out on the front porch, not ten feet away from him.

"Hey, Super Noah, what's new today?" Chloe takes a seat next to Noah, showering him with her undivided attention, as usual. They are two peas in a pod, those two.

Noah fills Chloe in on his school day and the All-About-Me project, giving her way more details than he offered me when he got home. I serve up cookies on two plates, then I pour milk for each of them. They chat away, taking bites interspersed in their stream of words. I lean back on the counter, cherishing the sight of my son and one of his favorite people on earth, both of them far more confident and outgoing than I am by nature.

"Hey, think I could grab a minute with your mom while you put away your backpack?" Chloe asks Noah after they've each devoured two cookies apiece.

"Sure, Aunt Chloe." Noah pops off the barstool and grabs his bag without another word.

"So ..." Chloe turns to me. "Everything okay?"

"Yeah. Why wouldn't it be?"

"No reason. At all. Really. Just ... checking on you."

"I'm fine. We have a new couple here today. Two more guests coming in whenever the late ferry lands. Are *you* okay?"

"I'm great. I just wanted to make sure. I'm glad you're good."

"You are acting weird. Even for you."

Chloe laughs. "Yeah. I am. Don't mind me. I'll just put these dishes in the washer and get to work. Oh! And what are you doing tomorrow night?"

"Probably the usual. Serving dinner here, putting Noah to bed. Grabbing my Kindle and a cup of tea and curling up with a romance novel."

"Sounds good. Only, could you change your plans if I wanted to ... let's say ... have a girls' night?"

"A girls' night?"

"Yeah. You know? A night where friends get together without guys and hang out together. Maybe watch a movie. Go dancing. Eat out. Something to break the monotony. What do you say? I think Alana's back in town. We could invite her and Harry."

Harry, as in Harriet, another friend I've known my whole life. She's a painter and she lives a few blocks over.

"Who will watch Noah?"

"One of your fairy godmothers. You know they will. Let me see if Jasmin can cover the front desk so you can get away for a few hours."

"I can talk to Jasmin. Don't worry."

"Okay. So, we're set. Girls' night. Saturday."

Chloe makes a little squealing sound and bounces on her toes. It's a little over the top, and out of character. Something's off with her today. I just can't tell what.

"You sure you're okay?" I double check.

"Yeah. Yeah. Just ... you know. Thinking about how life can change. And how things that aren't what you may have been expecting can happen. And if that's ever the case, I'm glad we have one another."

"Spill it."

"Spill what?" Chloe avoids my eyes, which means for sure she's hiding something.

"Whatever is changing that I'm going to need you to help me get through."

"Um. Nothing is changing for sure. It's just a rumor. So, let's … just forget I said anything."

"Which will be easy to do, since you haven't said anything. But you are going to say something. You can't just come in here all, 'Are you okay?' and then turn around and start cleaning rooms as if you didn't just set the stage for some mystery. I'll go bonkers. I mean, my mind will run the gamut from something amazing to something catastrophic. Like, what if Brad were coming back?"

I chuckle. The thought is preposterous, but my brain *would* go there. No doubt.

"So spill."

Chloe's face blanches.

"Good afternoon." My aunt, Phyllis, says from the kitchen doorway, saving Chloe from answering—for now. I'll circle back, for sure.

"Hey. What brings you here?" I ask Aunt Phyllis.

"I can't stop in on my niece?"

"You definitely can. It's just that you usually don't simply drop in out of the blue. Want a cookie? I just pulled a batch out of the oven."

"I'd love one. I could smell those from all the way out on the front porch. They're magic."

I grab a cookie for Phyllis as she slides onto a stool. She and Chloe exchange a look.

"What is going on?" I ask both of them.

"Just checking in on you," Phyllis says in a tone I'm sure is meant to be nonchalant, but comes off slightly high-pitched and very telling. She was in the movies ages ago. Her acting skills are far better than the show she's putting on right now.

"Funny, that's exactly what Chloe was doing. Why is everyone checking in on me?"

"Hey, everybody," Aunt Joan says from the doorway.

"Joan?" Phyllis asks her sister. "I thought I was coming over here."

"What do you mean? We decided I would be the one."

"No. We clearly said I would stop by Mila's place and you would ask around at Corner Market."

"Ask what?" I ask.

No one seems to remember I'm even here.

"Hey, sweeties!" My Aunt Connie sidles up next to Joan.

Joan looks over at Connie. "I thought you were going to C-Side to ask Clarissa what she knows."

"I thought you were going to C-Side and Phyllis was going to Corner Market and I was coming here. Remember? We sorted it by age."

"Yes. And I'm the oldest," Phyllis says. "I'm the one who was given legal custody of Mila when she came to live with us. So I was the one coming here."

"You're always pulling that card, Phyl. It's not right. We all raised her. Am I right, Mila?" Connie looks over at me with a pleading look.

"You all did raise me. And would someone, for the love, tell me what is going on around here?"

All four sets of eyes fix on me, as if I just appeared out of nowhere.

No one speaks.

I cross my arms and make eye contact with each of the women gathered in my kitchen in turn. These are my people. I'd do anything for any one of them. And they've got a secret, obviously —one they are doing a lousy job of hiding from me.

"It's just a rumor, dear," Phyllis says.

"Yes. Complete gossip. Probably unfounded," Joan adds.

"I'd guess someone has their facts wrong." Connie nods along.

I land on Chloe. She steps toward me, placing her hand on my shoulder. She takes a deep breath. Her face softens.

"Someone heard something about Brad. He's supposedly

expanding his second-hand sports equipment business to include watersports. And ... well ... Ashley heard from Dan. And then she told Brynn. And Brynn said something to Abbie. And Abbie told me. So ... it's basically a game of telephone. Probably nothing."

Brad. Noah's dad, aka, my ex. Not really Noah's *dad*, if by dad you mean someone who raises a child as a parent. But Brad is definitely the man who got me pregnant. We don't talk. We haven't talked since I was pregnant.

Brad and I married after college. High school sweethearts. We grew up here together. He and I had dreams. Those dreams never included children. And I thought I was okay with that. Until the day I found out I was pregnant. We had done all the things to make sure we wouldn't conceive, but Noah had other plans. He's too full of life not to be born into this world. He's a gift—one I didn't know I needed or wanted until that day. When I took that test and saw the plus sign staring back at me, my heart swelled with unexpected joy.

Naively, I assumed Brad would have the same change of heart. Maybe we had been selfish or unaware. We hadn't realized how awesome being parents could actually be. Things change. Plans change. We could change with this new information—this beautiful news. Up until I peed on that stick, the idea of kids was just that—an idea. But that morning, it became my reality. And I figured the reality would be something that would inspire us to pivot.

Only, Brad didn't react the way I had hoped. He was angry, asking if I had sabotaged our plans in secret. He accused me of skipping a pill. We tried to work through his initial reaction, which was beyond surprising to me. But his stance never changed. *I never wanted children, Mila. I still don't.* I can still hear his voice, see his face, the day he made that final declaration along with the announcement that he was filing for divorce and moving to the mainland to start a business—without me.

And just like that, I was a single mom who had recently inherited an island property she was converting to an inn. But I've never truly been alone. My aunts and Chloe and other people on Marbella have been alongside me from that day forward.

"Why would Brad branching into watersports equipment be of any concern to me?"

My voice is hushed. Noah is home. We never speak of his dad. I've regularly told him that he has a dad. I tell him his dad left because he was not the kind of man who knew how to keep his promises. I make sure Noah knows it had nothing—absolutely nothing—to do with Noah. But really, that conversation only comes up on occasion, because Noah has a full life with extended family and a sweet network of support, and Brad is not interested in being a part of it.

Noah knows in a general way that his dad left to choose a life for himself, but he doesn't know—nor will he ever—that his dad left because he didn't want him. That's Brad's loss. And I'll never let it be Noah's.

"Wellllll ..." Chloe's hand is still on my shoulder. "The rumor —and, again, it's just a rumor—is that Brad's coming here. Opening a watersports rental and resale on Marbella."

"Here?"

"It's just a rumor, dear," Connie says.

"Definitely. Most likely hearsay," Joan echoes.

"Agreed. Speculative at best," Connie adds.

And with each confirmation of improbability, I'm less convinced.

I don't know if I'm breathing.

Phyllis scoots one of the barstools over and I plop onto it. Numb. That's what I am. I can't feel my feet, my hands, my head. I'm a swirly mess of confusion. I'm floating over the room, looking down on this scene as if I'm being suspended over my own body.

Is this right? It can't be. Why would Brad come back to Marbella? Noah's here. I'm here. Brad doesn't want Noah. Why would he pick the one place he's bound to run into the son he disowned and the wife he abandoned? There are plenty of places along the coast where he can build that aspect of his business and flourish.

"Probably just a rumor!" Joan repeats overly enthusiastically.

"Yes! Yes! Agreed. You know how people are," Connie adds emphatically. "They hear one thing and then they add a little when they pass it on. Or they get confused. It's probably nothing. Or just a mix-up."

I expect Phyllis to say something equally dismissive and comforting, but she doesn't. She just stares at me.

"What do you think?" I ask her.

"I think it's never wise to go building houses in the clouds. We don't know what's happening. And we were *supposed* to find out the facts before we came to you." She glares lovingly at her sisters. The look she gives is still pretty intimidating, but there's no bite to her. "But we botched that royally. So now, we need to find out what's really going on. And you don't need to borrow trouble from tomorrow. Just serve your guests. Take care of Noah, and forget all about all of this. It may be hearsay. And if it isn't, who's to say you'll even see him if he builds a business here? He may not even come to the island. He may have someone else run it for him. The world is full of possibilities. We don't need to line them up and stress over each one in turn as if they are already happening."

I take a deep breath. Phyllis is right.

I'm going to be fine.

I look Chloe in the eyes. "I'll be fine."

"Of course you will. You're a boss babe. You own a freaking inn. You parent Noah like a champ. You'll be fine."

"Like a champ? Really?"

We both burst into much needed laughter.

"Whatever," Chloe says, still smiling with residual amusement. "I was under pressure. I wasn't prepared to have to give a spur of the moment pep talk. You're a great mom. Okay?" She pauses and gives my shoulder a reassuring squeeze. "And you will be fine. More than fine."

I smile at my best friend.

Most days, I don't give Brad a second thought. He's a part of my history—someone I left in my past while I moved forward to build a life for Noah and myself. Of course, the briefest thought of him flits through my mind on occasion, like today, when Noah said he was putting my name down under the section for "parents" on his project. Even then, I just thought, I *am* both your parents. Or, at least I do my best to fill in the blanks.

But now? Now, I'm thinking of Brad. I'll probably barely be able to think of anything else until I know the details of his plans for certain.

What if Brad actually is coming to Marbella?

THREE

Kai

I'm very much a homebody.
~ Liam Neeson

Club Descanso is loud and crowded. Or maybe I'm getting too old for this scene.

"Kai?" A woman I recognize from the resort approaches the high-top table where I'm sitting watching Ben, Summer, Riley and Cam out on the dance floor.

"Yeah. Hi." I don't use her name because, honestly, I forgot it.

"Gemma," she says, giggling lightly and pointing to herself with one manicured finger.

"Oh. Yeah. Sorry. I knew that." I politely nod toward the chair next to me.

Gemma takes the open seat, smiling widely. She sets her glass in front of her, swirling her drink and looking me in the eye like I'm an old friend, or maybe a conquest. I might be imagining the note of coyness in her eyes. Maybe that's just her way with people. I'm so out of practice I can't even tell if a woman is hitting on me. I'm not sure I want to hone my skills when it comes to dating. I'm pretty certain I'm ready to retreat, retire or tender my resignation —whatever a man does to bow out of the dating pool—and it's only my first night out.

"So, how are things at watersports?"

"Good."

Small talk hurts.

A slightly excruciating buzzing sort of pressure radiates from my throat to my chest as I try to muster up something interesting to say or ask.

Nope. I've got nothing.

"We're pretty busy at Chops," Gemma offers, not seeming the least bit bothered by my current lack of social skills.

Ah. Yes. The steakhouse. That's where she works.

"Nothing much changes for us even when the weather gets colder. People always want to have a fancy dinner while they're here on the island. Some people even ferry in for a night out."

"Sounds about right."

"So, what brings you out tonight?"

Gemma leans in a little, propping her elbow on the table and tilting her arm so her chin rests on the back of her hand. She's a beautiful woman ... confident ... seems nice. I don't know why I'm thinking about that mutt back at my place and whether he's ready to go do his business and get to sleep right now.

"I'm here with friends."

"Against your will?" Gemma's brows lift playfully and she looks over at me through her lashes.

I smile back at her. "Basically. I guess I'm sort of a homebody these days. Ben talked me into coming out dancing."

"And yet, you're sitting here alone."

"Not now, I'm not."

"No, you aren't." She smiles again. "Should we dance?"

"I ... don't know. I haven't danced in a while. Maybe I should just stick to keeping this chair occupied."

"Nonsense. You should dance. If I know Ben—and I do—

he'll give you all sorts of grief if you don't dance at least a little tonight."

She's got a point.

"You're probably right. I'd better get out there for at least one song."

Instead of judging me, or looking put out, Gemma smiles at me. It's not exactly a grin full of pity. But it's something akin to that—pity with a dash of compassion.

I look around. Men at the bar and at other tables are all eyeing Gemma. She's wearing jeans that fit her well. She's tall, but she's not afraid to wear heels. Her blouse is ruffled and tucked into the front of her pants in a way that looks stylish. And her brown wavy hair seems like she put some effort into it. Gemma's got an air about her that draws attention. And still, I'm thinking about how I can dance this one dance and graciously bow out as soon as I'm able.

Gemma leads the way, weaving her way between tables, looking over her shoulder occasionally, probably to make sure I haven't changed my mind and bolted for the exit. When she's on the dance floor in the middle of the room, she pivots toward me and begins swaying her hips as I approach. Her smile returns, comfortable and easy. I look over at Ben and make eye contact. He gives me a thumbs up.

When I turn my attention back to Gemma, she's dancing with her elbows tucked into her sides and her hands extended, fingers pinched like she could snap along with the music. She's moving to the beat, smiling freely and twisting her hips and shoulders. It all looks effortless, while I feel like a boy at his first junior high dance. I can dance. I grew up on Hawaii, learning dances for certain local ceremonies and at parties. And, I'm a surfer—ex pro. I know how to use my body.

The problem with me is mental. When my brain starts to loop and swirl in overthinking spirals, my body stops listening, and the two seem to war against one another rather than cooperating. So, I sway in place. It's a safe choice. I won't fall over and I don't look too foolish. Or, maybe I do. If I look as stiff as I feel, while Gemma looks like she was born to move on a dance floor, I definitely look foolish right now.

Gemma reaches out, placing her hands on either side of my waist. She presses lightly, moving me along with the beat of the song. It should feel intrusive or intimate. Instead, she makes me feel like I've got a friend, encouraging me to get over myself and have an ounce of fun. I give in at some point, and end up dancing three songs before I thank her and turn back toward my table and the comfort of the barstool I was sitting on before she approached me.

"Don't be a stranger, Kai," Gemma leans in and whispers in my ear before I step off the wooden floor onto the epoxy covered concrete that fills the rest of the room.

"Thank you for pushing me out of my comfort zone. I appreciate it." I smile at her.

"My pleasure." Gemma winks at me, dragging her hand slowly down my arm before she turns toward a group of women and joins them at the bar. The way they all light up when she approaches tells me she came with them, or they're her friends.

Back at my table, I don't bother taking my seat, but I do take a long sip of my drink. I almost make a clean getaway, but a voice behind me calls my name.

Ben.

"Hey! Hey! Hey! Look at my boss, out here dancing with a beautiful woman."

Summer walks up next to her husband and wraps her arm around his waist. Ben tugs her in close, placing a soft kiss on her temple. She smiles up at him.

"Want something to drink, Monroe?" Ben uses the nickname I've heard him call Summer even before she started giving him the time of day.

The comfort between them reminds me of my sister and Bodhi. It's the ease and familiarity of a good relationship, and the fondness that comes when you find your person among all the others in the world. I've been lucky to grow up in a family where my parents love one another. It's not the same electric type of chemistry common to couples around my age. Theirs is a love that's grown over time, mellow, comfortable, and certain. But my dad still looks at my mom like she's his world, and she returns the favor in her own quiet way.

"Okay. Well. I danced. And, I've got to get back to my sister's dog."

"Who is probably asleep on your couch. Why leave so soon? Gemma seemed into you." Ben nearly pouts.

"Did she?"

Summer smiles sympathetically at me. She turns to Ben, "Let Kai bow out, Ben."

Ben and Summer exchange some sort of secret couple conversation without uttering a word to one another. They simply stare into one another's eyes, while their expressions morph nearly imperceptibly.

When they seem to have come to some sort of understanding, Ben says, "Okay, I'll let you ditch us. But if you ask me, you're walking away from an opportunity. I know Gemma. She's nice and pretty easygoing."

"I enjoyed our dance." I'm already pushing my stool in and taking my first step toward the door.

"Well, you'll have to come out again another time."

"We'll see. You two go have fun."

The walk home is peaceful. A breeze blowing in off the ocean and across the beach brushes over my cheeks, bringing a welcome cooling after spending a few hours in a crowded dance club. Our house is only a few blocks south of the club, one block in from the ocean in a residential section of Descanso. I pause before turning up my street. Standing at the edge of the sand, I breathe in the ocean air.

I could have stayed, walked Gemma home, or at least danced some more.

But I'm not a twenty-something-year-old guy, out for a good

time. Something happened to me when I turned thirty. If I date, it's not merely to distract myself or find some temporary comfort and companionship. I'm looking for something serious. Or not. And I don't want to lead anyone on, especially not someone as nice as Gemma. She's not it for me. Knowing that means I don't walk her home. And I don't stay for another dance. I leave her there to enjoy the rest of the night with her friends while I go let a mutt out before that hairy beast climbs into my bed and curls up on top of my feet.

Not that I'm telling my sister about Shaka finding his way up onto my mattress at night. It's not like I want a dog in my bed. I just can't sleep with him whining some forlorn dog version of a sad song. He left me no choice.

I'm brushing my teeth, staring at myself in the bathroom mirror as if it holds the answers to life, when my phone vibrates on the counter, shaking me out of whatever thoughts I was having.

Mila's name and face flash on my screen—at 11:42 at night?

"Mila? Is everything okay?"

"Yes ... No. Well. No. Not at all, actually. I called Jason, but he's not answering. The kitchen faucet was dripping on and off this week but the main problem is that hanging sprayer. It won't turn off unless I use the lever to redirect all the water to the faucet over the kitchen sink. So, that's what I do every time. I use the sprayer, then switch the lever. I kept planning to call you or Jason." Mila pauses and a gasp comes through the phone. Then I hear a soft thud when she sets the phone down and shouts. "Oh! Gosh! Hold on Kai!"

Shuffling and clunking noises fill the background. Then Mila's back on the line. "Sorry about that. I've just been up to my ears with new guests and a project for Noah's class ... Anyway ..." Mila blows out a long breath. "I was doing some batch cooking after everyone was in bed. I turned the sprayer on to wash the mixing bowls and baking sheets. And, well, the top of the sprayer popped loose. I was drenched in an instant. The kitchen floor is covered in water. It just started spraying everywhere!"

"Just now?"

"A few minutes ago. I'm so sorry. Were you asleep?"

"No. Not at all. I was ..." *Out dancing.* "Just home getting ready to call it a night. I'm here alone with my sister's dog while they're on their trip. I'm coming right over. Turn off the water supply outside. You know where that is, right?"

"Yes. I shut it off already. But so much water already sprayed out of the sprayer. The kitchen is nearly a quarter of an inch deep right now. I've got a bucket and mop and towels thrown around everywhere." Mila sighs. "You don't have to come over. Just tell me what to do. Maybe you can walk me through it? I just have to turn the water back on before the morning for cooking and showers ... Except ... Oh! I don't know what I was thinking. My guests will need to flush toilets overnight. I don't want to have to have them relocate ..."

Her voice trails off as if she's nearly forgotten I'm on the other end of the line.

"Mila, I'm already grabbing a shirt and heading your way."

"You didn't have a shirt on? Oh. Kai, I'm sorry. You were in bed, weren't you?"

"No. I was just brushing my teeth. Don't worry about me. I'm not the least bit tired." I balance the phone between my ear and my shoulder while I shuck my pj bottoms and grab my pants off the chair and throw them on. Then I pull a clean T-shirt off a hanger in my closet and slip it on while holding the phone just a few inches from my face.

"Out the door already. I'll see you in a few minutes."

"I don't know how to thank you, Kai. You're the best."

"That's what friends are for."

"Well, I don't deserve you, but I promise to make it up to you in baked goods."

"Now who's spoiled? I'd repipe your whole inn for free coffee cake and those savory tarts you make. I'm already on my bike. See you in fifteen."

Mila and I hang up and I stuff my phone in my back pocket. Then I pedal to get to her as quickly as I can.

I keep a set of tools at Mila's. Local contractors and handymen do jobs for her when she needs something more complex or time consuming. But they charge a lot, so I insist on her calling me for smaller jobs. Besides, we're friends. It's the least I can do to help her keep the inn running smoothly.

She pays me in home cooking and the occasional paycheck. I keep telling her I'd pitch in for free. I do other jobs for a few other North Shore residents. They all pay me. But they aren't single moms trying to run their own small businesses while raising a young boy. Mila's not a charity case. She's a good friend. And I treat her like ohana—family.

The night air refreshes me, blowing off the heavy, uncertain thoughts I've been batting around all night. Heading to Mila's Place gives me a sense of purpose. Helping other people always does— especially her.

I park my bike in the racks Mila has out front of the white picket fence surrounding the inn. Then I take the porch steps in two strides. Mila opens the door before I knock, looking slightly frazzled, but still beautiful. Her long brown hair is piled on top of her head in a messy bun, strands hang loosely around the edges of her face in wet tendrils. She's wearing a vintage T-shirt and shorts. Her feet are bare.

While I felt nothing but a neutral appreciation for Gemma at the club, I can't help but notice the feeling I have whenever I see Mila. The same word always comes to mind: *home*. Mila is comfort, welcome, hospitality, and warmth. She's the type of person that makes others feel like everything will be alright. With merely a smile she sends me silent assurance that I'm doing just what I should and I don't need to change a thing about myself or my life.

Only, right now, her usual calm is tinged with an edge of

distress. One I'm going to alleviate, because I can't stand to see her rattled. I can do something to ease that look on her face—and I will.

"Kai." The way she says my name is everything.

She's relieved—because I'm here. One word from her in that soft, trusting tone was all I needed to settle whatever was stirring around in my head and heart all night.

"I'm here. Let's fix your faucet."

I brush past Mila, the familiar smell of cinnamon and vanilla enveloping me for a moment.

"Don't worry. We'll get everything back to normal. Your guests will never even know this happened by the time breakfast rolls around."

"What would I ever do without you?"

The way she looks up at me makes me hope she never has to find out.

FOUR

Mila

Learn what is to be taken seriously,
and laugh at the rest.
~ Hermann Hesse

K ai's here. I felt horrible calling him so late at night, but I know him. If he found out I had this disaster and didn't call him, he'd scold me relentlessly for days.

He rushes past me into the kitchen.

"I already got your toolbox out for you," I say, following behind him. "It's on the table. Watch out for the floor. It's still slippery."

It doesn't escape me—the way he looks right now, his hair rumpled, his face that certain type of drowsy that only comes at the end of a long day. I'm not dead. I know Kai Kapule could model surfwear if he ever got tired of his job at the watersports shack. He's muscular and fit—the sweet side effects of a job that keeps him physically active. Between the golden color of his skin, the amber of his eyes, contrasted with his dark hair, he's the type of man women stop to admire.

By necessity, I've had to shut down the part of my brain that looks at a man as anything other than a friend. Right now, while Kai focuses on my disaster of a kitchen, moving to grab a large wrench and then bending over the pile of sopping wet towels to check out the mess under my sink, that piece of me has a private moment where I allow myself to look at my friend and notice how beautiful he is.

Maybe it's the late hour. It could be the way he always steps up without hesitation to help me. Of course, I'll never act on anything with Kai. And usually, I don't even think twice about his looks. He's just Kai, my friend.

I've got Noah and the inn. And Kai and I aren't meant for anything other than the mutual friendship we share. I don't date men who live on the island. We're basically a small town, and our insular life is only heightened by the fact that we are surrounded by miles of ocean on all sides. If something went wrong between me and a man here on Marbella, I'd have to face him every day after our bad ending. And I'd have to endure the chatter and furtive glances that accompany the spreading of juicy news around town. I also don't date transients—guests, summer residents, or people with two homes, one of which happens to be here on Marbella.

Noah and I need stability, and it's up to me to provide that.

So, if you are doing the math, there are two dating pools in my world, and I'm not eligible for either of them. Which is fine. I'm not really in a position to do anything but mother Noah and run the inn for now. But, in another life, Kai would be ... Nothing. I don't have another life. I have this one. And I don't have the luxury of dreaming of anything beyond what's right in front of me.

Kai sticks his head into the cabinet under the sink. After a few moments he backs out and stands.

"Nothing looks like it's leaking down there. I'll just replace the sprayer head. We've got parts in the shed. It might be a crack in the washer or a loose C clip. More than likely the problem's in the spray head itself."

"Can you say that in English?" I stifle a yawn.

"Right." He chuckles lightly. "The spray heads are usually the problem when something goes wrong with your sprayer, but it could be a part in the connection between the head and the hose, so I'll replace all of it."

I plop onto one of the stools I keep tucked around the island, partly from exhaustion. Mostly, I'm overwhelmed. This situation will pass. Ongoing repairs are part of home ownership. An older building of this size means more repairs more often.

Kai stands and walks over to where I'm sitting. He places a strong hand on my shoulder.

"Why don't you go lie down on the couch in the main room. See if you can close your eyes and sleep or at least unplug. I've got this. You need rest."

"I can't just go rest while you fix my sink."

"Actually, you can."

"Kai."

"Mila."

He gives my shoulder a firm squeeze and stares into my eyes with a look that is both unwavering and kind.

"I can rest tomorrow." Kai assures me. "You have guests and Noah. Go. Lie down. I will wake you when the sprayer is fixed, before I leave to go home."

His hand never leaves my shoulder until I nod, against my own will. Then, without another word to one another, Kai heads out the back door of the kitchen, and I walk toward the couch in our main living room. I imagine I won't sleep at all, but somehow, after rearranging myself a few times, I must fall asleep, because I wake to the sound of Kai shouting in the kitchen. I spring up off the couch, slightly disoriented, wondering if I imagined the yelling, until he shouts again.

It's actually more a series of yelps and repeated outbursts of "No!" and "Agh!"

When I open the kitchen door, I burst into laughter at the sight of Kai, chasing down the spray hose which is flipping all over while water comes out the end that now has no spray head on it whatsoever. It's like he's the substitute snake-charmer, his first day on the job, and the snake is having a heyday while Kai tries to catch it. Water is spraying out in all directions like it did just before I called Kai, only this time there's no nozzle on the end of the hose, so it's worse.

I walk toward the sink without a second thought, hoping to help him grasp the hose. As soon as I'm a few feet away from Kai, I realize my mistake. Water sprays across me in a jet stream and then back the other direction as the hose flips and wiggles from the pressure of the spray coming out of it.

I gasp, drawing Kai's attention to my arrival. He backs up, bumping the back of his head on an open top cabinet door. He shouts, "Agh!" And then he reaches past the hose and twists the lever, switching the water flow to the faucet, effectively stopping the spray. The hose droops, defeated at last.

Kai's eyes meet mine. His shirt is soaked through, his hair wet, but he's grinning and his eyes are crinkling at the edges.

I grab a few of the towels I had left on the table across the room and hand them over to Kai so he can dry off. My foot hits a slick spot on the floor, and I lose my footing. Kai reaches out and grabs my forearm to steady me and I wobble forward, ending up flush against him in his arms.

I glance up to see an expression of sincere concern on Kai's face. But that only lasts a few seconds before something snaps between us and we both lose it, laughing hysterically. Kai drops my arms and I step back, fighting and losing against waves of uncontrollable giggles. Tears leak out my eyes and stream down my cheeks. It's the kind of laughter that overtakes you when you're slap-happy and exhausted, overwhelmed and finally at a breaking point. I could be crying, but instead, I'm barely catching my breath between gasps of laughter.

Kai finally speaks. "Mila. Didn't you say you turned off the water?"

"I did."

Kai looks at me, his hair soaking wet, T-shirt glued to his torso, see-through in places, and dripping. His mouth breaks into a full smile, showing off his white teeth in contrast to his tan skin. The sides of his face crinkle around his eyes.

"I don't think we'd get this kind of force if the water were off."

I shake my head. He's right.

"I'll go check." I stand, nearly slipping again in another puddle surrounding me.

"I'll double check the lever and put a bucket under the hose," Kai says. "Then I'll meet you out there."

Using my phone's flashlight, I make my way down the back steps and along the side of the house to the spot where all the controls for the sprinklers and water and gas are located. When I reach for the knob I turned before, I see it clearly: the engraved sign I placed over the faucet. *Sprinkler Shut-Off.*

The back kitchen door clatters shut and Kai walks toward me.

"Sprinklers are shut off. Just in case we needed that." I raise both my eyebrows and my hands in a show of apology.

"No worries," Kai says in a gentle voice. Then he chuckles and our combined laughter fills the darkness around us.

"I'll just turn off the water main and put that new head on. Then we just have to mop up the rest of the water."

"No. I'll do the mopping. You've done plenty."

"Many hands make light work. That's what my dad always said, anyway. I'm not leaving 'til the kitchen is ready for you to prep breakfast. Don't be stubborn, Mila. I'm here. Let me help you."

His hand is on my shoulder again. And we're facing one another, the moonlight playing off our features, making Kai appear unrecognizable and then familiar. A shiver courses through me.

"Are you cold?" he asks me.

"No. Just ... yeah. Probably a little. Let's get busy with the kitchen."

Kai fixes the spray head, tests it, and tells me we're good to go. While he does all that, I gather the towels and throw them in the wash. When I come back into the kitchen from the laundry, he's grabbed the mop from the cleaning closet and insists on being the one to finish mopping the floor. Between the two of us we work in silence for about a half hour. It's comfortable and yet I'm fighting the urge to send Kai home. He's done plenty. Once the mop is stored and the towels are switched to the dryer, I walk him to the front door.

"Thank you again, for everything."

"Anytime. You know that. Besides, I haven't laughed that hard in too long."

His eyes flit down over me and back to my face. "Well, I'd better go. You need to clean up and get some rest. I'll stop by tomorrow to double check that everything's good."

"You don't have ..."

My sentence doesn't even end before Kai cuts me off. "I don't have to. I want to. See you in the afternoon. I'll leave Ben to cover the shack and swing by."

"Okay."

He smiles at me, standing in my doorway until the moment trails on possibly longer than either of us expected. And then he turns, saying, "Get some rest, Mila."

I nod, watching him walk to the bike rack and then I shut the door and head to bed.

FIVE

Kai

You feel alive to the degree
that you feel you can help others.
~John Travolta

"Heya, Shaka," Ben practically coos when the mutt shows up in the doorway of the watersports shack with me the next morning.

Shaka wags his tail effusively and trots into the shop like he owns the place.

"Nope. No," I say to the dog ... and to Ben.

"No, what?" Ben asks while he bends to scratch Shaka behind the ears.

"No dog in the shop."

"Awww. But he's so cute."

"Cute or not, he can't be in here."

"Why'd you bring him to work then?"

"I didn't."

Ben looks at Shaka. Shaka stares up at Ben with the dog version of an innocent smile. Trust me, that dog is anything but

36

innocent. Then the dog and Ben glance at me with identical expressions of confusion.

"If you didn't bring him, how did he get here? On your heels, no less."

"He ... followed me."

"Uh huh." Ben stares at me as if to say, *go on*.

"He was whining and scratching at the door from the inside after I shut it behind myself. And I resolved to keep walking. He's going to acclimate, right? But then he kept at it. And I thought of ... you know ... the damage to the house."

"The house. Right. So you opened the door and let him follow you."

"Yeah." I can't look Ben in the eye.

"You know what you are?"

"Hrmph." I mutter out some sort of noncommittal sound.

"You're a softie. And you love this dog."

"Don't you start in on that too."

"Too?"

"Kala and Bodhi insist that I secretly love that mutt. I don't love him. I barely tolerate him. If he didn't make my sister so ridiculously happy, he'd be back on the streets."

"Mm hmm. And yet, here he sits, looking at you like you're Zeus and he's an adoring Greek citizen."

I arch an eyebrow at Ben.

"I tell you what," Ben says. "Why don't we have him lie down behind the counter? The first sign of disobedience or disruption, and I'll take him outside. Okay?"

"Whatever. The dog's already taken over my house, my yard, and my bed, why not my workplace too?"

"Your ... bed?" Ben starts laughing. He even bends a little, holding his finger up as if he needs a moment to regain control of himself. "Wait. Wait. Wait! Your bed? The dog is in bed with you?"

"It's that or get no sleep."

"Ahh. Right. So that's why you look so worn out despite leaving the club far too early for a man your age."

"I couldn't sleep. I was up late."

"Snuggling Shaka in your bed."

"Something like that."

"Gemma did not leave with anyone else—just the friends she came with," Ben unhelpfully offers.

"Not my concern."

"What's wrong with her?"

"Absolutely nothing."

"So why did you bail on her?"

"I didn't bail on her. I just went home."

"While a beautiful, friendly, available woman disregarded the attention of every other man in the room to practically force you onto the dance floor."

"We danced. It was nice. I was ready to leave."

"Could you be less of a grandpa?"

"A grandpa?"

"Yeah. You're so stodgy. Don't you ever want to settle down, or even have, I don't know ... fun?"

"I have fun. You know I do. When you started here, I helped Bodhi prank you for your whole first week. That was fun. I teach surfing for a living. It doesn't get any more fun than that."

"I just think you could do more with your nights than going home to a dog you secretly love. You could have shaken things up a little. I still think you need female companionship—someone to help you let loose a little. You and Bodhi used to throw barbecues and host the bonfires. Whatever happened to that? You barely had one night out in the past month, and you cut it short."

"Trust me. My night was full enough."

Mercifully, customers walk in before Ben has a chance to grill me about what I mean. It's not that I don't want him to know I was helping Mila, but he and Bodhi always make more out of the relationship I have with her than is real, so I'd rather he think I

38

was home snuggling that wiry mutt than out past midnight fixing Mila's plumbing.

"How can we help you, ladies?" Ben asks the two women in his usually genial tone.

"We're meeting Stevens here."

"I'm sure he'll be here any minute," Ben says with a smile. "Let me know if I can do anything for you while you wait."

Stevens is a marine biologist who lives on Marbella. He runs educational tours of the kelp beds teaching about marine life. We book things for him and he keeps his boats moored in the harbor on the north side of our pier.

The women meander through the shop, thumbing through racks of surfwear, trying on sunglasses, giggling and chatting, and effectively keeping Ben from prodding into my personal life.

Stevens arrives about ten minutes later, true to form. He's one of those guys that spends so much time up in his head, he rarely knows what time it is. Sometimes he'll get so lost in a project he forgets to eat. His idea of a fun night is playing Words with Friends and solving physics problems. Sometimes, in the course of a perfectly normal conversation, he'll bring up topics like neutrino mass, matter–antimatter asymmetry, and the concept of dark energy. Ben entertains himself poking good-natured fun at Stevens, who rarely realizes he's being taunted until at least a few sentences into an exchange between the two of them.

But the man has a heart of gold. He's an animal-lover, and he's great on tours. You'd think all his nerdy brainiac conversational skills would render him inept at taking the average tourist out on the water, but somehow, once he's on a boat, he tones it down to sub-genius level and is able to engage people in the things he loves most—like sea cucumbers.

Stevens introduces himself to the two women.

"Hi, I'm Stevens. I hope you weren't waiting long."

They have the same reaction most females have to Stevens—starry-eyed, staring, tittering nervously, and more unabashed gawking.

"Um, no. It's fine," the taller blond says, literally batting her lashes in a very obvious display of flirtation.

"Totally worth the wait," her brunette friend adds with a tip of her shoulder in Stevens' direction. "*You* are the marine biologist?"

"That's me."

"No one told me marine biology could be so attractive," the first woman says.

Her friend giggles nervously.

"It's fascinating. You'll see." Stevens smiles congenially, completely oblivious to the blatant non-verbal—and verbal—signals these women are sending his way.

Want to know the mating habits of the California sea lion? Stevens is your man. Ironically, the female of that species acts a lot like these two are behaving right now—practically throwing herself at the bull of her species. When it comes to his own kind, Stevens is so oblivious it's nearly comical. His reaction to female attention is usually something along the lines of carrying on about Gorgonian sea fans or some other oceanic marvel, unintentionally shutting down any romantic advances.

Stevens hands the women their waivers, and once they've signed the paperwork, he leads them out to his boat, leaving me alone with Ben again.

Before Ben can pick up our previous conversation, my phone rings. I recognize the number right away. The caller ID says *Mom and Dad*.

I hold a finger up to Ben while I step out the back door to take the call.

"Kai!" My dad's voice booms through the phone. "We're all here and we wanted to call you before Kala and Makoa leave for Maui."

Makoa is the name my father calls Bodhi.

A chorus of "Hi, Kai!" makes me smile so broadly I feel my cheeks stretch. I discern the voices of my mom, Kala and Bodhi in the mix.

"How are you Kai?" my mom asks.

"I'm fine. Good. A little tired today. I was up late helping a friend. But I'm good. How are you?"

"We're all well. So happy to have your sister and her future husband here with us. We miss all of you."

"I miss you too. I'm at work right now, though. Can I call you later?"

"Of course. We just wanted to include you in their visit. I wish you were here."

"You'll be here for the wedding and we'll see one another then."

We talk a little longer, Bodhi and Kala telling me about a few local Hawaiian friends who send their greetings. They fill me in on the surfing conditions and waves they've ridden since being back in Hawaii, Mom gives me an update on her life over the past week since we last spoke, Dad is mostly silent until we all wish one another well and then we hang up.

The day moves forward, customers trickling in and out of the shop here and there, but nothing like they do in the summer months. Both Ben and I have surf lessons at various times. A few hours after lunch I inform Ben that I'm going to take off early.

"I've got some follow up from an odd job I did on the North Shore."

"At Mila's Place?"

"Just a job I did."

"Hmm. No problem. Cut out early. I've got things covered here. Want me to keep Shaka with me and walk him back to your place when I lock up?"

"Would you?"

"As long as you won't miss him too much being separated for those few hours." Ben winks, amused with himself.

"I think I'll survive."

Ben chuckles.

I bend to scratch the dog behind his ears before I realize what

I'm doing. Then I hightail it out of the shack before Ben can tease me for going soft on that mutt.

I borrow a golf cart from the corral at the resort. It's a perk of being an employee here, since cars aren't allowed on Marbella. The day is sunny by now and people are out walking, riding bicycles, and gathering on the beach to my right. I drive away from the south side of the island where Alicante Resort is situated, past residences, and into the distinctly different area we call the North Shore. The shops here are quiet and smaller, not suited for tourists, but staples for the local residents. The whitewashed wood fronts give off a traditionally beachy vibe. Then I steer into the neighborhoods with houses on lots with smaller yards. Beyond these is the section of homes which used to belong to the wealthier families who first inhabited Marbella.

On one corner sits the inn. A sign hangs over the white picket fence surrounding her property: Mila's Place. The full wraparound porch has a swing and several seating areas. The steps, the same ones I ran up just last night, are broad and welcoming. And the double front doors open into a great room where she has her reception area and some furniture for guests. Board games and books are tastefully set on various side tables and coffee tables throughout the room.

I park the golf cart and walk up the stairs, into the main room. No one is at the reception desk, but I hear noise in the kitchen, so I walk through, calling out for Mila as I approach the doorway.

SIX

Mila

You've got someone standing beside you
that's stronger than the one standing against you.
~ Steven Furtick

"Now I just put in the chocolate chips!" Noah exclaims.
He grabs the open five pound bag and begins to dump far more than the required cup into the dough.

"Whoa. Whoa. Whoa. Not so many."

"Mom. You can never have too many chocolate chips. Trust me."

"Noah." I laugh. "Where did you come up with that?"

"Auntie P."

"Of course. Well, you can't believe everything Phyllis says to you."

"Cookies?" Kai's voice interrupts the moment between Noah and me. He's leaning against the doorjamb between the kitchen and the main room, smiling.

"Hi, Unko. We're making cookies. Wanna help?"

When Noah met Kai, he was only three years old. One day, I

can't even remember how long it was after they had met, Kai told Noah to call him Uncle Kai. But Noah couldn't say his Ls very clearly, so it came out, *Unko.* Somehow, that stuck. Noah doesn't remember a time when Kai wasn't in his life. They share a bond that's as close as family, often making me feel like I'm intruding on a private joke they've shared.

"Help you make cookies? You don't have to ask twice." Kai pushes off the wall and walks to the sink to wash his hands.

He turns on the sprayer, tests the lever, and opens the cabinet to check the pipes under the sink, obviously looking for any sign of residual issues after last night's flooding.

"Looks good," he assures me.

Then he glances around at the floor. "Call Jason and have him assess the water damage as soon as you can, okay? Just to be sure."

"I already called him this morning."

Kai steps up to the island at a spot between me and Noah where we've got all the flour, butter, salt and other ingredients spread out for our baking project. He looks down at me and smiles warmly.

"Sorry. I should have known you'd be on top of that. It's your business."

Noah looks between me and Kai, and a rush of embarrassment floods through me. I don't know why.

Kai came and fixed the sprayer last night. That's all.

"I appreciate you following up." My voice is softer than usual until I clear my throat.

I'm not sure why thanking Kai nearly chokes me up. He's the only man who checks up on me. Sure. I have other contractors and workers who help out, but Kai's different. He's always insisting we're like family to him. He rarely accepts pay from me. And then he does things like this—coming by in the middle of the afternoon to make sure we're okay, and advising me to have Jason assess potential damage.

I'd say Kai's like an older brother, but it's different with us. I never had a guy friend. Brad and I dated from high school on, and he didn't like the idea of me being friendly with other boys, so I stuck to my girlfriends. Kai's the first man I have had a genuine friendship with.

"Can we make cookies, or what?" Noah asks, obviously eager to get the first batch in the oven.

"Definitely," Kai says. "Tell me what to do, boss man."

Noah giggles, but his chest puffs in a way it never does with me. I could be jealous, but I'm not—not at all.

"Are you sure you have time?"

It seems like a man in his early thirties would want to spend an afternoon doing anything besides baking cookies with a single mom and her son.

"I've got nothing going on. I cut out of work early."

"To check on us?"

"To bake cookies with my favorite seven-year-old." Kai winks at me.

"Tell Mom more chocolate chips makes them better, Unko."

"True story." Kai nods at Noah. "I think more chocolate chips makes most things better."

We form balls of cookie dough out of the batch Noah and I just finished preparing and plop those on sheets which we place in the preheated oven. Then Kai and Noah make another batch together while I prep supper for my guests.

"What are you doing for dinner?" I ask Kai.

"Leftovers with that dog."

"Shaka?" Noah asks.

"Yeah. That's the one."

"I loooove Shaka." Noah's eyes go all dreamy. "I wish I could have a dog."

"Well, I wish I could give you that one, but I think my sister would miss him. You could come play with him, though."

"Can I, Mom?"

"We'll see. You need to clean your room first. And then we can talk about privileges."

"Awww."

Kai gives Noah a look and shakes his head lightly. Noah straightens up and says, "Okay, Mom. But can I ask Kai my important question first?"

I nod.

"What's up, buddy?" Kai leans his elbows on the island and lowers himself so his head is level with Noah's.

Noah drops his voice to an almost conspiratorial level. "I want to learn how to surf."

"You do, huh? Did your mom say yes to this?"

Kai looks over at me. I nod again. "Yes. If he takes lessons with someone I trust."

"In other words, not Ben or Bodhi?" Kai laughs.

"They're fine. I know they are both great surfers ... and good teachers ..."

"Well, I wouldn't let anyone teach you but me," Kai says, beaming at Noah. "I wouldn't want to miss the first time you pop up on a wave."

Noah's smile fills his face. "Can we start today?"

Kai looks over at me. As usual, he reads my expression without me having to say anything.

Then he tells Noah, "I'm honored to teach you to surf, boss man. I think a school day might be pushing it. How about we go out next weekend?"

"Yes!" Noah's hand shoots up into the air in a fist pump and I wonder when my baby started looking like he's only a few years shy of adolescence.

"I better clean my room now," Noah announces. "Just so Mom doesn't change her mind."

Kai chuckles as Noah hops off his stool and dashes into the main room and down the hall toward his bedroom.

I put the salad I prepped back into the fridge and then I wipe my hands on my apron.

"So, I have to ask ..." I say, settling on one of the stools across from Kai.

"Hmm?"

"Were you really at home when I called last night?"

"Yeah. Why?"

"Chloe said she thought you were out dancing at Club Descanso. I would hate to think I interrupted a date to have you come crawl around under my sink in the middle of the night."

"Chloe? How would she know if I went out dancing?"

"Marbella. You know how people talk."

"Hmm. Right. Well, I was out with Ben and Summer earlier last night. Not on a date. But I ended it early. By the time you called I had been home for a while."

"Good. ... I mean, good I didn't interrupt a date."

"Not a chance, since I'm not dating anyone right now."

A silence settles between us for a few seconds. Then I hear the front door of the inn open, so I step out into the main room in case it's my guests or a delivery. Kai doesn't follow behind me immediately, probably taking a moment to double check the plumbing.

When I look across the room toward the front doors, I nearly faint. My knees go weak and my mouth goes dry.

"Brad?"

"Mila."

"Whaa ... what are you doing here?"

I hate that my voice quavered. After all these years, I never thought I'd see Brad again. On a rare occasion, I'd imagine running into him when I was on the mainland. Those fantasies always involved me coming off pulled-together and very confident. Stammering wasn't in the picture. As it is, I'm lucky my knees are holding me upright. I'm possibly three seconds away from collapsing into a puddle of embarrassment.

"I came to see you because I'm pretty sure you wouldn't take a call. From me, that is. And that's understandable. I'm just ... I want to ... talk."

"To talk?" My voice squeaks out.

I wonder if Ebenezer Scrooge felt like this when the ghosts actually came as predicted. Or, better yet, when Marley, his old partner, showed up in the form of a ghost. I am looking at a ghost of my former partner and I can barely breathe.

The kitchen door opens and shuts. I barely register the soft swoosh and creak. My eyes are locked on Brad, but I feel him—Kai—come up behind me. And before I know it, he's standing so close, the warmth of his body seeping into mine. We've been near one another before, of course, passing in the kitchen, or at times when I insisted on helping him with a repair. This feels different —like finding shelter in a squall.

Then, before I know what is happening, Kai has slipped his arm behind me and around my waist in a move that could only be called possessive. Music streams from down the hall in Noah's bedroom—his favorite Kidz Bop songs motivating him to do the chore he resists most—and I nearly gasp at the thought that his father is in the house and he could stumble out here and find us all here ... Kai with his arm around me, Brad staring at us with a look of confusion.

"Let's take this out onto the porch," Kai suggests in a voice I barely recognize—commanding, unwavering, pure strength.

Brad doesn't say a word. His eyes keep bouncing between me and Kai, and then he says, "Yeah. Okay." and backs out through the front doors.

Kai looks down at me, only shifting his arm the slightest to place his palm on my back. It's been almost seven years since Noah's birth. I was three months pregnant when Brad left. In all that time, no man has touched me, let alone placed his hand on the small of my back in a show of comfort and support. If I thought my knees were weak from the sight of my ex in my inn, the way Kai is touching me right now might be my undoing.

"I'm here, Mila."

That's all Kai says before he softly nudges me and leads me out to face Brad.

I don't know why I lean into Kai. His hand remains on my back as we join Brad on the porch, his strong presence like a pillar. Maybe I should step away, handle this interaction in private, send

Kai off to do whatever single men do when their lives are free of complications like ex-husbands showing up in the middle of an afternoon. But I don't. I cling to Kai, silently, willing him to keep his hand or arm attached to me, as if removing it would sever something vital.

If I had known what Kai would say next, I might have backed away, or done something—anything but stay in his arms, allowing him to act as a buffer between me and Brad. But it's too late. Once the words are out of Kai's mouth, we both have no choice but to barrel forward.

SEVEN

Kai

I could never pretend something I didn't feel.
~ Marilyn Monroe

"Who's this?" Mila's ex asks once the three of us are standing on the porch with the doors shut behind us.

I'm still acutely aware that Noah could come bounding out the doors any moment. I don't know the full story about Mila's ex, except he left her when she was pregnant. Do I really need to know more? Whatever else I might be lacking in details was written on her face when I walked from the kitchen into the main room of the inn.

And now, I'm standing here, with my arm around my friend, facing down the man who abandoned her and Noah, hoping she feels my solidarity.

Only, the way Mila's ex asks that question—*Who's this?*—sets my teeth on edge. He almost seems accusatory and possessive, as if he's been gone on a long trip and returned to find Mila in another man's arms. And something snaps in me. I can't explain it, but my mouth takes on a mind of its own.

"Her boyfriend," I say, staring him down with a look of challenge I feel all the way from the top of my head to the tips of my toes. "Kai."

I extend my hand. "And you are?"

Mila gasps for one brief moment, and I'm not sure if her shock registers with her ex or not, but the way she leans into me tells me I didn't misstep as much as I feared. She needs this—a temporary ruse—someone to stand up to this man who appeared out of nowhere on her property, throwing her for a loop the day after she got so little sleep.

She clears her throat and says, "This is Brad, Kai. My ex."

"My pleasure," I say, extending my hand further toward him until he takes it, which he does, reluctantly.

His eyes continue to dart between me and Mila and then to the spot where my arm is looped around her. I stand firm, holding my friend up, fully committed to this fabrication now that I started it. I'm not one to lie. Most people who know me would define my life as one marked by integrity.

I don't know what came over me. But we're in this now. At least it's only one small fib. As soon as Brad is finished here, we can go back to life as usual. I'll apologize to Mila, and from the way she's still leaning on me like I'd better never let her go, I know she'll get past my overstepping. I did it for her. I'd do anything for her, especially when she's facing something alone or when she's in need.

"I came ..." Brad looks at Mila, obviously trying to ignore the fact that I'm here, intruding on this moment between them. "I came to let you know I'm opening a branch of my business here on the North Shore. And ... well ..." He looks at me and back at Mila. "Do you think we could talk alone?"

"No," I say at the same time Mila does. She finishes her sentence. "Whatever you have to say, you can say in front of Kai."

She glances up at me. I've never seen her so uncertain. Her face, which is usually glowing from time spent in the kitchen or the usual way she busies herself running the inn, looks nearly ashen. Her eyes plead with me.

I smile down at Mila, hoping she can read my unspoken thoughts: *I'm not leaving you.* Then I return my attention to Brad. I don't say anything to him either. I just stare into his eyes, man to man, letting him know he won't be getting time alone with Mila on my watch.

"Okay." Brad lets out a breath. "I want to ... I would like ..." He runs his hand through his hair, looks at me, and then focuses back on Mila. "I want to get to know Noah."

The sentence hangs in the air. Mila stiffens in my arms and I instinctively give her side a squeeze.

"You want ..." Her voice trails off.

"I know. I know."

Brad's face looks contrite. I'll give him that.

"I really was hoping we could sit somewhere to discuss all of this. I have this whole speech ... Not a speech. Just words. I planned to explain myself. Not that there's any excuse. Mila."

He says her name, looking at her like he could dredge up whatever they shared in the past, as if that shared history could erase his absence throughout her pregnancy and the years she's raised their son without him.

"There's no excuse." Mila's voice is colder than I've ever heard it. Detached, but solid.

"I know. I was young and foolish and determined. And angry. If I could take it back, I would. And I should have come sooner. I've wanted to. But I told myself I lost my chance. I chose to walk away. Why would you let me back?" Brad shakes his head and looks off toward the picket fence and down the street leading toward the inn.

I almost pity him for a moment, but then I feel every point of contact between me and Mila. I feel the way she's leaning on me, the way she's barely holding herself up right now.

"I don't know, Brad. This is a blindside," Mila tells him.

"I know," he admits.

"Give me ... time." She pauses and looks up at me. "I need to think about everything."

"I have more to say," Brad offers. "If it will help. I'm not here to interfere in your life. Noah doesn't have to know I'm his dad at first. I'll play by your rules, Mila. I just want a chance."

The man is begging. His previous strength when he challenged my role in Mila's life has shrunk like a deflating balloon.

"I'll think about it. I don't know. I can't make any promises right now," Mila tells Brad.

He nods.

"You should go. Noah's inside. I don't want him to meet you until I have time to think this over."

"Do you have a number where we can reach you?" I ask.

Brad looks at me, his face reflecting the awareness that he's not dealing with Mila alone. I won't keep carrying on as if we're dating after today, but I will support her. She's not alone in this, and I won't let Brad have an inkling of a thought that she is. Not unless she tells me that's what she wants. Then I'll back down and leave her to this. But only if she's the one telling me to.

Brad pulls a card out of his wallet and hands it in our direction. I take it, sending an unspoken message. I hand the card to Mila and she smiles up at me.

"Okay. Well. I'll be going. I'm staying at the Alicante overnight if you need to reach me. I'll take the ferry back to Ventura in the morning."

"Okay," Mila says.

Brad turns and walks down the steps and out to the street. My arm remains securely looped around Mila until he's at least a half block away. Then I drop it and she turns to face me.

"I'm sorry," I blurt at the same time as Mila says, "Thank you."

Then she starts laughing. I look down the road. Brad is no longer in sight.

Mila laughs and laughs. I stand back, arms folded across my

chest, watching her as the adrenaline mixed with the absurdity of my claim wash over her in waves.

Between gulps of air, she says, "Oh my gosh! Kai! My boyfriend!"

"I know." I shake my head. "I'm sorry. I just saw your face ... and him ... and I don't know what happened."

She chuckles, wiping a tear from her eye. "Well, you saved me, as usual."

The front door opens and Noah peeks his head out. "What's so funny, Mom? And why are you out here? The cookie timer is going off. They're going to burn."

"Oh! The cookies! I forgot!" Mila rushes past me into the kitchen and I stay on the porch, questioning my own sanity.

Well, what's done is done. We put up a front. Mila's obviously not mad at me. We can move forward from here. No harm, no foul.

I walk back into the inn, waiting for an opening so I can talk to Mila about what happened. We can clear up what she'll need from me—if anything—going forward with Brad.

Her boyfriend. As if.

I'm lucky to be her friend after that move.

When I push through the kitchen door, Mila's smile is the first thing I see. She's scraping cookies off the baking sheet into the trash.

"Burnt," she announces. "But we have another batch in the oven already, so all is not lost.

"Never leave the kitchen when you've got cookies in the oven," Noah scolds me. "That's what Mom always told me."

"My bad," I tell Noah. "I asked your mom to step outside for a minute. Sorry we burnt the first batch."

"It's okay," he says easily.

I wince at my second lie of the day. Lying to Brad felt justified, mostly. Lying to Noah leaves a bitter taste in my mouth. He trusts me, and I've always given him every reason to believe I'm honest and reliable. It's not like I can tell him the truth right now. But still, the lie makes me squirm—as it should.

Mila's eyes meet mine, soft and warm. I smile back, trying to keep myself from apologizing again—and again and again. *What was I thinking?* She's obviously okay now, thankfully. If you were to take a snapshot of this moment, you'd never know her ex had just shown up on her porch not fifteen minutes ago. And you'd never know she's left wondering whether to allow him to meet his son.

Her strength inspires me, as always. She's resilient and steadfast. I don't think I could find a better woman if I searched the world over. That's why I stood up for her. And I'd do it again, only maybe without the farce next time. I could have just as easily said, *I'm her friend.* But I had to put my foot in it. Maybe "friend" wouldn't have felt like a strong enough line to draw. Something in Mila's vulnerability, the way she looked like she was on the verge of collapsing, made me snap. I don't know if I could have done anything differently. My urge to protect her overrode my good sense.

"Stay for dinner," Mila says, snapping me out of my review of our interaction with Brad.

"Oh. No. That's fine. I just wanted to take a look at the pipes. Everything looks good. I'll let you get to your guests. I can eat at home with Shaka."

"Awww." Noah pouts. "I want you to stay, Unko. Pleeeeease."

Mila glances at me with an unspoken plea nearly as strong as the one on Noah's face. I don't have it in me to turn her down when she looks like that.

"Okay. Okay. I'll stay. If I'm staying, you'd better put me to work. What can I do to help?"

EIGHT
Mila

*It is easier to build strong children
than to repair broken men.*
~ Frederick Douglass

"Okay ... so ... not a rumor." Chloe propels the bench swing, flexing her foot on the porch, swaying us lightly. "Brad's actually here."

Her voice sounds as stunned as I still feel. Even hours after Brad left my property, I'm essentially numb with shock. You know those dreams you wake from, convinced they actually happened? That's my encounter with Brad, only I know I didn't conjure him up in a sleep-induced mirage. He's here, mere miles away, at the resort, right now.

Noah's finally asleep, the dinner dishes are washed, my guests are out on the other side of town or retired to their rooms. Chloe and I are on the porch and I'm reviewing Brad's unexpected appearance with her—minus the detail that Kai said he was my boyfriend. For some reason, I don't want to share the momentary farce we pulled off with my best friend—not yet. Chloe might not

56

understand Kai's motive. And she would, for sure, get all excited and try to push me into making our charade into a reality. She's always been "Team Kai," as she designated her stance a few years ago. There's no "team anyone" I always tell her. I'm team Mila and Noah. That's it.

Not that Kai has any real feelings for me other than friendship. And, while I admire his strong body and beautiful face, and even moreso, his kind heart, subtle sense of humor, and the way he's always here pitching in without even being asked, I can't have romantic feelings for any man, so I don't have any for Kai.

All of those factors haven't changed simply because my ex showed up unannounced this afternoon.

"Have you called him?"

"No! Of course not." I look over at Chloe, who is stifling a laugh at my outburst. "I have to think."

Her face morphs into an expression of soft concern. "Of course you do, but if you don't hear all the details of what Brad wants to say—what he has in mind—you'll still be in the dark. I think you have no choice but to talk to him. Do you want me to go with you? We could go tomorrow after breakfast is served—while Noah is at school."

"I ... don't know."

"Davis is still away through the weekend," Chloe says.

Davis is Chloe's husband. He's a commercial pilot. Their untraditional rhythm of life means she's home alone for days on end, and then Davis reappears as if he's on vacation, filling their home and overtaking her routine day-in and day-out before he takes off again to fly around the world. He's hilarious, larger than life, and ambitious. When Davis is around, you know it. When he isn't, Chloe has this whole other Davis-free life which includes her being fully available to any of her friends at the drop of a hat.

"I know you're right." I curl my legs up onto the bench swing, letting Chloe lull me with the sway of her gentle push-pull on the floorboards of the porch.

"Duh. I'm always right." Chloe winks at me, but her eyes are warm and filled with compassion.

"I really want a Door Number Three. You know?"

"Ah, the elusive third option. Like, if confronting your ex and avoiding your ex weren't the only two paths forward."

"Exactly. I've driven myself half-mad trying to think of another choice all day."

"And?"

"I've got nothing. I have to talk to him. And, while I'd rather phone him, I think we have to meet while he's here. I'll hear him out. I don't have to do anything. Not yet."

"You don't have to do anything ever. I'd like to remind you that you have full custody of Noah. That man, who I was convinced loved you with this earth-shattering love—whom I know you loved deeply—signed off his rights to Noah while you were still pregnant. I still can't get over it. I think you've moved on more completely than I have, and I wasn't even the one he abandoned."

Chloe stares at the other end of the porch as if an outdoor movie screen just unfurled to replay the demise of my marriage frame by frame.

"He left," Chloe says in a monotone voice. "I didn't even recognize who Brad was after you told him you were pregnant. It was this whole other side to him I never would have expected." Then she turns to me and her whole demeanor transforms to something far more determined. She's all mama bear when she says, "That's a done deal. He doesn't have a say in anything where you and Noah are concerned. The ball is one hundred percent in your court."

I shut my eyes, allowing the evening breeze coming in off the beach to caress my cheeks and blow strands of my hair around my face. I don't even lift a finger to swipe the errant wisps away. My breath is steady and purposeful. I need to stay in the moment. It's too easy to run ahead down one hundred rabbit trails of thought ... What if Brad starts to dominate our lives? What will Noah think? How will I adapt? What will change? What if Brad wants me too, not just a connection with Noah? ... Instead of indulging my anxious inner ramblings, I allow the island to calm me: the sweet night air, the occasional sound of a gull, the distant roll of the waves a few blocks down at the beach.

I am here. I am safe. I can do this—whatever it is—one step at a time.

Chloe sits quietly, giving me space to process my thoughts.

"Okay." I dig my phone out of my pocket and sit upright. "I'm going to text him."

"Do you want me to text for you?"

"No. I've got this. I just want you on standby afterward, in case I'm ... I don't even know."

"You've always got me—before, during, or after you see him. I'm here, Mila."

I'm here, Mila.

Kai said those exact words before we faced Brad together. I feel the corners of my mouth turn up in a soft smile when I remember the way Kai placed his arm around me, the way he stood next to me like a tower of strength—a shelter from the storm.

I shake my head. Then I pull out the business card Brad gave Kai, enter the number into my contacts, and type out a message.

> Mila: I can meet tomorrow morning after Noah is at school. I'll come to the resort. We can meet in the restaurant off the lobby— Horizons.

Not even five seconds pass before my phone buzzes with a reply.

> Brad: Thank you. I appreciate this more than you know. Does 9:00 work?

Mila: 9:00 works.

The reply dots show on my screen and disappear a few times. Nothing more comes through, so I pocket my phone and look over at Chloe.

"We're meeting at nine in the morning."

"You are so brave, girlfriend. I'm in awe of you, as always."

I yawn, feeling the full impact of this day in one fell swoop. Chloe takes that as her cue to stand.

"I'll be on standby. My phone will be on and in my hand or pocket all morning. Just text me at any point and I'll show up, or call me after you two meet, or whatever. But don't ghost me, or I'll hunt you down." She points at me to emphasize how serious she is about that last declaration.

I smile up at her, and then I stand, extending my arms. When she pulls me to her, I collapse into a much-needed hug from my best friend.

"Thank you."

"You're kidding, right? This is what we do."

"Still ..." I mumble over Chloe's shoulder while she continues to hold me tight. "There aren't words for what you mean to me. So, thanks."

Chloe starts humming *Bridge Over Troubled Water*, and I try not to smile, but I can't help myself. We sang that song for our seventh grade talent show, and, to put it bluntly, we stunk. Badly. Like, if that had been a week Simon Cowell was staying on Marbella, he would have been pushing all four Xs and saying things in his condescending British accent like, "That was abysmal," and "Worst singers in the world," or "I would have rather listened to a shrieking banshee. You two have given me a headache."

I can actually sing. Chloe cannot. But in junior high, singing a heartfelt hippy ballad was not in my wheelhouse—at all.

Chloe pulls back from our hug, her eyes dancing with mirth as she shifts from humming to singing—no—*belting* out the chorus. She's like a drunken sailor—a tone deaf sailor who privately hit the stowed casks of rum, and is crooning to anyone and everyone about how she'll lay herself down like a bridge across the troubled waters of their lives. When she forgets a word, she just improvises, which only serves to add to the absurdity that is my best friend.

When she inserts my name into the song, "Oh, Mila, I'm a bridge! I'm your bridge ..." I can't help myself. I snort. Then we both devolve into a much needed fit of laughter.

I half whisper, "You'll wake Noah, or my guests."

To which Chloe answers, "I'm a bridge, baby!"

Which only makes me snort again—more proof that I am so beyond being dating material for anyone, which is super-A-okay by me. I've got everyone I need in my life. The last thing I need is a man to complicate matters.

Chloe and I laugh with tears coming out of our eyes. Every time I start to regain my composure, she belts out a new line of the song, hamming it up on purpose. And I double over, gasping for breath, eyes squinted and my whole face aching with the best sort of strain from smiling too hard.

My bestie, ladies and gentlemen. I hit the jackpot.

After spending far too long staring into my closet trying to decide what to wear today, I make my way downstairs to prepare breakfast for our guests and Noah.

My outfit hopefully says, *I'm a confident woman who has moved on with her life and is rocking her role as an innkeeper and single mother.* If outfits can talk, that is. I'm wearing a cream-on-cream blouse that has layers of soft fabric with a sheer overlay, embossed with flowers and butterflies. I paired that with dark jeans and wedge sandals.

After I dressed, I pulled my hair up, but then let it fall back down. Then up. Then down, and then I looked myself in the eyes in my mirror and gave myself the kind of pep talk I give Noah when he's about to do something new or scary.

After breakfast, Phyllis shows up to walk Noah to school. I don't mention my plans for the day. If Phyllis knew I was meeting Brad, I might not make it out the door. I certainly would not make it out alone. "Flora" would call Fauna and Merriweather, and I would have a whole blue-pink-blue-pink fiasco on my hands. Those three bicker over me when situations threaten my wellbeing, and they often do it as if I'm not even in the room. They'd insist on coming along to protect me, or even to talk to Brad. We'd invariably be asked to leave the resort property, possibly thrown out, depending on how far things went. Nope. I'm not talking to my aunts until after I speak with Brad alone.

And now, I'm walking into the Alicante, through the grand double doors, across the marble floor, past palms and the airy decor that says refined beach affluence. I smooth my hands down my thighs as if I'm going on a blind date instead of meeting the man who ripped my heart out seven and a half years ago. My heart beats so rapidly, you'd think I ran here instead of driving the inn's golf cart. I glance toward the restaurant just as my phone buzzes with a text.

Chloe: No need to answer. I just wanted to send you this.

A GIF of a bridge over a raging stream comes through and I smile a private smile, even chuckling softly to myself. Leave it to Chloe to make me laugh when everything feels heavy and daunting.

I'm too flustered to notice him at first, but then my mind catches up to the fact that Brad is standing just outside Horizons waving nervously at me. He's wearing pressed jeans and a dry-fit shirt that shows off his affinity for exercise. His blond hair is styled. He used to look so carefree and confident. A typical island boy, without a care in the world except when and where the biggest swells were hitting.

Today, Brad's brows are drawn up. He's not smiling, but he's watching me intently as I approach him—this man whom I thought I'd spend forever with. The first guy I kissed. My first everything. My only everything.

I take a cleansing breath just before I reach him.

"Good morning, Mila. You look beautiful."

I shake my head. "Don't. Okay? Let's just keep this focused on Noah."

"Okay." Brad nods lightly, his lips forming a pensive line.

He makes the instinctual move to place his hand on my back to guide me into the restaurant and I almost let him before I realize what I'm doing and sidestep his gesture. He looks down at his own arm quizzically, as if it popped out to lead me of its own volition.

The hostess grabs two menus and walks us to a table near the back of the second room where it's secluded and quiet. I'm immediately grateful. I hadn't considered the potential of bumping into other islanders inside the resort. If Brad and I are seen together, people will talk.

"So," he says, taking the seat adjacent to mine.

"So," I echo.

I pull my napkin onto my lap and study the menu, even though it may as well be written in Sanskrit right now. The words blur and I finally give up, setting it to the side of my place setting.

"So," Brad says, again, mirroring me and laying his menu down. "I know I threw you off showing up unannounced yesterday. I'm sorry."

"It's fine. I mean ... yes. You did. But I'm here now. You said you had a speech ... or words ... something more to say?"

My hands begin wringing my napkin under the table and I will them to flatten on my lap, one over the other.

"I ..." Brad stares at me. His Adam's apple bobs. "I can't really explain what happened ... back then. I was young. Stupid. Selfish. Afraid." Brad purses his lips and scrunches his brow in. "There aren't enough adjectives to describe the foolishness of a man who can't celebrate ... or at least man up when his wife announces she's pregnant." Brad looks down into his lap. Then he lifts his chin and our eyes lock. "I wish I could take it all back, Mila. I would, in a heartbeat. If I could go back, I would grab younger me and shake him."

He's so familiar. Different, but the same. And the parts of him I fell for are still here, only so much has changed. Irreparably altered by his choice.

I'm unsure what's keeping me glued to my chair. I could jump up and dash out of the restaurant, straight through the double doors and out into the salty air. My lungs feel tight, this room too small. I've neatly shut the door to the past like a linen cabinet after the towels are warm and folded from the dryer. In less than twenty-four hours, Brad has single-handedly yanked the cupboard open, tearing through haphazardly, leaving everything strewn helter-skelter.

There were months, maybe even a year total, when I would have done anything to hear Brad say the words tumbling out of his mouth right now. But at some point, shortly after Noah was born, I made a decision. Any man who couldn't find it in himself to stay and support his new wife and son didn't deserve me. And he sure didn't deserve Noah.

I'd never classify Brad as a mean person. Even the day he left me, the only unkindness between us were his repeated declarations of suspicion—as if I had tricked him by purposely getting pregnant. As if I would ever do something so underhanded. Before that season of our shared life, Brad was always upbeat, adventurous and generous. He and Davis were close and the two of them were known for being the life of the party, but also for being the kind of men you only hoped to spend your life with. And Chloe and I thought we had won the guy-lottery, both dating such unattainable boys in high school, and then going on to marry them just after we graduated college.

Brad meant it when he said he never wanted kids. I'm not sure what made him so staunch on that point. He had a loving family and a decent childhood. To me, those are the key elements in causing someone to naturally want a family of their own. So, even though we had agreed we wouldn't have kids—we'd run the inn and travel, unencumbered—I guess I always thought we were somewhat open to the option if it happened to come our way. We weren't trying, but we weren't so bitterly opposed to children that we would tear our marriage apart over a pregnancy. Or, so I thought.

I never wanted to rope Brad into something he didn't feel ready for, and I surely wasn't going to beg him to stay.

A question has been buzzing in my brain ever since Brad showed up at my inn yesterday. So, I finally take a breath and ask, "What made you wait? You could have come back anytime." My voice tightens. "You stayed away over seven years. Seven years, Brad." The tone of accusation makes both of us flinch.

I don't apologize. He's the one who left. I have the right to ask. I forgave him. That doesn't mean he has an open door to return into our lives—or even just into Noah's. Who am I kidding? If Brad is in Noah's life, by default he'll be in mine.

He lets out a long breath before he attempts to explain. "I know this is going to sound ludicrous. It's like the time we skipped school in tenth grade. And then I talked you into skipping just one more day because the weather was beyond perfect and I wanted time alone with you. After that first day, you were determined to go back and act like nothing had happened. But after a second day passed, and then I convinced you to take one more day to lay on the beach and kayak instead of going into school, it felt awkward and nearly impossible to casually return to all our classes. We did go, of course, but the fear mounted exponentially with each hour we stayed away. The excuses as to why we missed a half a week seemed increasingly flimsy the longer we allowed ourselves to be truant."

His eyes search mine. "I didn't realize the magnitude of my decision at first—leaving the two of you like I did. I felt justified. I honestly believed you had tricked me."

My face must reflect what I'm about to say because Brad rushes in to say, "I know you didn't trick me, Mila. I was so lost and foolish ... confused and upset. That's how I felt at first. But the more time I stayed away, the more I thought about you and the fact that we had a child—our child. And then I realized how badly I had messed up by abandoning you to raise Noah alone. I knew I couldn't just waltz back into your life. So I threw myself into building my business. And, the more time passed, the harder it became to reach out or come back. But I thought about you—and Noah—every day."

"Brad ..." I start, but he keeps talking.

"I know I lost you. I realize that was my own doing. And I never got to know Noah. And that's my fault too."

Brad's face contorts and his eyes glass over with unshed tears. He clears his throat.

"It's crazy what can trigger a person. About six months ago, a man came into one of my stores to pick up an elliptical. He was dressed in a coaching uniform. Guys like him come in all the time. And they sometimes bring their kids. This wasn't a first. But the man had his son with him—his seven-year-old son—and they were laughing and talking about baseball while one of my employees rang them up. A thought slammed me as if someone had actually socked me in the gut: *That could be me and Noah.* I had to go back into the storeroom before I lost it right there in front of the customer and my employees."

The waitress arrives at our table before I can respond. Not that I know what to say. I don't have the first clue as to how to navigate any of this.

"Are you ready to order?"

"Uh. Yeah. Yes." Brad picks up his menu again.

He looks at me.

I hand the waitress my menu. "Just water for me. Thanks."

"Are you sure?" Brad asks me.

"Yeah. I already ate—at the inn."

"Of course. Okay. Well ..." He looks at the waitress. "Just coffee, black. And an avocado toast on whole grain bread. Make it an egg white scramble, please."

I smile faintly, remembering how diligent Brad always was about his diet. In everything else he was very in-the-moment and easy-going, but when it came to fitness, he was determined and regimented.

"What is it you want now?" I ask, smoothing one of my hands over the other in my lap to still the trembling. "You can't just introduce yourself as Noah's dad. He has a life—routines. He's used to the people around him. He doesn't know you. You don't know him."

"I get all of that. I don't know, Mila. I just ... I want to get to know him. If you'll let me."

I look out toward the lobby. People are milling about, coming into the resort to get away from the heaviness and responsibility of life. Others are checking out, refreshed from a stay in paradise. Here we sit, a study in contrasts, two people who used to be in love, trying to navigate a situation that has no manual or guide book. The weight of our reality presses in on us despite our luxurious surroundings.

"I need to think about this," I tell Brad.

"Of course. I expected you would."

"And, you're opening a business here? Why here?" Again, my tone sounds accusatory and defensive. It's a foreign sound compared to my usual way of approaching people. Even during our breakup, I never yelled or raised my voice at Brad. It's just not in me.

"I love Marbella. It was my childhood home. And the market is good here for watersports. People come here to the island for vacation. Others live here part-time or full-time. People need watersports equipment. There's the shack at the resort, but what if someone wants to buy something—to have a stand up paddleboard to ride every day in the cove? What if they want to learn to surf, and they don't want to pay lesson fees and rental fees every day. I'm filling a need in a place I love. And ... if you give me a chance, I'll be closer to Noah. It will be easier for me to spend time with him."

"And if I don't?"

"If you don't, I'll hire a manager to run the shop here and I'll spend more time on the mainland."

"Just like that?"

"Yes. Just like that."

I nod. My head is swimming and I don't feel any closer to a decision than I did when I woke up this morning, but I do have more information.

Brad's toast and coffee arrive. I sit with him while he finishes eating. He tries to make small talk, asking about the inn and about my three fairy godmothers. He even refers to my aunts that way, reminding me how deeply entrenched and entangled our lives were so many years ago—how well he knew me, better than anyone. I answer him politely. I don't ask him any personal questions. When he's finished eating, he pays the bill and we walk out into the lobby.

NINE

Kai

A lie leads a man from a grove into a jungle.
~ Marcelene Cox

I'm leaving my meeting with the other resort managers when I see someone out of the corner of my eye. At first, I think my mind is playing tricks on me. A second glance tells me I'm right. Mila's standing in front of Horizons with ... Brad?

Before I can think through my actions, my feet are moving in her direction.

I should probably turn and walk away, but I feel drawn to her —to make sure she's okay. Maybe I'm also a little curious. Why would they be at breakfast together when Brad believes I'm Mila's boyfriend? I'm not, but a strange rush of possessiveness fills me anyway. Mila's my friend. I replay the way Brad disarmed her yesterday. Thoughts of how it felt to be the man who stood by Mila follow close on the heels of that flashback. She needed me then, maybe she needs me now.

"Kai?" Shaw, the manager of guest services, calls my name.

"I'll catch up with you later," I shout over my shoulder.

And then I'm across the lobby, standing in front of Mila and Brad.

"Hey," Mila says, a look of confusion crossing her features.

"Hi. I was just in a meeting. Managers. All the resort managers. We meet once a week."

"Oh, yes. Your meeting."

Mila acts like she knows about it. Of course she does. We're supposedly dating. She would know these things.

"Right. Yeah. My meeting. That's the one. The meeting. Of managers. Weekly. The one you know about." *Shuuuuttt up, Kai.*

I smile, hoping it covers the stream of words that just erupted out of me like word lava from an over-informative volcano.

Mila's eyes flare momentarily wide. And then she's nodding repetitively like a bobble-head version of herself.

"Yep," she says, smiling at me. "That's right. Your weekly managers' meeting."

A laugh starts to bubble up at the absurdity of this moment, but then I glance at Brad and remember the depth of what Mila's up against. She needs me. I can't mess this up for her.

I take a cleansing breath and steel my features.

"Good to see you again, Kai," Brad extends his hand, looking far more confident and at home with Mila than he did yesterday when he blindsided her.

I nod at him, not taking his hand at first, but then I do when he continues to hold it out to me.

"So, uh ..." I don't even know what to say.

"We were just talking about Brad's request," Mila informs me. "About Noah."

She surprises me, stepping away from his side and moving over so she's next to me. In a moment of genius or stupidity, I'm not sure which, I wrap my arm around Mila and place a soft kiss on her temple.

She smells like coffee and cinnamon and her familiar warmth —*home.*

The kiss is for show, of course, but the moments my lips meet her skin, I'm thrown off. It's been a long, long time since I kissed anyone. Kissing Mila feels different. Probably because of my dry spell. I shake all those thoughts and force myself to focus on the situation at hand.

"You okay?" I murmur into Mila's hair, truly wanting to know, but also fully committed to this unexpected encore of our farce.

Mila looks up at me. "Yeah. I am. I'm okay now."

My head swims. Is she okay now because she talked with Brad, or because I showed up? Or is she just saying that to make our play-acting seem more convincing?

Brad looks between the two of us. His face is inscrutable. I'm sure it's not easy for him to see his ex-wife in someone else's arms, but I'm not here as his therapist or emotional support animal. I'm here for Mila, and apparently my loyalty to her will take me to great lengths—ones I never imagined I'd be capable of or willing to go to.

"So, I'd better ... pack," Brad says, still looking from me to Mila, to the point where my arm rests behind her back.

"Okay," Mila says, and I think she sinks into me just a little more when she says it. "I'll be in touch."

"Thank you."

Brad steps forward like he's going to hug Mila, but when she remains tucked into my side, he steps back, running his hand through his styled hair.

"Okay. I'll be hearing from you then."

"Yes. I don't know when," Mila tells Brad. "I'll text you when I've had time to process everything."

Her voice is steady, but I feel a slight tremble running through her, so I give her a gentle squeeze of assurance on her waist where my hand is resting.

"Sounds good." Brad quickly gives us a curt nod and then he turns and walks toward the bank of elevators on the other side of the lobby.

Mila and I stand together, unflinching, until Brad is safely inside an elevator. Then, I drop my arm.

Just like yesterday, I apologize, and at the same moment the word, "Sorry," comes out of my mouth, Mila says, "Thank you."

"I probably should have left the two of you alone."

"No. It actually couldn't have been better timing. It was fine —meeting with him, I mean. But I was nervous and jittery the whole time. Seeing you helped. Having you here settled my nerves. So, thank you. You're a good friend, Kai. I appreciate you."

"Anytime," I assure her. "I told you I'm here for you. Only, I didn't mean to extend our charade."

"I know. Neither did I. But honestly, I don't mind Brad thinking I'm taken. He says he only wants time with Noah, but he doesn't even know Noah. And ... Well, anyway, I just feel better knowing he thinks I'm not an option right now."

The way she paused makes me think there was something else she was going to say before she thought better of it. Did Brad give her the impression he's here to reconnect with her too?

"I don't mind filling that spot for you. It's harmless. It's not like we're telling a bunch of people we're dating. Just your ex. Consider me tribute."

Mila laughs. It's a sweet sound, especially after how tense she obviously was from having to meet with Brad.

"Well, I'd better get back to the inn. I have a couple checking out midday and another couple checking in for the weekend this afternoon."

"Yeah. I have to get to the watersports shack too. How's the water running in the kitchen?"

"Perfect. You saved the day, as always."

"Glad to help."

Mila smiles at me, and then we start walking together toward the main entrance of the lobby.

When we're outside, Mila turns to me. "Oh! I nearly forgot. Were you serious about surfing lessons for Noah this weekend?"

"Of course. If we've got your stamp of approval."

"It's all he's talking about. If I bring him by once I finish cleaning up from breakfast tomorrow, would that work?"

"Around ten?"

"Yes. If that's okay."

"I can't wait."

Mila smiles again, and this time it's the smile I'm used to seeing on her beautiful face—not one tainted by the intrusion of her ex-husband.

We part ways at the street, me crossing to step onto the beach leading toward the watersports dock, and Mila walking to the golf cart corral to retrieve her own cart so she can drive back to the inn.

I'm not even halfway to the dock when my phone vibrates with a text.

> Shaw: You and Mila, huh? Can't say I'm surprised.

I stop dead in my tracks. It's one thing to have to pull off a farce for Brad. He won't even be on the island after today, as far as I know. If I tell Shaw the truth, and somehow it leaks to Brad that Mila and I are not actually dating … that would be a disaster. Does Shaw know Brad? They both grew up on Marbella. It's a small enough community. The odds are good that they attended high school together at the very least.

Mila and I are going to need to talk.

I pocket my phone and head to work, my mind preoccupied with who else may have seen us. I was careless. All strategic thinking left my mind as soon as I saw Mila and Brad together outside Horizons. I should have kept my distance. But it's too late now. We'll just have to troubleshoot and hope Shaw was the only one paying attention to our little display.

Instead of walking straight to the shack, I turn, strolling toward the water's edge. I'm in a pair of dress slacks and a button down shirt. These meeting days are the one time each week I dress in anything but board shorts and a surf T-shirt. I shuck my loafers and stuff my socks inside them, letting the shoes dangle from my hand as the sand slips between my toes, grounding me. Staring out at the horizon, I try to consider the best course forward. I don't want to burden Mila. I'd rather come to her with some idea of what we ought to do and what we need to tell Shaw.

I stand there, letting the foam drift over my toes and back out to sea repeatedly for probably fifteen or twenty minutes. Before I walk over to the shack, I pull my phone out and send Mila a text.

> Kai: Are you free around lunchtime?

> Mila: Yes. Is everything okay?

I wish I had the answer to that question.

> Kai: Everything's fine. I just need to run something by you.

> Mila: Come on over. I'll make you a sandwich. I just whipped up chicken salad and I have fresh fruit.

> Kai: You don't have to feed me.

> Mila: I don't mind. Besides, I owe you from the kitchen sink repair. And don't say I don't owe you.

> Kai: You don't owe me. But I'll gladly take one of your chicken salad sandwiches.

> Mila: Stubborn man. ;) And I'm glad you'll let me cook for you. See you in a few.

> Kai: See you then.

I stroll across the sand, smiling. Between Mila and me, I'm sure we'll figure out how to handle Shaw witnessing us in the lobby.

When I open the door to the watersports shack, Ben is behind the cash register.

"Something you want to share with the class?!" he asks, an impish expression on his face.

"What? What are you talking about?"

"You and Mila. I thought that should happen. You kept telling me it would never. All that talk about only being friends. Well, I'm glad for you—for both of you. She's a catch, and you're good for her. You two have a solid friendship to build from. My mom always said that was the best way to build a romance. Not that I listened. I had to go all rogue and try to date my enemy ... but this isn't about me and Summer. It's about you. And Mila. Man, Noah's going to be over the moon about this."

Ben's babbling rapid-fire and grinning like he's never been so deliriously happy. Each word out of his mouth feels like a BB pelting my skin.

"Whoa. What?"

"Sorry. Does Noah not know? I assumed he would, but of course you might be keeping this quiet from him for a while. You'll want to put some time into this before you rock his world. I get it. Just say the word and my lips are sealed, bro."

"Uh. No. No. Noah doesn't know." *Whaaaaaat?* I quickly amend that. "Because we're not dating. Officially, that is. We are still friends. And we're not dating. Because we're friends."

"Friends can date."

"Well, we aren't."

"Uh huh. Huh. That doesn't add up."

"And why is that, exactly?"

"Welp. Bree at the front desk just called over to tell me she saw you and Mila and some guy outside Horizons. She wanted to see if I knew anything. According to her, you put your arm around Mila. And then you kissed her temple. And then your arm remained around Mila while the three of you—Mila, you, and this unknown guy—talked. From what Bree said, it all looked very much like you and Mila are together."

"She what? Bree? Who is Bree?"

"She's a girl who works at guest services, but mostly the front desk end of things. I met her through Cam. She's been to your barbecues before."

Note to self: stop hosting barbecues.

"Well, she's wrong. Mistaken. She's mistaken."

"So you didn't have your arm around Mila? You didn't kiss her temple?"

"Why would a front desk hostess call back here to let you know what she saw in the lobby, anyway?"

"Are you kidding me right now?" Ben looks seriously confused.

"No. Not at all."

"It's like the Pony Express. News, my friend. News. This is the way we spread it."

"News?"

Ben just nods. "So, confirm or deny. Did you have your arm around Mila? And, did you kiss her face?"

"That's out of context. And ... we're at work ... so, I'm done talking."

Ben cups his hands in front of his mouth and announces, "That would be a yes, ladies and gents. Kai Kapule did, actually, have his arm around Mila Mitchell. And he placed a loving kiss on her temple, like the doting boyfriend he is."

No one is here to hear Ben's ridiculousness, but I still find myself telling him to be quiet.

"Bro, calm down. We're not dating."

"So, it's under wraps. Gotcha." Ben makes a zipping motion across his lips, but his eyes crinkle with amusement. "Sort of a secret relationship? Clandestine meetings? You throwing pebbles at her window at night?"

"She lives on the first floor of the inn." I nearly roll my eyes.

"And you know this because ..."

"Because I'm over there doing repairs at least once a week."

"Which was the way ... you ... fell ... for ... her." He emphasizes each word, punctuating them with an infuriating smile. "It all makes sense now: Why you weren't into Gemma. I see it all. And, don't worry, Kai. I won't tell anyone. I won't even tell Bree what I know. Or Kalaine or Bodhi. I'll be like a vault."

For one ridiculous, out-of-my-ever-loving-mind moment, I consider telling Ben everything. But that moment passes, and I come to my senses. The only person I can talk to about this is Mila.

"How about you inventory those snorkel sets that came in yesterday and add them to the stock list online." I give Ben my serious boss face.

"Gotcha, loverboy." Ben makes that zipping motion across his lips again while wagging his eyebrows playfully at me.

Normally, I'd be amused. This is how we roll out here. We prank one another. We tease. We basically act like junior high boys with one another half the time, only the more grown-up version. If this situation with Mila's ex weren't so serious and concerning, and our need to fake a relationship weren't growing faster than a rash from a man-o-war, I'd be laughing too.

At least I'm getting away for lunch.

Mila and I definitely need to talk.

TEN

Mila

The biggest fool is the one who
thinks they have fooled everyone.
~ Unknown

I'm placing lettuce in the homemade chicken salad croissant sandwich I'm making for Kai when the front door opens and closes. Kai's in the doorway of the kitchen moments later, looking slightly frazzled. He's changed out of the dress pants he had on this morning into shorts and a T-shirt. His dark hair is mussed, as if he's been running his hands through it. He places a palm on the back of his neck and fixes his gaze on me before walking further into the kitchen.

"Did you eat?" he asks me.

"Not yet. But don't worry about me. Here. Sit." I point to one of the stools around the island.

"Thanks. Please, make yourself something and join me. You know I don't like eating alone, and you need lunch."

I consider resisting him, but then I think better of it. "Okay," I say with a smile. "If you insist."

"I do."

Kai doesn't take a bite of his sandwich until mine is made and I'm seated across from him. When he finally does dig in, he smiles over at me. "This is delicious. Everything you make has that special something about it. I don't know how you do it."

"It's just a family recipe."

"Nope. It's you."

I feel myself blush slightly. I've never been great about accepting compliments, and with the recent increase in touches from Kai ... and especially that unexpected kiss to my temple this morning, his words hit me in a different way. A good way—like a cup of hot cinnamon tea on the porch swing at night, or the first firework over the water on the Fourth of July.

"Did you come over here just to make me squirm under your compliments, Kai?" My voice is meant to come across teasing, but there's an airiness to it that surprises me.

Kai's face grows serious. "No. Actually, we need to talk."

"Okaaaay. Is everything alright?"

"Mostly. I'm sure it is. It's just ..." Kai looks over at me, setting his sandwich down and running his hand through his hair, mussing it up even more.

Then Kai goes on to tell me about Shaw texting him and Ben's teasing because an employee at the front desk called to gossip about seeing us outside Horizons. I sit quietly, listening to Kai. My mind whirls. I didn't intend for him to declare himself my boyfriend in front of Brad in the first place, but up until this moment, the farce seemed harmless and helpful. If I can keep Brad from thinking I'm available, it will simplify things if I allow him into Noah's life, which I will have to do somehow. He is Noah's father, after all.

But now, people are talking. Granted, they are people at the resort, which is on the other side of the island, but news here travels. It's one of the reasons I've avoided actually dating all these years.

"Does Shaw know Brad?" Kai asks.

"They went to high school together. We all did."

"That's what I was afraid of."

"Okay. So." I start to say something definitive, to offer up an idea as to how we can move forward, but I come up blank. So, I just look at Kai, hoping he's got an idea even though I'm at a loss.

"I've been thinking about this for the past two hours." Kai reaches over and places his hand on top of mine.

My eyes drift down to where his light golden skin engulfs mine. It's not like Kai and I never touch. We occasionally bump into one another when we're working on a project together. We've hugged. He's nudged me playfully. But this touch is one of comfort, and it reminds me too much of what it felt like to be nestled into his side, held up by him when my world was falling apart.

"I think we can go about this a few different ways," Kai says. "And we ought to think through each option and the ramifications if we choose that course of action. Then, maybe, the way forward will be clear."

"Sounds logical."

He gives my hand a gentle squeeze and returns to eating his sandwich.

"First," he says. "The obvious option. We can call this off, clear things up with Shaw and Ben, and move forward like nothing happened. I'd just text Shaw and say, 'Mila and I are not together. I was just helping her talk to Brad.' And then I'd tell Ben, 'Mila and I really aren't dating. Trust me.' To be fair, knowing Ben, he won't buy it at first, but over time, when he saw us still acting as friends, he would."

"Okay. Yeah. That sounds good."

"Does it?"

It's funny Kai should ask that, because something in me feels ... disappointed? Why? I should feel relieved that we'd be calling our farce off and ending it sooner than later. I'm smart enough to know any lie breeds lies. And those lies breed lies. This would be no different, would it?

Maybe it's just that the words, *call this off*, sound too much like a break up, and I don't relish the idea of anything that involves losing Kai. Not that I'd be losing him. He's right here. He'll still be my friend like he's always been.

"Yeah. I think so," I finally say. "What's the downside to this option? It seems the most direct and obvious."

"Right. Well, the main downside is Brad. You said this morning that you liked the idea of him thinking you were attached to someone. Do you need to put up a front with him?"

The question feels intimate. I don't usually talk about my marriage, not even with Chloe. I shut the door and moved forward years ago. But now it's all right in my face, demanding attention since Brad showed up and rocked the foundation of the life I've built for Noah and myself with one simple request—to see his son.

"He hasn't said as much, but I know Brad. Maybe I'm crazy ..."

"You're not. Trust your instincts, Mila. You were married to the man. You do know him. Is he interested in more than seeing Noah? Is this whole thing possibly a ploy to get to see you too?"

"I don't know if I'd go as far as to say it's a ploy, but he told me I looked beautiful this morning."

"You did."

Kai comments on my appearance like he's observing the weather. *There's a storm blowing in. Also, you looked beautiful.* But something in me thrills at his compliment. What woman wouldn't? Here's an attractive, kind man, sitting alone with me in my kitchen telling me I looked beautiful. Anyone would feel goosebumps and a little flip in their belly. It's natural.

"To answer you," I steer us back to the point at hand. "I'm not sure. He seemed like he regretted letting me go. He said things like, *I think about you every day.*"

"He said he thinks about you every day."

"I think so. Yeah. Sorry. My brain was so overwhelmed and I

was full of nerves. It's hard to recall the exact words he used. But, yes. He said that."

"Mila." Kai's hand slips across the table and over mine again. "A man doesn't tell a woman he's thinking about her daily unless she's on his mind. Brad never got over you."

Kai's expression is serious. "Take it from a man. When a woman gets under our skin, we're determined. And we'll play the long game to win her back. From what you're telling me, Brad may want to connect with Noah. I'm not second-guessing his motives in that area. But there's no doubt he's got ideas about seeing you again, maybe even reunification."

"That's not happening." My tone is forceful, absolute.

Kai grins. "Okay, tiger." He chuckles.

I shake my head and drop my gaze to the plate in front of me. "Sorry. I'm just never getting back with Brad. It's not an option. He ..." I blink, unsure where the tears are suddenly coming from. When I look up, Kai has the most compassionate look on his face. His amber eyes search mine. He gives my hand a reassuring squeeze. "He left me, Kai. When I was pregnant."

We sit quietly. Kai doesn't press me. His hand remains over mine, like an anchor—a soft, warm, strong anchor.

"I forgive him. I forgave him a long time ago."

"I know you did. It's one of your most remarkable traits. You are very forgiving and so hospitable. Those qualities go hand in hand. You open yourself up to people easily—and you make them feel wanted and welcome."

I search his eyes. He's so sincere. We've been friends for almost four years, but Kai's usually here on business, checking up on me, on the inn. This is the most personal conversation we've ever had. It could feel awkward, but instead, I feel safe.

"Thank you."

My voice is soft, still soaked in the emotions of talking about Brad, and also these unusual reactions I'm having to my friend right now. Obviously, this fake dating thing has played with my head, and Brad's appearance has made me more vulnerable and emotional.

"So, you may need a beard. Is that what they call it?" Kai strokes his chin. "Because I'm all about the beard."

"Oh my gosh!" I bust out laughing. "Kai!"

"What?" he plays it up, flexing his biceps and then slowly dragging one hand through his thick, dark hair. "I'm a great beard. What guy has a chance against all this?"

I giggle. Like a flipping schoolgirl. What in the world has come over me? This is *Kai*—my friend. I've just never seen him turn on the charm like this. It's a bit disarming.

As if he didn't just put on that show, Kai's voice turns serious. "If you need Brad to keep thinking you are in a relationship, this gets trickier, but not impossible."

"I really don't want to lie."

"I'm not a fan of dishonesty either. Not at all. You know that. But desperate times ..." Kai pauses. "Would Brad accept it if you told him you were unavailable?"

"Honestly, I don't know. I think, knowing Brad, he'd feign acceptance, maybe he'd even convince himself he was fine with it, but he'd start to push his luck."

"And how do you feel about that?"

"Exhausted." The mere thought of having to fend off Brad's possible advances while navigating how to let him into Noah's life wears me out so much I want to walk down the hall and curl up in a ball on my bed.

"Well, that settles it. We have to keep pretending. It's a protection for you—one you need."

"Are you sure?"

"I'm sure. Besides, I don't think I can stand by while that guy tries to reconnect with you. So far, both times I've seen him with you I went into some sort of automatic reaction."

I smile. I'm as pro-woman as the next gal. But I'm not going to lie. A man who gets feral when he sees me struggling and in need of support? That might just be my kryptonite. I loved both times Kai stepped in to protect me from Brad. He didn't overstep or treat me like I couldn't handle myself. He just came alongside me with a strength I lacked in the moment.

"I noticed that automatic reaction," I smile. "Kai in caveman mode. Watch out, ladies." My comment is meant to be teasing.

Kai's eyes darken momentarily, his pupils nearly swallowing the amber of his irises. He clears his throat.

"Okay. So. We'd better get a game plan together," he suggests. His tone is all business now.

"Yes. A game plan. Right."

I take a bite of my croissant. "We need drinks."

"It's not even one o'clock," Kai teases.

"Ha. How about some sweet tea? Or I made strawberry lemonade?"

"I'd love some of your lemonade."

I pour Kai a lemonade and myself an iced tea, and rejoin him at the island.

"So, if we are going to pull this off for Brad, ideally, we could wait until he comes back," Kai says. "If no one else knew, we'd be able to put our charade on ice. But it's complicated now that Shaw and Ben and this wahine, Bree, all know."

Kai lapses into Hawaiian terms when he's upset or nervous. I've watched this over the years. It's pretty darn cute, and I'll never call him on it, just like I never called Noah on saying bisgetti. I knew he'd outgrow it, and it tickled me every time he'd say it. Kai won't outgrow this habit, and I'm secretly glad of that.

"Right," I agree, taking a sip of my tea.

"So, we can play it by ear?" He says it half as a question and half as a statement.

"What would that look like? And we have to think of Noah."

"Of course. Noah comes first. Always. I'm just thinking, I only really see Shaw once a week. I don't even know Bree. Ben said I just need to tell him to zip it and he will. He actually used that motion so much when we were talking I wanted to reach over and see if I could find an invisible zipper to make him stop talking."

I chuckle.

"You laugh. You weren't there. He was like a toddler hyped up on Cap'n Crunch. No. A sugar-amped toddler who's been watching Cocomelon all day long."

"Not Cocomelon!" I fake a horrified look, putting my hands on either side of my face, raising my eyebrows and pursing my lips in an O.

"Right?"

"That show was banned after a while around here."

"Rightfully so. Anyway, the point is, despite Ben's inappropriate exuberance, he'll zip it if I tell him to keep things under wraps. So, we don't have much to worry about. Then, if the situation calls for it, we will fake a dating relationship. Only, not in front of Noah. Every adult who thinks we're dating needs to know we're not telling Noah. That's a line they'll gladly honor."

Before I think better of it, I'm blurting out, "Oh, you're right. Whenever my aunts would try to tell me what a cute couple we'd make, they'd always say, 'We won't tell Noah until things are serious.'"

Kai stares at me a beat too long. Then he says, "Your aunts thought we'd be cute together?"

"In a metaphorical, hypothetical, completely fantastical, not real, imaginary way ... Yes."

"Hmm." Kai just hums.

He studies me from across the table.

Then he says, "Okay. So, what do you think of that plan?"

"I think it sounds too easy."

"Am I missing something?"

"Well, unlike you, who only reads surfing biographies and crime thrillers, I read romance."

"I know. What do our reading habits have to do with this, if you don't mind me asking? I'm missing the correlation."

"In romance, people fake date all the time."

"They do?"

"They do. It's a thing. Anyway, the key to pulling off a fake romance is having rules."

"Rules."

"Yes. You know." I cross my arms over my chest, looking at Kai seriously now that I'm the one laying out parameters. "Rules. Like, no kissing unless absolutely necessary. Only kissing in front of other people. No catching feelings. Things like that."

"Oh. Yeah. Okay. That makes sense. Well, since you are the one with all the research, write some rules. I'll follow them."

"Unlike the men in my books," I say under my breath.

"What?"

"I said, I think you'll do a far better job of following the rules than the men in my books."

"I am a rule-follower."

"That you are."

ELEVEN

Kai

You've got to have a motive, you know.
There are only five important ones.
Fear — jealousy — money — revenge —
and protecting someone you love.
~ Frederick Knott

I hear voices inside the shack when I come back to work for the afternoon. Mila and I have a plan. I'm still not quite sure how we got here, but she needs me, and that's all that matters now.

Ben's at the back of the shop, talking with a couple and their teen son when I walk in.

"Hey, Kai!" Ben shouts. "Folks, this is Kai, the one I was telling you about. He's an ex-pro surfer, and one of the best teachers on staff. Also, my boss, but I'd still say all that good stuff about him even if he weren't."

I wave at the family. "Nice to meet you."

The teen boy has a slightly awestruck expression on his face after that introduction. It's been a while since anyone looked at me like that. The dad steps away from Ben and over to me.

"Jack Snider," he says, extending his hand. "We're here for two weeks. Visiting from Kansas. Not much surfing there. I'm military, so we move around every few years. My wife, Shelly, homeschools our kids. Cody here has always wanted to learn to surf. So, we'd like to sign him up for lessons with you while we're here."

"Sounds good. Though, Ben's a fantastic teacher too. It might be good to have him with me for a few lessons and then with Ben, just so he gets exposed to a variety of approaches to surfing. The basics are going to be the same, but we each have our style. My future brother-in-law works here too. If he were going to be around, I'd have Cody pair up with him as well."

"Bodhi Merrick?" Cody asks from across the room.

"One and the same."

"Wow."

If I thought Cody looked a little starstruck when he saw me, that was nothing. He's nearly drooling at the mention of Bodhi's name.

"We'll take good care of you, Cody. Do you play any sports back home?"

"Yes, sir. Football, basketball, and I swim."

"That's all going to help. I'm betting you'll stand up and catch a wave your first lesson, but there's no pressure. Some people get the hang of it on day one. Others take a few sessions."

"I'm looking forward to it, sir."

Military family from Kansas. Still, the way Cody says, *sir*, makes me want to check the mirror for gray hairs. I'm not getting any younger, that's for sure.

I pull out the shop calendar and Mr. Snider and I line up a week's worth of lessons. He wants two weeks, but I assure him Cody may not need them, and if he does, we can schedule them later. Mr. Snider pays, and his family leaves with Cody set to go out with me tomorrow at eight in the morning. After his lesson Noah will come—with Mila.

Thinking of her feels new and strange. After all we've been

through in the past two days, something shifted. I've never found myself picturing her as a man imagines a woman. I can't stop myself from conjuring up the way she looked stepping out of Horizons wearing that flowing blouse, her hair down in brown waves. Even as distressed as she was, her warmth and natural beauty drew me to her from across the lobby.

I can easily recall the way she relied on me when she was stressed, tucked into my side where I'd do anything to keep her safe and help alleviate her fears. I picture the way she blushed when I told her I thought she looked beautiful. It was a simple compliment, but something felt different in the delivery and in the way she reacted.

We're going to have to be careful with this charade. We're two single adults. All this touching and pretending feels precarious at times. I'll just have to remind myself she's off limits—just like I always have.

"So, how was lunch? Did you go to Mila's?" Ben's words mercifully snap me out of my daydream.

He makes his way through the store until he's standing only a few feet away from me. The man has no concept of personal space.

"Yes. As a matter of fact, I did. She made chicken salad croissants and lemonade."

Ben's smile says, *Told you so.*

"So?" he asks.

"Okay. You got me. Mila and I are ... sort of dating. But we're keeping things quiet. Noah's not used to the idea of his mom seeing anyone. We don't want to upset him unnecessarily."

So far, most of that statement is at least slightly true. Mila and I are sort of dating, as in fake dating. That's *sort of*, right? And we are definitely keeping things quiet, though Marbella residents and Alicante staff aren't known for keeping juicy details about relationships quiet. We can only hope for the best. And, it's true, we don't want to upset Noah. He isn't used to his mom dating. I feel pretty good after saying all that to Ben. None of it was a direct lie.

Ben literally rubs his hands together like he can't contain his excitement. Then he lets out a whoop. "This is awesome!"

"Could you not? I thought you said you'd keep this on the D.L."

"I am. I am." He makes that infuriating zipping motion across his lips again. "I'm a vault. But right now, it's just you and me out here, and I'm so stoked, bro. This is awesome. You and Mila. Think of it. If this gets serious—which, why wouldn't it?—you'll be Noah's stepdad. Will you live at the inn? What will you do with Shaka when Bodhi and Mavs are traveling? Don't worry, man. I'll talk to Summer. We can pitch in with the dog. Unless Mila lets you take him to the inn with you. I don't know how having a pet works when you're living at an inn. Just know we're here for you—me and Summer."

I stare at Ben, feeling like I just got off the teacup ride at Disney. I don't even know what to address first in that slew of insanity he just spewed out of his supposedly zipped lips. The worst part? I can almost see it. When he says all those things about me moving in with Mila, me taking care of Noah ... it's not impossible. Only, it is. And I need to remember that—big time. Like she said earlier about the rules: No catching feelings.

I won't. This is just new. It's an adjustment period. I'll get used to touching her—kissing her. She did say kissing, didn't she? I'll deal. And I'll remain firmly planted in the friend zone where I belong.

Ben claps me on the back. "I'm so happy for you, Kai. Really. This is just what you need. I told you—female companionship. But this is way better. Mila. You and Mila." He shakes his head in disbelief.

"Okay. Well. Celebration time is over. Let's get to work."

"Man. You are a puzzle. If I were you—when I was you, and Summer finally caved and admitted her feelings for me—that's a time to let all that oxytocin and dopamine fly free. Soak that stuff up! Indulge in all the gooshie feelings while you're in the honeymoon stage. It's like nothing you'll ever feel again. Sure, you'll love her for the rest of your life, but this early dating season, it's special. Stop being so self-controlled and let yourself enjoy this."

Honeymoon period? Gooshie feelings? Only Ben.

I do love Mila. But not the way Ben's implying. I love her like a sister—like a good friend. What he's describing ... I don't think that's ever happened to me. I wonder if it ever would. Maybe that kind of experience is only for men like Ben who are over the top and full of bubbling emotions by nature.

"I'm not in love," I clarify.

"Yet. Maybe. I'm guessing you might be and you haven't given yourself the memo yet. Just don't hold back. When you find a woman like Mila and she's into you, you go for it. Don't waste this opportunity."

"Is this what it's going to be like now: You acting like Dr. Phil every day? Is this your version of the zipped lip?"

Ben's making me beyond nervous—on so many levels.

"Sorry. Sorry." Ben holds his hands up. "This is me, going outside to rinse off the boards from today's group lesson, boss."

He gives me one more zipper motion for good measure. I'm going to have post-traumatic-zipper-disorder. I'll flinch at the sight or sound of a common, everyday zipper. I wonder if I'll even be able to fasten my own pants after today's episodes with Ben.

Once Ben's outside and I'm alone in the shop, I head to my small nook of an office at the back of the shop next to the dressing rooms. It's so small only a tiny, two-drawer desk and a stool fit in here. But, it has a door, so I can shut myself in when I've had enough of everyone in the shop.

And that's just what I do right now.

I'm working through payroll when a text from Mila comes through.

I smile at the sight of her name.

That's not new. I always smile when she calls or texts. She's my friend. It's normal to smile.

Mila: I left you a message because my text was getting waaaay too long.

Kai: Thanks, checking it now.

Mila: Is this weird? I don't want it to be weird.

Kai: Our arrangement is unconventional. But we have our reasons. Don't second guess it. We had a good talk at lunch. Our plan is solid. I told you I'm here for you, and I meant it.

Mila: Thank you. You're the best. Snickerdoodles for life.

Kai: I'll hold you to that.

Mila: K. Go listen. Let me know if everything seems good.

Kai: Going now. I'll text you after I listen.

Mila: Thanks, Kai.

As soon as we stop texting, I push the button to hear the message Mila left me.

Her voice fills my office, so I turn the volume down and put the phone to my ear.

"Hey, Kai. It's me, Mila. Of course, you know that. First of all, thank you—for caring, for being there for me these past two days, and for being willing to pretend to be my boyfriend. Am I crazy? Are we crazy? If you had told me I'd be doing this even a week ago, I'd have sent you to bed with some soup and taken your temp—not in that order, and probably not soup in bed. But you know what I mean. I would have never believed this. But here we are. So, like I said, we need ground rules. It will help us stay on track and keep our story straight.

"The basic rules mostly concern physical contact. You can put your arm around me like you've been doing if Brad is here, or if someone needs convincing that we're dating. We may even have to kiss in front of someone at some point if the occasion calls for it. A simple peck should do it."

There's a long pause, a deep breath, and then she continues.

"So, the rule is only touching when we're in front of other people, and only when needed to convince others. Okay? I'm sure that's okay. It's not like you're going around thinking about touching me." Another pause. "Sorry. This is a bit awkward."

My brain unhelpfully starts thinking about touching Mila. I squeeze my eyes shut as if that would fend off the thoughts that seem to have been loosed like a bull out of a pen at a rodeo. I'm lassoing those inclinations and giving a strong tug to the rope to bring them to their knees.

Mila goes on. "And, I'm sure I don't have to say this, but just in case, there's the rule that we won't catch feelings. We're in this as friends. We'll walk out of this as friends. I couldn't bear to lose your friendship. So, let's agree to keep our friendship strong and to protect it through this little farce of ours."

She'll never lose my friendship. I'll make sure of that. Mila's been an amazing friend to me. She's one of the best people I know. I'm going through with this whole ruse *because of* our friendship. No worries there.

"Then there's the matter of Noah. We have to keep this from him at all costs. I don't ever want to be in a position to lie to my son. I've never lied to him before, and I won't start now. We just need to protect him from our charade. That should be obvious, but I needed to say it. I'm sure you agree.

"And we need a deadline—an end date. But I have no idea how to decide on that. There's one book where the woman needed a fake date for a wedding. Another where the man was trying to make his ex jealous. Oh! I read a few where they fake dated for an inheritance. But that's not us, of course. I guess we'll have to figure a deadline later since our situation isn't one I've seen before in any of the books."

I smile. Mila's adorable—especially when she's all flustered.

"Oh! One last thing. We can't tell anyone we're faking. Not unless we both agree that person can be completely trusted to keep a secret for us. And we both have to agree on any person we tell. I think that's it. If either of us need any other rules, we can put them in place. Let me know what you think." Mila blows out a long breath. "Bye, Kai. And thanks again."

I almost set my phone down, thinking she's finished. Then her voice comes through after at least a five or six second pause. "Wait! Kai? If you want to back out or quit, it's fine. You don't have to do this for me. It's a lot to ask. I know that. There's no hard feelings if you decide this is too much. Okay. Thanks."

The line truly goes dead after that.

I set my phone on my desk.

Ben knocks.

"Come in."

"Was that Mila? I thought I heard her voice."

"I thought you were out rinsing surfboards."

"I was. I finished. Did Mila leave you a voice message? So soon after you were there for lunch? That's a good sign, man."

"She did."

"And you've got the goofy look of a man in love."

"Love? I already told you, it's not love. Dude, slow your roll, okay?"

"Say what you will, but you look like your head is in the clouds. She's got you whipped already. And that's a good thing."

"A thing you are keeping under wraps," I remind him. "And don't make that zipping motion again. Just zip it. Without the motion."

Ben lifts his hand like he's going to make that movement. He holds his pinched fingers together at the side of his mouth. Then he wags his brows playfully.

I clamp my lips shut, pocket my phone, and send up a silent

prayer that Ben gets laryngitis. And his hands are simultaneously paralyzed so he can't even pantomime about our secret. Not that I want Ben suffering. I just need him bound and gagged—gently, in a not-too-harmful-but-definitely-effective way. For a while. Until this ruse is over.

A group of men enter the shop. I nod toward them and Ben takes my cue to go see what they need. While Ben is distracted, I send Mila a text.

> Kai: Got your voice message. Everything's good on my end. Don't stress. This will be fine. And I'm not backing out. You shouldn't have to face your ex trying to ease his way into Noah's life and him trying to pursue you at the same time. I'm here. We're doing this.

> Mila: Sorry for the way I rambled. And, thank you. You'll never know how much relief that gives me. I just don't want you to feel like you have to do this.

> Kai: Understandable. But you don't have to worry. This is me, Mila. I'm the same man who's been your friend for the past four years. I'm here for you.

> Mila: How did I ever get so lucky?

> Kai: I could say the same. Now go about your day as if everything's as it always has been. Brad's not here. You and I get a respite before Act II of this show.

> Mila: Thanks, Kai.

I type, *anything for you,* but then I consider the current blurred lines between us, and I change my text at the last minute before hitting send.

Kai: No problem.

TWELVE

Mila

I'm always secretly disappointed when
a liar's pants don't actually catch on fire.
~ Unknown

"Yoooo hooo!" Phyllis' voice carries through the main room to the kitchen where I'm preparing a lasagna, garlic bread and salad for dinner.

She appears in the doorway, followed closely by Connie and Joan.

"I take it I'm being converged upon."

"We're not converging, dear." Connie smiles a very unconvincing smile.

"We were ..." Joan starts.

"... out walking," Phyllis fills in too quickly.

"Yes. Walking," Connie says with a rapid bob of her head. "And we started thinking of you ... talking about you ..."

"... about you and how you are doing ..." Joan adds.

"... since Brad came to town." Phyllis gives me a pointed look.

"Ahhh. You heard about that, did you?"

I dump the ground sausage into the tomato sauce and stir.

"We heard, alright," Phyllis says. "We heard a lot of things."

"Such as?" I continue stirring.

"Such as you were at the Alicante with him this morning for breakfast."

"Wow."

I look at each of them and then return my focus to the sauce, adding dried basil, oregano and a pinch of salt.

"And, Bernice said she heard Kai showed up," Joan says, with a twinkle in her eye.

"Kai has a management meeting at the main building every week. Today was his management meeting."

"Which explains why his arm was wrapped around you?" Phyllis asks.

I stare at the sauce, stirring slowly in circles to the left, and then to the right.

"Excuse me," I say, grabbing the boiling noodles off the back burner and walking to the sink to drain them.

"Well?" Phyllis presses.

"Well, what?"

"Did Kai have his arm around you at the resort this morning? Darla said she heard something about a kiss. That's what she told Connie when Connie went to get her hair washed and curled this afternoon."

"How do Bernice and Darla know what was supposedly going on at the Alicante?"

"It doesn't matter, dear," Connie says. "The point is someone said he had his arm around you and someone else claims there was a kiss involved. And there's another story going around that you two snuck out by the golf carts for a ... well ... I can't really comfortably repeat that one."

"For a what?" My voice raises just the slightest in volume and octave.

"A private, passionate moment. I'm just quoting." Connie blushes and shakes her head lightly. "Can you imagine? I'm sure that one was embellished. But the other things ... well ... we're just so tickled."

"Joe at the Corner Market said Kai came to the inn for lunch," Joan says. "I stopped in to pick up some of that muscle rub I use on my hands at night. Joe brought it up while he was ringing up my order. He said, 'Nice to see Mila's finally letting herself enjoy a man's company.' So, of course, I had to ask him whatever he did mean. And he told me. I don't always trust him as a source, but he said he heard it from Suzanna—about Kai being here for lunch."

"Wow."

My mind is spinning with how fast news has traveled and how many people have nothing better to do than talk about Kai putting his arm around me or coming here for lunch. I shouldn't be surprised. There's a double-edged sword to small-town life, and island life is small-town living with few options for getting away from said small town.

On one hand, people treat one another like family. The islanders have been here for me while I set up the inn, when I gave birth, and to pitch in while I raise Noah single-handedly. But then again, just like family, the people of Marbella are up in one another's business, and today is my lucky day, because it seems like half the island is up in mine.

The bigger problem, aside from my overly involved neighbors, obviously, is what to tell the three women who raised me. They are my family. I can't remember a day I lied to them in my entire life. That one week when Brad talked me into skipping school for three delightful days on the beach was the exception. I ended up confessing to my aunts at the end of the third day. And the secret burned in me until I finally came clean.

But this is different.

"Kai and I ..." I start.

But I don't know what to say after that. The words get stuck in my throat.

"Oooooh!" Connie claps her hands excitedly and bounces a

little on her toes. She looks nearly childlike with giddiness, despite her gray hair and wrinkles.

"I knew it!" Joan adds. "The two of you always have had such a fondness for one another. You're well-suited. Is that still what they say these days?" She looks to Phyllis to clarify.

"I think she knows what you mean. Don't you, Mila?"

I start to speak ... but Connie beats me to it.

"Of course she knows. She's so bright, our Mila. And good, and kind, and beautiful. Of course Kai would want to date her."

"Of course, he would," Joan agrees. "What man wouldn't?"

Phyllis just nods, studying me.

"We're so excited for you two!" Connie starts bouncing again.

"Very excited," Joan adds.

Phyllis still studies me.

"We're ... um. We can't let Noah know," I say, my deepest concern finally finding its way into words.

"Oh, of course not, dear," Connie says.

"Mum's the word," Joan agrees.

Phyllis finally speaks. "We know you'll want to keep your relationship private until you are more serious. I just wish you had told us. We didn't like finding out from everyone else."

"It's ... complicated." I finally say something fully true.

"Oh, romance always is!" Connie nearly busts at the seams with that statement. "And to think, you were always so dead set against romance. Well, I had a hunch that Kai would be the one to snap you out of that dry spell. He's a looker. And if any young man could do it, my money was on him."

I'm surprised she doesn't whip out a measuring tape and start sizing me up for a wedding gown on the spot. She's the epitome of the heart-eye emoji, only a bouncing one who's slightly hard of hearing and takes arthritis meds.

"I'm sorry," I say.

And I am. Sorry that I'm not telling them everything. Sorry they think everyone knows something and they're the last to find out. Sorry I'm even in this situation.

"Nothing to be sorry about. We thought it might be a silly rumor at first," Phyllis says. "But the more we kept hearing, the more we knew some parts of it must be true. That's why we came over."

"On your walk?" I tease. "Spontaneously?"

"No matter," Phyllis smiles at me. "We came and now we know."

"There's more," I pull my lasagna pan out, spray the bottom with oil, and start layering noodles.

"What more?" Phyllis asks, taking one of the seats around the island while Joan walks over to the fridge and pulls out the jug of tea.

"Brad wants to meet Noah. He wants to be a part of his life." I collapse onto a stool.

"Oh, dear!" Connie says, taking a glass of tea from Joan.

"Yeah. He said he knows he messed up and he wants to be a part of Noah's life now."

A silence falls over the four of us, my three aunts exchange glances in a way I've grown accustomed to over the years. There's a whole discussion being shared wordlessly between them.

Phyllis finally speaks. "You probably need to consider Noah's right to know his dad."

"Not that you have to rush into this," Connie adds, attempting to soften the harsh reality of my situation.

"Inch into it," Joan adds. "Maybe you bring Brad in as a stranger. I think I saw a Hallmark movie about this. Or, maybe it was Lifetime. Anyway, the man wanted to come back into his son's life. Of course, in that one, the woman let him come around as a stranger, and they fell back in love and got remarried." She sniffs. "It was beautiful, really. I love a redemption story, don't you?"

"Oh for heaven's sake!" Phyllis scolds Joan. "Do you really want Brad and Mila back together?"

"Goodness, no!" Joan says.

Connie adds, "Never. Besides, Mila has Kai now. Brad isn't an option."

And that solidifies it for me. I do need Kai. With him in the picture, Brad will know he's not an option for me—everyone will.

Phyllis looks over at me. "You might want to start priming the pump over time with Noah. Ask him what he would feel like if you found his father. Ask if he'd ever want to meet him one day. Don't talk too much about it, but you need to get him prepared. He's spent all these years never even missing the man. But you have to build a bridge eventually."

"Not right away, though," Connie adds.

"Definitely not. Just let him come around as a stranger at first. See how things go."

I nod, unable to think of anything except what it will be like for my ex to be around my son—and me.

At least I'll have Kai as a buffer.

THIRTEEN

Kai

To show a child what once delighted you,
to find the child's delight added to your own -
this is happiness.
~ J. B. Priestley

My lesson with Cody wraps up. We paddle in on the next waves. Just as I predicted, he stood after his first few attempts in the shallow water, and then he moved on to more sizable waves for the rest of the lesson. He fell off the board a good number of times, but he also caught his fair share of rides.

I feel alive after our hour in the water. The ocean always resuscitates me, clearing away the debris of life on shore, putting everything into perspective.

"That was awesome!" Cody shouts over to me as we lift our boards from the shallow shore pound and walk side-by-side onto the beach.

His family is waiting, a younger brother and sister building sand castles, while his mom reads in one of the loungers provided by the resort. His dad, who never sat down the whole time we were out in the water, as far as I can tell, walks toward us and thanks me. Mrs. Snider calls Cody over to share the videos she took of him on her phone.

"Can we get in the water now?" Cody's brother asks their dad, interrupting our conversation.

"We're going back to the resort so your mom can have her massage." Mr. Snider tells his son. "We'll come back down here this afternoon. In the meantime, you can swim in one of the pools."

Mr. Snider thanks me again, and I leave the family to pack up while I remind Cody how to turn his wetsuit in at the shack where our weekend part-timer, Jamison, can take care of it for him.

I instinctively look over toward the shack in time to see Mila and Noah walking this way. Cody's loaner board and mine lay on the sand, ready for Noah to have his first lesson from me.

I watch Mila and Noah share conversation, her smile visible even at this distance, her long brown hair blowing recklessly in the onshore breeze and the skirt of her sundress following suit.

About half the way across the sand, Noah breaks into a run. He never slows, and when he's about three feet away, I sense what he's planning. I spread my arms wide and brace my legs just in time to catch him as he flies at me.

"You're getting too big for that maneuver," I say, spinning him in the air despite what I just said, and then plopping him back on his feet.

I've known Noah since he was three. He's run into my arms like that for nearly as long as I can remember. Today may be the first time I realized I won't always be able to lift him and propel him in a broad circle.

"I am getting bigger, right?" Noah puffs up just a little to prove his point.

"Big enough to start learning to surf."

"Yep." He beams.

I ruffle his hair and he ducks away like he's too cool to be messed with.

Mila catches up with Noah.

"Hey," she says, smiling up at me.

"Hey," I smile down at Mila. "Good to see you."

She's wearing a light coverup over her dress and her beach bag is slung over one shoulder. I turn my attention to Noah to keep myself from staring at her.

It's warmer today than it's been in a while. The sun is out and the waves are just right for learning. I couldn't have asked for better weather if I had ordered it.

"Thanks again for doing this," Mila says. Her eyes soften and her smile feels like a gift I could never earn.

"My pleasure. It's a privilege, really." I look at Noah. "My dad took me out surfing when I was one.

"Years old?" Noah's eyes go wide.

"Yeah. I don't even think I was actually one yet when he had me on the board with him. And I rode my own board by the time I was two and a half with my dad overseeing me."

"Whoa."

"It's a little different in Hawaii," I explain.

"Do you just come out bigger?"

I chuckle. "No. We come out the same size. Most of us do, anyway. But we're a surf culture—at least the part of the islands where I grew up—so we get our children in the water young."

"No wonder you're a superhero."

I send Mila a help-me-out-here look. Noah definitely looks up to me, but I'm pretty sure he doesn't think I'm a superhero.

"A professional?" Mila asks Noah.

"Yeah. That. You got to surf for your job. Like a superhero."

I chuckle again. "Yeah. Sort of like Aquaman, huh?"

Noah cracks up.

"Okay, boss man, let's get you surfing."

Mila drops the beach bag from her shoulder and spreads out her blanket. I spend the next hour teaching Noah the fundamental principles of surfing, starting with a lesson on the sand with basic safety measures followed by how to paddle and pop up. He's boogie boarded over the years, so some of this is repeat information—and he's quick to tell me everything he already knows.

We paddle out into the white water, practicing standing where the water's shallow. Once he's had enough practice in the slush, I remind him about what he's going to do in the glassy waves further out.

"What do you do if you fall?" I quiz him as we float side by side, our legs dangling off the edges of our boards while we sit upright.

"Don't put the board between me and the wave so it doesn't smack my face. Fall to the side of the board. And wave my hand overhead before coming out of the water so I don't bonk the board on the way up. And don't swallow the ocean. Hold my breath when my head is under."

"Perfect. I think you're ready."

"Oh, yeah! I was born ready!" Noah shouts over to me.

"Where do you get these sayings of yours?" I smile over at him.

"School, of course."

"Of course."

He's too much, this kid. And I love him.

We paddle further out. I send Noah into a few waves. He misses the first few, falling off the board, but he's a champ about it. And he's leashed to his board, so we don't have to chase it down and start paddling out from shore. After a few fails, another sweet wave comes toward us. It's the perfect size and shape for a beginner.

"This one's all yours, buddy," I tell Noah.

The look of determination on his face makes me wish I were wearing my GoPro. Mila would love to capture this moment on film from my angle.

Noah follows my directions step by step, and when it's time to pop up, I shout, "Now!"

Noah jumps up, and he's standing. I can't count the number of people I've taught to surf over the years. Only a few of them mattered like Noah does. He's like a nephew to me—calling me Unko before he could really make sense of who I was to him. As far as I'm concerned, Noah is my ohana, and today I'm the one who gets to teach him how to ride the waves.

"I'm up! I'm surfing! I'm surfing!" Noah shouts.

His grin nearly splits his face in half.

He starts waving his hands around in his excitement, which causes him to lose his balance and fall into the water. I'm right there to guide him back to his board.

Once he's on the board and recovered from the fall, he turns to me and asks, "Did you see that?"

"I sure did. You rode your first wave!"

"Next time I'll save the celebration for the beach."

I chuckle. "Good plan."

We paddle out again and Noah catches the next wave, following my prompts as to when to aim his nose in and when to stand. He rides that one a good distance toward shore. After that wave, he catches a bunch more, falling every so often, but riding a lot more than he misses.

When I finally tell Noah we need to take the last wave in, he pouts. "But I'm having so much fun!"

"And that's a good time to call it quits. Believe me, you'll be feeling this tomorrow as it is."

We catch the next waves. Noah goes ahead of me, and I ride right behind him, landing in the shallow surf near the sand. I coach him as to how to lift his board to carry it onto shore. He's got it going on until he hits the place where the water isn't holding the board up for him, so I give him a hand and tote both boards. Noah runs to where Mila's waiting for him on her beach blanket with a smile that takes my breath away for the briefest moment.

"Did you see all that?" Noah asks his mom.

"I sure did. I watched every minute of it. I'm so proud of you!"

"It was awesome. I did great, huh Unko? Didn't I?"

"You sure did. You did just as great as the teenager I taught just before you."

Noah beams at the compliment.

"When can we learn again?"

"How about I talk with your mom about that while you run over to the shack and give Jamison your wetsuit?"

"Okay. I think we can surf next Saturday too. Huh, Mom? Right?"

"We'll see." Mila smiles at Noah.

He doesn't wait for either of us to say anything else before he's off and running toward the shack.

Mila starts packing up her bag. I grab two corners of the blanket and we fold it as a team, meeting in the middle, her staring up at me while I hand my edge to her. Our fingers brush together in a touch so feather light I could almost miss it. The problem is, I don't. I never used to catalog the small moments with Mila. I'm sure I'll get back to some sort of neutrality with her in a few days or so. We simply need to adjust to this new arrangement.

I leave the boards for Jamison to retrieve and rinse. He's the low man on our totem pole in the shack, and that means he gets the grunt work. We've all been there—recipients of the initiation weeks where we test the new guy with pranks. And then he's brought into the unspoken hierarchy of workers. When I came on, the two guys who had been there longer than me put me through that same rite of passage even though I was ex-pro and came in at a management level. They couldn't have cared less if I bought the Alicante. In the shack, we have our own culture, and if you want to be a part of that family of workers, you earn your way in and up.

We walk toward the dock. Mila smiles over at me and thanks me again.

"Being with your son is never something you have to keep

thanking me for. Teaching Noah is my honor. Best hour of my week so far."

Mila's smile widens. A gust of wind catches her hair and whips it around her face. She moves to swipe it away. I watch her like a man watching a woman. What is wrong with me? I'm an idiot. I spent nearly four years in her presence, all but numb to her beauty and her tender, compassionate heart. I know why. She made it clear to me early on where she stood with men in her life. We could be friends or nothing. Knowing her stance on dating flipped a switch inside me, keeping me safely unaware of her— unaffected and relatively oblivious. Nothing about her stance has changed.

"Here, give me that beach bag so you have both hands free," I tell Mila when she shifts the weight on her shoulder.

"You don't have to ..." her voice trails off when I give her my serious look. It's the same one I use with Ben when he's goofing off at work and I've had my fill.

"The dad face!" She laughs, her finger pointing at me. "You have that down pat."

"It's my boss face," I correct her.

"Well, here's my bag, boss." Mila bumps her hip into me playfully and hands the bag into my hands.

"That's more like it," I tease.

"Man, I thought surfers were supposed to be chill." She smiles up at me through her lashes.

"I'm so chill. I just spent two hours in the ocean. There's nothing more chill than that."

"Teaching. You spent two hours teaching. I'd bet you were on high alert that whole time, watching for the safety of your other student and my son."

"Yeah. I was. But it was a super-chill kind of high-alert."

I make the shaka sign with the hand that's not carrying her bag to emphasize my totally relaxed personality. *Hang loose. All's well.* It should be my motto, considering my heritage, but I've always carried a burden for the people around me. It's just part of my makeup.

Mila's laughter fills my chest like helium. She is sun through clouds—her misty rays piercing the sky with light. She's simultaneously sharp and ethereal. Captivating and elusive. I'm aware of the muscles in my throat as I swallow the lump forming there.

Mila.

Talk about a complication.

Noah's voice carries out from inside the watersports shack. I can't contain my smile. He's like any surfer, boasting about his waves, reveling in the thrill of the ride. One morning sesh and he's already hooked on my favorite sport—the passion I devoted my life to for years.

He's a storyteller too. His animated voice has both my employees' rapt attention. "And then I stood up! But that time I got so excited I flopped right off."

Noah laughs hard at himself, with his typical childlike resilience. Ben and Jamison laugh along with him.

Noah sees me and Mila enter through the front door. "Mom! I was just telling the guys here how I surfed!"

"You were, were you?"

"Yeah. Show them. You got a video, right?"

"I got more than one, but they aren't super clear."

"That's okay. They still wanna see it. Don't ya, guys?"

If you could plug Noah in right now, he'd power the shack and most of the boats in the harbor.

"We definitely want to see it," Ben says. "I don't think I can move on with my day without seeing this video."

"I left the boards on the sand," I tell Jamison.

"Let him see the video first, man," Ben says.

"Fine. Watch the video. Then get the boards."

No one will bother the boards. This is Marbella. Our crime rate is basically non-existent. We leave doors unlocked, bikes out in racks, golf carts parked with keys still in the ignition. It's one of the perks of living on this kind of island.

"I thought you and Mila had something to discuss … alone … out front … anyway." Ben punctuates each of his statements with a slight lift of his brows.

Subtle. So subtle.

As if he hadn't made his point, he says, "You know. Since you two might need time alone to say those things, we've got Noah here showing us videos. So, take full advantage of the opportunity to get those words out." He smiles at Mila, then me, like he's some sort of genius.

Noah looks up at Ben. "You're acting weird."

"Yeah, bruh. I'm weird. Now show me that video." Ben looks over at us. "You two, shoo. Go have your adult *conversation* while we're watching the next big name in surfing show us his first waves."

Mila blushes. I wonder if I'm blushing too. But, to her credit, she turns and walks out the front door.

I follow behind, unsure what we're actually supposed to do now that we've basically been sent into the adult version of Seven Minutes in Heaven, minus the closet.

"Well, this isn't awkward," I say, as soon as we're outside the shack and out of earshot.

Mila giggles. "Ben is so over the top."

"He's the poster child for over the top."

"Is he watching?" Mila asks, her head tilted up toward me.

It's the exact posture a woman would have if she were waiting for a kiss. My eyes flick toward her lips—soft and rosy, tilted up in a smile, the bottom one just slightly fuller than the top. And that Cupid's bow at the peak of her mouth. Did she always have that? Why didn't I notice it before today?

"Kai?" Mila's words draw my eyes back to hers.

"Yeah?"

"Is he watching?"

"Who? Noah?"

"No. Ben. He thinks we're dating. I don't want to stand out here looking like friends if he thinks we're more. If anyone could blow our cover, it's him. He wouldn't mean to, but ... you know him. Sometimes his mouth starts speaking before his brain has engaged."

"Sometimes?" I smile down at Mila.

Then I glance over my shoulder into the shack. All three of the guys in there, Jamison, Ben and Noah, have their shoulders bent so they can huddle close with their eyes fixed on the video playing on Mila's phone.

"They're all watching the clip of Noah surfing."

"We'd better hit a happy middle ground," Mila suggests.

"Middle ground?"

"If Noah looks out here, we need it to appear like we're our usual friendly selves. If Ben glances over, we need it to seem ..." She pauses. "You know, like we're taking advantage of the opportunity he gave us. That's what we'd do if we were newly dating."

"How about a hug?" I suggest.

Mila smiles up at me and then she wraps her arms around my waist. I loop my arms behind her and tug her close. Her cheek rests on my chest and I hold her there, hoping she can't feel the uptick in my heartbeat. I rest my chin on top of her head, and I swear I hear her sigh.

"Okay." She breaks away abruptly. "That should do it."

"Okay. Yeah." I run my hand through my hair. "Seems like we need more rules, or a guidebook. Or maybe it's just me. Do you feel out of your depth yet?"

"I'm sorry, Kai."

"No. No. It's not that. Forget I said anything. We're laying the groundwork here. Brad will be back when he starts developing the business. We have to get a reputation for being together before he shows up, otherwise we won't be convincing."

"Are you sure?"

"Totally. I'm one hundred percent sure. We'll just take each situation as it comes."

"Okay! That was great!" Ben's voice booms from inside the

shack. "Noah's going to come out to interrupt that *conversation* now."

Mila and I look at one another and burst into laughter.

Ben. There's only one Ben. Thank goodness. I don't know if I could handle more than one.

Noah comes bounding out of the shack with Ben on his heels.

Ben pats Noah on the shoulder. "Proud of you, kiddo. Next time, I want to be out there with you."

"You can! We might go next Saturday. Right, Mom?"

"We'll see," Mila says softly.

"That always means yes. Usually," Noah says with unbridled confidence.

"Good deal." Ben raises a fist and Noah bumps it with his.

Ben turns to Mila. "Kai told me about your development. I'm so happy to hear about it. I should tell you, my boss has been smiling a lot more these days."

"Hey, boss man," I say to Noah, intentionally cutting Ben off. "Let's look at the break right now before you take off with your mom. You can point to a wave and tell me when you'd pop up. It's a game I used to play with my dad when I was learning to ride."

"Okay!" Noah heads for the end of the dock before I say another word—and more importantly, before Ben does.

I hear Ben from behind me as I follow behind Noah.

He's saying, "Don't worry, Mila. I'm keeping everything between you and Kai zipped up tight."

I glance over just in time to see Ben make that ridiculous zipping motion in front of his lips.

Oh, yeah. He's a vault alright.

FOURTEEN
Mila

There is nothing I would not do
for those who are really my friends.
I have no notion of loving people by halves;
it is not my nature.
~ Jane Austen

S ome people come in like a gentle rain, others like a squall. My best friend is the latter—rarely subtle, always making her presence known. She holds within her the capacity to be as fierce as she is fun.

And today, Chloe is on the warpath, or so it seems, as she storms through my front double doors, letting them fall shut with a bang behind her.

"Mila Rose Mitchell, what on earth?!" Her voice echoes off the old wood paneling and high ceilings in the main room

"Calm down," I whisper hoarsely, even though it's midafternoon. "You'll upset the guests."

"Upset the guests? Upset the guests?" Chloe pops her hands on her hips and stares at me, her eyes narrowed.

"What is going on?" I walk around from behind the reception desk and approach her like I'm nearing one of the wild monkeys that inhabit our island.

Yes. Wild monkeys. As you may know, a movie was filmed here years ago that called for wild animals. After production finished, the animals were left to roam on the back side of the island. Only, being animals, they multiplied. And they don't always know they're supposed to stay on the uninhabited portion of Marbella. Sometimes they end up in shops—or my trash cans.

Right now, my bestie looks as feral and dangerous as one of those primates when he's got a whopping chunk of my garbage in his hands.

"What is wrong?" I ask in my most unoffending tone of voice.

"You're kidding, right?"

"No."

I can feel my brow furrow in confusion. What is she so ... ?

Oooooh. Nooooo.

Chloe must have heard about me and Kai. From someone else. I truly hope that's not what this is, but one more appraisal of Chloe's face and I know. She thinks I started dating Kai and didn't tell her.

"Kai?" Chloe moves her hands from her hips and crosses her arms over her chest. "Really, Mila? You started dating Kai and didn't even bother to tell me."

I reach my hand out to rest it on her shoulder assuringly, and she shrugs it off. Yep. She's mad. I don't blame her. I would be upset too.

"It's a long story ..."

Chloe's eyebrows raise, and her lips purse. "Is that why you didn't even call me? It would take too long to tell me this long story? About your new *boyfriend*?"

"Chloe, please. Trust me. You're my best friend. I tell you everything. Do you really think I'd keep it from you if I were dating Kai?"

"So, you're not dating Kai?"

"Not exactly."

"Not exactly?"

"Right. Here. Sit down. I'll tell you everything."

And, without even a second thought, I decide she needs to know. Chloe has been my best friend my whole life. She has kept every secret I ever told her. And I've kept hers.

She sits on one end of a sofa and I take the opposing end, swiveling to face her.

"So, that day Brad came by?"

Chloe nods, her arms still crossed over her chest, but her face softening just the slightest.

"Kai was here, at the inn. And before I knew it, he had stepped onto the porch and introduced himself as my boyfriend."

"He whaaa ... ?" Chloe's expression shifts from confused to hopeful in less than a second. "Oh! Okay, now. This we can work with."

"No. No. Uh uh. We cannot work with this. *This* is me and Kai doing what's necessary. That's all."

I go on to tell Chloe about the day I had breakfast with Brad, only this time I share all the parts I left out the first time I told her: how Kai showed up and stepped in, how he put his arm around me and kissed my temple, how we talked that afternoon and agreed to put up a front to keep Brad at bay.

"So, let me get this straight. You and Kai are only pretending to date because of Brad? Kai's not secretly into you? Are you sure?"

"Yes. That's it. I'm sure. And I just broke a rule."

"A rule?"

"You know. Like they set rules in the romance books—when there's a fake dating trope?"

"Mmmm. I love those. Simply delicious."

"Right. Well, I borrowed a page from the books and we made rules—guidelines, like no catching feelings, stuff like that."

"Why on earth would you set that as a rule, Mila? Kai is hot. Yes. I said it. He's a darn good looking man. I mean, those eyes alone. And then you add in the surfer bod ... my heart is completely devoted to Davis. But I'm not dead. I know a handsome man when I see one. And Kai's handsome in a way that makes you look—like when you really look at a Dutch painting, like one by Rembrandt, and it just gets more and more beautiful the longer you stare at it, or those rare sunsets where every single shade of pastel and neon vie for your attention in a display that makes you ponder things beyond this earth. You simply have to look. Tell me you can at least see Kai's attractive."

I nod, not appreciating the fact that Chloe noticed Kai, or that she has such a poetic way of describing his uncommon beauty, then chiding myself for caring. Why should I care? Kai is handsome. It's not like that's a secret. After Chloe's rant about Kai's looks, I'm unfortunately assaulted by images of Kai—helping in my kitchen, laughing, surfing with Noah, running his hand through his hair, his dad face, the way he looked down at me like a man who wanted to kiss a woman.

Chloe continues her campaign. It's like *Kai for President*, only it's *Kai for the most eligible bachelor in your life.*

"And he's kind. He's good with Noah. Plus, he's always over here pitching in. I don't know why you haven't caught feelings already."

"And, this?" I wave my hand in her direction. "This is why I hesitated to tell you. It's not that I don't trust you with my secrets. I know you guard my confidences with your life. It's just ... I can't fall for Kai. And I don't want him falling for me. And I don't want you getting all excited about a potential love match when this is strictly a practical decision to keep lines clear between me and Brad."

"A practical decision? Is that what the kids are calling it these days?" Chloe laughs.

"You mock me. But, seriously, I can't have Brad thinking he's got a chance with me."

"So, tell him. Tell Brad you'd never date him again if it were the zombie apocalypse and it were up to the two of you to perpetuate the human race."

"I don't think that's the exact phrasing I'd choose."

"Whatever, just make it firm. That's what adults do, Mila. They set boundaries. They talk. They don't ... fake date a hot guy just to keep their ex-husband from making a move."

She's got an expression on her face that's half annoyed, half compassionate. I'll admit I haven't always been the most direct communicator. I love peace. I could wear a T-shirt that says something like, *Why can't we all just get along?* Or *Play nice.* Come to think of it, I do own two graphic T's that say, *Be Kind.* That's really the way I like to do life—non-confrontational and agreeable, with a side of baked goods.

But having a peace-loving personality doesn't mean I can't set boundaries. Maybe it used to, but Chloe knows me. I've grown. I have limits and I set them kindly and firmly. Going through a divorce and owning my own business where I serve all manner of customers has sent me through two orientations by fire. I've learned my limits and how to communicate them diplomatically.

I look at my best friend, so grateful for her mama bear tendencies when it comes to me and my life. She'd take a bullet for me. Knowing her, though, the bullet would take one look at her when she's all riled up, and retreat to shoot in the opposite direction.

"So, you think I should just tell Brad he doesn't have a chance? And he'd just accept it? He'd leave me alone? He'd honor that line if I drew it?"

Chloe pauses. She knows Brad. "Okay. Yeah. You're right. He'd act like he accepted your wishes, and then he'd double down, trying to win you back."

"And that won't ever happen."

"I know. Because if there were even a smidge of a chance of anything happening between you two, I'd be over here in his face —and in yours—tackling that mess like a linebacker."

I chuckle. "Yeah. You would. But you won't have to. I'm never going back to Brad. I'm not even dating any man until after Noah is out of the house. I've already decided that. It's too complicated. And Noah needs me. The inn needs me. But even when I do start dating—if I do—Brad is on the list of men I will never date, not even then."

"Decisions can change." Chloe's face looks so unfortunately hopeful, not about Brad, obviously, but about me dating before Noah leaves.

"Not that decision."

"What about the rules?" Chloe's arms have lowered at some point. She's relaxed back into the cushions of the couch, making a playful face.

"The rules are there for a reason. Kai and I want to preserve our friendship. And we need the guidelines to help us carry this off. And we can't let Noah suspect anything."

"Of course not." Chloe nods emphatically.

We stare at one another, the weight of Noah's situation hanging between us. The unknown influence of Brad's sudden reappearance like an anvil overhead, dangling by nothing but piano wire and hope for the best.

"Well, my lips are sealed," Chloe promises me. "I'm in on this charade now. I'll just act like you and Kai are dating. Is this just in front of Brad? Or ...?"

"Oh. Yeah. Right." I sigh. "Well, it was supposed to be. But then someone saw me and Kai with Brad outside Horizons. And then people talked. And it got back to my aunts."

"Oh, no! What did you tell them?"

"Thankfully, they assumed the rumors were true, and I didn't correct them."

Chloe smiles warmly. She's not upset at me for duping my aunts. I feel a little guilty, but it had to be done. In time, I'll explain everything to them. I'm not sure when, but I will.

"So, I'm the only one who knows?"

"Yep. You, me, and Kai."

~

The day rolls on with dinner preparation and service for my guests, then they take off to places I've recommended where they can enjoy island life. And finally, after the inn is quiet and empty for the evening, Noah settles in for his bedtime routine. I convinced Chloe to bring a book over and read in the main room while I run to Kai's. I need to talk to him about my choice to tell Chloe about our fake dating situation, and that's not a conversation that feels right to have over text or even a call.

The night air whips my hair around as I cycle through our neighborhood, then up and down a few hilly streets with the ocean's inky glow off to my left, sometimes barely visible in glimpses between houses and then suddenly in full view when I pass a cove, the moonlight reflecting in luminous lines along the peaks and valleys of the water's surface.

I pedal toward the resort side of Marbella. Something about riding my bike brings back childhood memories, and not one memory in particular, but all of them, in one blurry haze of bliss. It's the feel of freedom, the rush of air past me as I glide forward. Nothing can touch me when I'm coasting down a hill. I can outrun responsibility, decisions, and deadlines with each depression of my pedals. I'm lighter and nearly giddy by the time I make my way along the street that runs between the beach and the resort.

I reach Kai's neighborhood in fifteen or twenty minutes, park my bike outside his house, and walk up the walkway toward his porch toting the dessert I packed in my bike bag.

Kalaine's dog barks repeatedly, alerting Kai to my presence, and the front door opens before I even have a chance to knock.

Kai stands on the other side of the screen door, shirtless, framed in light. There's a sheen of sweat across his brow and maybe his pecs. I'm trying not to count his one ... two ... three ... Yep. Six pack of abs. Whew. It's been a long, long time since I've been this close to a shirtless man who wasn't on a beach at a decent distance from me. That's what this is. A case of overexposure, plain and simple.

I clear my throat.

"Mila? What are you doing here? Are you okay?"

I was, until you answered the door like *that*.

I'm not dead. Chloe's words echo through my head. Well, apparently I'm not dead either.

Shaka's tail is wagging and he's pressing his wet, pink nose to the screen door separating me from Kai. That door feels like a buffer—one I apparently need right now. It's late. Chloe filled my head with all this *Kai's attractive* propaganda. That's all this is.

"Mila?"

"Oh. Yeah. Hey. I'm here. On your porch. As you can see. From looking at me, you could tell it's me. Out here. At your house. I'm ... sorry."

"You're sorry?"

Kai's mouth turns up in a half-grin, crooked smile that does nothing to still the thoughts I'm having about how he looks right now. Muscles, muscles, muscles, and that golden skin. I look up at the porch light and back at Kai who is still sporting an amused smirk.

I feel like I need to get on my bike and fly down a few more hills. I could use the ocean breeze on my overheated skin right about now.

"Sorry. I should have called."

"No. No. It's fine. I was just exercising." He looks down at Shaka, who is rubbing against Kai's calves on one side and then the other, wagging his tail effusively like he's the luckiest dog in the world.

Can't argue that. Gah. *Get a grip, Mila.*

Kai sidesteps the dog.

Shaka follows along, not willing to put one centimeter between himself and Kai.

Kai makes a grimacing face down toward Shaka.

The dog gives him the most adoring look in return.

"After surfing today? You still have energy to exercise?"

"I couldn't settle my brain tonight. Exercising relaxes me.

That or playing guitar," Kai says, as he pushes the door open. "Want to come in?"

"Um. Yes. I brought you dessert. Apple cobbler."

Suddenly, I feel beyond awkward about bringing Kai dessert. I've never been awkward about sharing my baking with him before.

"Awesome. Thanks. I love your cobbler."

Kai takes the outstretched container of dessert from me as I step over the threshold.

I walk past Kai, who should smell at least a little offensive from working out, but he doesn't. He's sunshine and tropics, earthy, but warm. Manly.

Shaka saves me from this weird mental trail I'm on about my *friend*. Shaka's wagging his tail even harder now that I'm inside the house, and he's obviously about to jump up to greet me when Kai firmly says, "Hey! Off."

Shaka sits, his tail wagging on the floor like a swiffer in overdrive.

"Hey there, good boy. Who's a good boy?" I say to Shaka, scrubbing his head and under his chin.

"Not that one. Don't let him fool you," Kai says in a grumbly tone that makes me smile.

He walks into the kitchen, setting the bag on the dining table and then coming back into the living room. Shaka follows Kai.

"What did Shaka do?" I ask.

"He's just everywhere I go. And he's ... well, look at him."

I do. Shaka smiles the way some breeds do. An actual dog smile. Then he lets his tongue loll out for an extra dose of adorableness. Shaka's obviously oblivious to the way Kai feels about him because he looks up at Kai as if no one else in the world exists.

"Well, the feeling sure isn't mutual. That dog adores you."

"Hrmph." Kai makes a grumpy old man noise.

I burst into laughter. "I've never seen this side of you."

"It's that dog."

"Mm hmm. Well, you're a saint for putting up with him. I can see that he's absolutely horrible."

Kai gives me a side eye.

Then he waves his arm toward the couches and overstuffed chair. "Come in. Make yourself at home."

Kai looks around as if he's trying to size up whether the house is guest-ready. It's immaculate. Surfing magazines are stacked neatly on a side table. Blue and white abstract paintings of the ocean line the walls, interspersed with a collage of surf photos of Kai, Kalaine, and Bodhi. I walk closer so I can see them better.

I've never been in Kai's space alone. I've attended a few barbecues, but then I was only out back in the yard, entering through the gate from the alleyway behind the houses like the rest of the guests. I came in to use the restroom once during a party, but I never ventured into the living room.

"Wow." I breathe out my awe in one word that doesn't do justice to what I'm seeing.

Kai on a wave. This photo looks like it was taken by a professional with a high-quality camera. The details are vivid. He's surfing in Hawaii or somewhere tropical. The wave is twice as tall as Kai, and he's riding down the face with his body bent. I can feel the intensity of his focus, the way every inch of him is engaged in the ride. I study the next photo. Kai's on the top of a wave like a skier on a slope. His board is aimed with the nose out of the water, spray arcing behind him. Every muscle flexed. The smile on his face is broad and free.

He's gorgeous. Most days I forget Kai was a pro-surfer. He's just Kai to me.

"Do you miss it?" I ask.

"Sometimes."

He walks over so he's just behind me. We stand there, silently absorbing the photos together.

Kai points at one. "That was the best day. I won all my heats. Took first in the whole contest."

"You're a superhero," I nearly whisper.

He chuckles low and deep. "Like Aquaman."

I make the mistake of turning to smile at him. He's right there, a light dusting of end-of-the-day stubble covering his jawline, dark and inviting. His golden-amber eyes find mine. We're locked in this moment, so close I can hear his breath, for one ... two ... three seconds that feel like they defy time, and then I come to my senses, and it seems like he does too.

Kai steps back. "You never said what brought you knocking at my door this late at night. Surely it's not so you could take in the history of Kai Kapule's pro-surfing days."

"No. Actually, I need to talk to you."

"Okay. Everything alright?"

That protective edge is back in his voice and it hits me in a way it never had before we started faking a relationship. I've always known Kai excelled in providing for and protecting those he loves. I've been the grateful recipient of his care over the years. Right now, his protectiveness feels more masculine. And this dormant feminine side of me can't help but wake up and stretch in response.

Go back to sleep, I try to coax myself. *It's not time to wake up.*

It's late. Kai's shirtless. I'm confused.

In the light of morning, I'll be less vulnerable, I'm sure of it.

"Can I get you a drink?" Kai offers.

"Sure. Water, or nothing. Or whatever."

"Water coming right up. Have a seat, Mila. Make yourself at home. But be forewarned. That dog will climb up next to you."

"Thanks for the heads up. I would hate it if a dog were to snuggle up with me without warning."

Kai turns around and raises his eyebrow. "You're making fun of me, right?"

I hold my fingers up in a pinch. "I mean, Kai, look at him. He's so well behaved. And cute. And he obviously loves you."

I take a seat on the couch. Shaka jumps up next to me, turns around once, and curls himself into a ball at my side. Then he lifts his fluffy head and rests it on my thigh.

I run my fingers through his hair and he lets out a whoosh of breath and settles in even more.

"The mutt's alright. I wouldn't have him here if it weren't for Kala. But you know how I am with her. She's my baby sister. I'd do anything for her."

I smile. *The mutt.* I've never seen this side of Kai before. It's amusing.

"I do know how you are. Best big brother in the world."

"Tell Kala that. She thinks I'm overbearing."

"Sometimes we don't see what's right in front of us. Deep down she knows you're the best."

"So, what's got you on the other side of the island after dark?" Kai walks back into the living room with two glasses of water. "You seemed a little flustered when I opened the door. Did something happen?"

Besides you walking around shirtless? Not much.

Kai sets his water on the side table next to mine. Then, as if he read my mind—which I'm begging and hoping he didn't—he grabs his shirt from where it was draped over the back of the love seat and puts it on. Unfortunately, putting on a shirt is nearly as sexy as walking around without one. His muscles bunch and his hair is tousled in the process, and then he runs one hand through his hair to tame it, but that movement isn't any less offending.

I grab my water and take a big gulp. Then I nearly choke.

"You okay?" Kai's face fills with concern.

"Yeah." I sputter-cough a little. "Just a long day. I'm always a little less pulled together by this time of night."

I take a big breath, running my hands over Shaka's back in soothing motions. "We need to talk."

"What's up? Does this have to do with Brad? Did he contact you again?"

"No. He didn't contact me. But Chloe came by today. She heard we were dating—and she didn't hear it from me."

"Oh. That can't have gone well."

Kai knows Chloe.

"She was upset. But I made a snap decision. And then I realized I broke one of our rules."

"Fine."

"Fine? You don't even know which rule I broke."

"I'm assuming you told her the truth."

"I did. In the moment it was either lie to her and damage a lifelong friendship, or come clean with her."

"That's fine. I'm glad she knows."

"Really?"

"Of course. You trust Chloe. This is your thing. We're fake dating for you—to protect you. I'm just pitching in. If you want to tell someone, tell them. I know Chloe is your best friend. It makes sense."

"Thank you."

"No problem. Hopefully that's the biggest hurdle we'll face."

The words, "Yes. Hopefully," are what I say. But in my heart, I have a feeling we've only barely started clearing the hurdles we'll be facing with this charade of ours.

FIFTEEN

Kai

My family is my strength and my weakness.
~ Aishwarya Rai Bachchan

"Hey, big brother!" Kala's face fills my phone when I click the green button with the video camera icon on it.

"Hi. I'm at work."

I turn the screen to scan the watersports shack as if my sister doesn't know what my work looks like. My mistake becomes evident before I even finish panning the phone.

"Heeeeyyyyyyy! Hi, Kapule Fam!" Ben's face smooshes toward the screen, he's literally five inches from my cell—okay, maybe eight—beaming at my family like a clown on laughing gas—which sounds incredibly creepy, and also describes Ben to a T right now.

My family waves at Ben. Their warm smiles fill my phone screen when I turn my cell so my face is now the one in the little picture-in-picture.

"How's Kai really doing?" Kala shouts as if Ben isn't so far into my personal space he could be my Siamese twin.

I shudder at the thought of me and Ben attached at the hip.

"You'd have thought he was a lost puppy when you first left,"
Ben chuckles, his voice booming next to my ear. "But I made him
go out dancing ... That was before ..."

I shoot Ben a look. He makes his classic zipping motion,
thankfully off camera so my family doesn't see him.

Kala asks, "Before what?"

Ben looks at me, wide-eyed. Then he answers Kala. "Before he
adjusted and ..." Ben looks around the shack. "... started bringing
Shaka to work. Yeah. Shaka. He's bringing your dog to work."

I stifle a groan at Ben's attempt to cover how he nearly leaked
everything to my entire family.

"What?!" Kala has the sweetest smile on her face. "Are you
serious?"

Bodhi's next to her grinning with an I-told-you-so smile on
his face.

"Kai, you're bringing Shaka to work," Kala nearly coos.

"I have to."

"You have to, huh?" Bodhi goads.

"The dog is relentless. I'm not leaving him home to destroy
my place. I have no choice."

Ben rolls his eyes in sync with Bodhi.

"You softie!" Kala beams. "I knew you loved my dog. It was
only a matter of time before you admitted it."

"Yeah. Yeah. So, tell me what's new with you two." I greet my
parents. "Aloha, Makuahine and Makuakāne."

My mom and dad say hi and fill me in on things going on in
their life in Hawaii. Kala and Bodhi remind me it's their last day
on Oahu. Tomorrow they leave for Portugal. They bring me up to
speed about their surfing, which is unnecessary because I've been
watching their YouTube channel for updates religiously every
night before I fall asleep. I don't confess that little detail to them,
especially not in front of Ben.

"Only one more week, big brother. Then we'll be home."

My mom clucks her tongue slightly at my sister's use of the

word *home*. Of course Oahu is home. I'm just glad Kalaine feels like my place is another home for her.

"I'm so happy for you," I tell Bodhi and Kala. "And proud."

"Oh!" Ben says, butting in as if he belongs in a conversation between me and my ohana. "Kai taught Noah to surf."

"Noah, Mila's Noah?" Kala asks.

I nod. And I can't help but smile at the memory of that morning—all the memories, including the walk Mila and I had to the shack after Noah ran ahead of us, and the way it felt to hold her when she hugged me.

"Yeah. You should have seen Noah," Ben goes on. "He was nearly coming unglued with excitement ..."

I let Ben ramble as if he were the one in the water teaching Noah. It is exciting whenever someone local learns to surf. It's more special than teaching a guest at the resort because we'll have the privilege of watching an islander continue to mature as a surfer over time. And the people here matter.

While Ben raves about the video Noah showed him and Jamison, I run through options as to what to tell my family about Mila —or not tell them. If I keep our supposed dating life a secret, no one will go absurdly crazy over me finally dating. But Kala and Bodhi are bound to hear rumors when they come back. I don't want to be in the position Mila was with Chloe. It's better if I'm the one to leak everything. At least I can maintain some control over the narrative that way.

Ben's still rambling, while my family stares on patiently, warm smiles on all four of their faces. They don't have to work with this ball of charismatic energy day in and day out. Well, Bodhi does. But he's always been more chill than I am. He finds Ben amusing. Which he is, but in small doses. Besides, Bodhi gets a reprieve from life here whenever he and Kala leave for another surf trip.

"So," I cut in.

Ben looks at me with a half-smile on his face. "Bro, I wasn't finished."

"Okay."

"No. No. Go ahead. It's your fam. You talk."

Suddenly, I wonder if I'm thinking clearly. Should I tell them? My throat feels tight and my mouth a little dry.

"Well, it's nothing really. I just wanted to say I'm dating someone. Casually. Not that it's a big deal. I'm a grown man. I can date. I just ... wanted you to know."

Bodhi wags his eyebrows and smiles at me. Kala starts jumping around and squealing, and my parents exchange a look with smiles that are so sweet I have to look away. I got their hopes up. It feels wrong to lead them on.

I remind myself why I'm carrying off this farce in the first place. Mila needs me. I can patch up the damage after we "break up," whenever that is. I'll just say it didn't work out, and we'll all move on.

"Who is it?" Kala asks, her giddiness bubbling straight through the phone and into my heart like an arrow.

Bodhi looks down at her. "Pretty obvious, isn't it?"

"Mila?" she asks him.

"That's my guess. I'd put money on it."

"Yeah, bro!" Ben shouts from right next to me. "You nailed it. It's so perfect, right? I saw it coming too."

"And you two went dancing?" Kala asks, clasping her hands together, her eyes crinkling at the edges with her big smile.

"Nah. I messed that up," Ben answers for me. "I asked him out not knowing he was into Mila. Well, I thought he was, but he denied it. Then he left early, ditching Gemma. After I heard about him and Mila, it all made sense."

I shake my head. What a mess.

"I love the idea of the two of you together." Kala smiles this particular smile of hers at me. It's familiar and warm, and it makes me want to book a flight to Hawaii, just to spend one hour in the middle of my ohana—the four most important people in my life.

Kala turns to my mom and says something I can't quite decipher. Then my mom looks into the camera and says, "She's a lucky woman, Kai. You are a strong man. A fierce protector and provider. A man of integrity. I hope she is worthy of you."

Man of integrity. Well, in some ways, what I'm doing is because of who I am. I can't let Mila face her ex alone. Integrity might be a stretch here, considering I just lied to my closest friend, my parents and my baby sister. And I allowed Ben to carry on in the charade, even though he has no idea he's complicit.

Why can't this be more simple? If only Mila and I could just act like we're dating when Brad is around. It seemed like a cut-and-dry solution when I opened my big mouth a few days ago. Now, I'm not so sure.

Add to that the way I'm more aware of her all the time ever since we started this pretend relationship, and I'm pretty sure I'm going to need a long vacation somewhere isolated and unreachable when we finally come clean—like the South Pole, or deep in the Amazon jungle where some cannibal tribe can put me out of my misery. They can place my dehydrated head on a pole as an example to all men who think they're being chivalrous and kind when they're actually lying to an entire community. Not that men in the deep Amazon fake date. I'm relatively sure they don't.

I snap myself out of thoughts of half-naked men chasing me through a jungle with poisoned spears just in time to hear my family saying their goodbyes.

"Love you!" Kala shouts last.

"Love you too. All of you. Aloha."

I click the camera icon on my phone screen and set my cell on the counter.

"Well. Well. Well. Telling the fam. That's big, bro."

"Not big. I just wanted Kalaine and Bodhi to hear it from me. It's still new."

Ben grins like the Cheshire Cat.

"Back to work. Stevens is coming in to do that tour. You need to ... do whatever you do to get ready to go out with him."

"Exactly nothing. I do nothing to get ready. I just ride along and he does all the talking. I'm the muscle, he's the brains."

Oh, the things I could say right now.

Ben rests his arms on the counter and stares at me. I turn away from him and walk to my cubby of an office. And then I shut the door.

In one week, my sister and soon-to-be brother-in-law will be home and I'll have to pull off a burgeoning relationship with Mila in front of them. What have I done?

SIXTEEN
Mila

I am a drifter without you,
you anchor me when all the world
is spinning around.
~ Unknown

The inn phone rings at the reception desk midday. We have caller I.D. and my breath catches when I see the name on the display.

Brad.

He said he'd give me space to decide about Noah. I'm not completely surprised that he isn't waiting for me to be the one to call. For one thing, Brad never was known for his patience when it came to getting something he wanted. He wasn't mean or selfish about it, just insistent and relentless. I used to see those qualities as admirable. And, on one hand, and in certain circumstances, they are. But when it comes to my son, Brad should know better. I need time. He bowled me over by showing up unannounced. I shouldn't have to answer to him so soon. And our next interaction should be on my terms.

After the fourth ring, I take a big breath, release it in a whoosh, and pick up the phone.

"Mila's Place, may I help you?"

"Mila's Place? That's a cute name, Mila."

When Brad and I were originally dreaming about the inn, we had a name. It flashes in my mind like words on a marquis: *Swanson Place.*

Brad's last name.

Our last name.

Not my last name anymore.

Or ever again.

And not Noah's last name ever. I gave Noah my name— because he's mine.

"Brad?" I act surprised. It's the best reaction I've got when he's ambushing me for the second time in a week.

"Yeah. It's me. Listen, I know I told you I'd wait about Noah. And I will. I just wanted you to know something. I think you have a right to know."

I sit down in the chair behind the reception desk. Something tells me I ought to be seated for whatever Brad's about to say.

"Go ahead," I tell him.

"Well, you know how I'm planning to expand the business?"

"Yeah?"

"I got a call from my realtor on Marbella. You know that old Boy Scout camp at Outriggers Cove?"

My stomach starts to roil and I wonder if there's enough air in the room because it's a little hard to catch my next breath.

I manage to say, "Yeah."

"Well, that place is up for sale. Not the whole camp, but the bait shop and the dock area with that other little outbuilding. You know the one. We snuck down there ..."

I cut him off, not needing to place one foot on memory lane, let alone take a stroll down it.

"Yeah. I know the buildings. So, you're buying them?"

"I am. I had to. It's too good. I thought I'd have to find beachfront property and develop it. This way, I only have to do renos. And, what's even better?" He doesn't even pause to let me guess, which is honestly mostly a relief. "I am buying the house on the back part of the property. You know, when you walk past the cabins where the Scouts used to stay? That house up the hill, the one with the ocean views? That's the one."

"You're ... moving here?"

Now I know the oxygen has left the room. I'm actually feeling dizzy.

"Not full time. I'll still keep my home in Santa Barbara. It will be more convenient while I'm setting up the business if I have a home on Marbella. And, anytime I need to come oversee the project, or later on, the business, I can stay in my island house. I'm going to eventually turn that into an AirBnB listing. Or Vrbo. Whatever. I'll have my property management company oversee it. Then I can just rent it out the rest of the time I'm not staying there. It's basically an investment."

"An investment," I echo like a dying parrot.

Brad's voice lowers. "I'm not trying to crowd you, Mila. I'll stay out of your way. But ..." he has the decency to pause. "If you do decide I can be in Noah's life, it will also make it more convenient for me to see him. I can stay over at my Marbella place on days you agree to let me see our son ... or whatever."

Our son. The words feel like a bitter pill.

"Stay over," I repeat.

"At my house, of course. Not yours. Not the inn, I mean." It almost seems like he has more to say.

I feel his unspoken hope hanging in the air.

"Well, of course, not here. I mean, I have a boyfriend."

I shouldn't throw my fake relationship with Kai around so freely.

"I know, Mila. I met him."

The memory of the day Brad met Kai settles me a little, as if Kai were right here, his arm around my waist, holding me up. It's probably not right to rely on him for strength like I do, but I can't help my reaction to Kai. He's strong and protective, and I need all the reinforcement I can get. After all, Kai was the one who told Brad he was my boyfriend in the first place. I didn't stop him, though. And I haven't stopped him since. Now, I'm pulling that lie out of my pocket so easily it's a little frightening.

"Well, thanks for letting me know," I say, hoping to wrap up the call sooner than later.

"Right. Well. There's one more thing."

"What's that?"

I don't think I can take one more revelation from Brad today.

Brad says, "I have a timeline."

And then the door of the inn swings open and Kai walks in. He takes one look at me and his casual gait turns into long, purposeful strides. He's at the reception desk before I even blink.

"What's wrong?" he mouths to me.

"Brad," I mouth back.

Kai rounds the desk and sticks his hand out as if he expects me to hand the phone over so he can step in and take the call for me.

I shake my head. "I've got this," I mouth.

Kai places a reassuring hand on my shoulder and my whole body relaxes so instantly it's like I just got a massage.

Kai.

He did that.

And I don't know what to do about the fact that he matters so much to me. As a friend, yes. But I'm starting to wonder about the other layer of feelings that flit around in my belly these days whenever he's near, or when I reminisce about him teaching Noah to surf, and especially when I think about how Kai held me outside the watersports shack.

"What?" I say to Brad, realizing he's been elaborating on his timeline while I've been fully distracted by Kai's arrival.

"Is someone else there? Do you have guests? Want me to call you back?"

"No. Yes. Actually. Yes. And, no. Don't call me back. Kai just walked in. Sorry. You were saying?"

Kai smiles a smirky grin. He seems pleased with himself for throwing me off, or maybe he's just pleased that I mentioned his name and acknowledged his presence to Brad.

I smile back. I can't help it. Kai always makes me smile.

Brad lets out an audible sigh. "I was just saying, the agent representing the seller is in a hurry to push the sale, so we're in a remarkably short escrow. My down payment is cash, and my businesses are part of the assets I'm bringing into the equation, so all that helps speed things along. I'll start work on the property in two weeks. And I'll be out that way sooner to finalize the deal, to walk the property for inspection ... you know. All the details that go into a sale."

"Two weeks," I say the words while looking at Kai.

Kai's brow furrows. He squeezes my shoulder in reassurance, even though he doesn't know what two weeks I'm even referring to.

My body warms from his touch and I clear my throat.

Kai's eyes lock on mine and I say the next sentence to Brad without looking away from Kai. Those honey-gold flecks embedded in cinnamon brown feel like a lifeline to me.

"Okay. Thanks for letting me know," I say.

Kai's face is warm, but serious, like a guard dog standing next to his owner, ready to pounce if only given the signal.

"I want to be upfront with you, Mila," Brad says. "I know I threw you off when I first came around, but I want you to know I'm not trying to get away with anything. I've changed. And I regret the foolish choices I made years ago. I hope you can give me a chance."

Foolish choices years ago? Those foolish choices continued every single day Brad didn't attempt to reach out. For each week, month, and year he stayed away, those choices dug a deeper hole. And now that trench plummets fathoms beyond what I can see. He didn't make a choice all those years ago. He continued to make that choice every minute of the past seven years.

Kai's eyes are still on mine and the crease in his forehead

deepens in response to whatever my face is doing. He obviously senses my mental spiral.

"I'm okay," I mouth to Kai, even though I don't know what I am. Okay isn't anywhere near what I am.

Brad says he wants me to give him a chance, but I hear the unspoken "us." He wants me to give *us* a chance. And that's not happening—not today, and not ever.

It's just like Brad to see Kai as a little wooden roadblock rather than an impassable stone wall. It's not that Brad would condone cheating. He'd never expect me to see him and Kai at the same time. Not if Brad's anything like he was in the past. He was always prone to seeking adventure, but ethical in most things. But, knowing Brad like I do, he still has some twisted idea that I'm his. He obviously hopes that he'll be able to convince me the past choices he made were a mistake and now he's a new man—one I should consider dating again. And that means he sees Kai as a lapse on my part—a placeholder until Brad comes back to win my heart. Not happening. Ever.

Brad and I finish out the call and I hang up. Then I collapse back into my chair and Kai's hand slips away. I scold myself for missing the contact. I shouldn't want Kai's touch or miss it when we separate. I've got years to go before I even entertain the idea of actually dating a man.

"What was all that about?" Kai asks, his face filled with concern.

"Brad bought the Boy Scout camp."

"The ... ?"

"It's a property on Outrigger Cove."

"I know the place. That's a huge outlay."

"Yeah. Well, apparently the used sporting goods business has done well for him. And, as a bonus, he bought the house at the back of that property."

I explain the whole conversation to Kai. He listens intently.

When I'm finished, Kai says, "This doesn't change anything. We're committed to faking a relationship. And Brad will see when he comes here that you aren't available. At least he informed you instead of just showing up on the island without warning."

"Yeah. I guess that is considerate," I concede. "And he's not demanding time with Noah."

"And, if he mainly stays in Outrigger Cove, you may not even know he's here on Marbella."

"Right."

Something tells me that's wishful thinking.

I try to sound optimistic when I say, "Besides, once Brad's got the business up and running, he will only come to the island sporadically. He'll have to rotate his time here between checking in on the other locations. It won't be enough for him to even notice if we're together or not. Then you and I can call things off."

Kai nods. An expression flashes across Kai's face. It almost looked like regret. I hope he'd tell me if he regretted setting this whole ball in motion. I'd let him off the hook. I'm sure he knows that.

"What brings you over here anyway?" I ask.

"Oh. My family. Kalaine and Bodhi Facetimed me with my parents today. And I told them we're dating."

"You did?"

"I didn't want them to come back and hear it from someone else."

"That makes sense."

"Especially now that Brad's coming here so soon."

I nod. Kai must pick up on how overwhelmed I am. As always, he jumps in to reassure me.

"I've got you, Mila. Don't let Brad throw you off. I'm always a phone call or text away. You aren't facing him alone."

Kai smiles down at me. Then he asks, "Did you eat lunch?"

"No. I've been busy going over reservations and making sure the confirmation emails went out to next week's guests. I'll grab something from the fridge in a bit. Or I'll just have a protein bar."

"Let me take you to Sebastian's for sandwiches," Kai suggests.

"Right now?"

"Yeah. Or I could go pick them up and bring them back here?"

"No. I should get out of here and clear my head. Give me a minute?"

"Sure. I'll just wait on the porch."

SEVENTEEN

Kai

*Parents often give middle names just so that later,
when they're yelling at the kid, they can drag it out.
'Henry David Thoreau,
you come in here this instant!'*
~ Paul Reiser

Mila steps onto the porch, leaving the inn unattended. Her guests know they can come and go, and she leaves a sign dangling on the reception desk that says, "Back in ..." with the amount of time she estimates she'll be gone. On days when Chloe's cleaning, Mila runs errands. And, when Mila's here alone, she locks the kitchen and shuts down the computer before she leaves. Otherwise, she doesn't think twice about taking a break with me.

I stand from the porch swing and walk over to her, instinctively placing my palm on her back in a way I never would have a week ago.

"Are you okay?" I study her face for a sign of what she might hide with words.

"Yeah. I think so. Don't worry about me."

"I'll worry if I want to. You're not the boss of me, Mila ... What's your middle name anyway?"

"My middle name?"

"Yeah. It sounds better if I can say *Mila June Mitchell,* when I'm telling you that you're not the boss of me."

We head down the porch steps together and I let my hand fall off Mila's back once we're walking.

"June?" She scrunches up her nose in this adorable way that gives a glimpse of what she must have looked like growing up.

"Not June?"

"No." She giggles, which makes me want to continue bantering with her.

Anything to lift the mood I caught her in when I walked in on her phone call with Brad.

"July?"

She laughs harder. "No!'

"January?" I wink at her. "February? March? Now that would be a name. Alliteration freaks would go mad for a name like that. Mila March Mitchell. Say that five times fast."

She tries and bursts into more laughter when "Mitchell" comes out "Mishell." And then the words get even more jumbled from there.

"MeeyaMarMimshell." She pauses in the street and places her hand on my shoulder. "Wait! Wait! I can do it. Give me another chance."

"Okay, Meeya. Go for it." My smile feels so full it reaches into my chest and fills it with a warm bubbly feeling I don't think I've ever felt before.

Mila starts saying, "Mila March Mitchell," but her lips are pursing and she's enunciating every syllable so intentionally with the effort to get it right. "Mee-lah March Mitch-ell. Mee-lah March Mitch-ell."

I start to imitate her and she bursts into another bout of giggles.

"No fair! You can't mock me in the middle of this challenge."

"I didn't know there were rules."

"There are," she says, trying to make her face serious, but utterly failing.

Mila's laughter only serves to fuel me. "April, May? Oh. There's another winner. Mila May. It makes you sound southern."

"Well, I declay-ah," Mila says with a perfect lilt that reminds me of *Gone With the Wind*, a classic movie Summer made a bunch of us watch with her a few months ago. She's obsessed with old films.

"You can't just go using an accent like that on a man without warning," I tease. Or at least it's meant to sound teasing. My voice comes out deeper and slightly scratchy. She affects me. There's no denying it. I just have to work around the fact—for her sake.

Mila looks up at me, her cheeks going suddenly pink. I stare down at her, unable to force myself to look away from her warm brown eyes and the light freckles dusting her nose, her rosy lips, the curve of her cheeks, the way her wavy hair frames her face.

I shake my head. "Okay. Not a month?"

"Maybe," she teases. "You haven't asked if it's October."

"Is it?"

She smiles up at me. "'Fraid not."

"Hmmm. Food? Is it a food item? Mila Burger Mitchell? Mila Gummy Bear Mitchell?"

She puffs out a laugh and shakes her head.

"Mila Pizza Mitchell? That's a fave. If it's not your name, I think you ought to consider a legal change. Noah would be in heaven."

"In that case, it should be Mila Snickerdoodle Mitchell." She says it so matter-of-factly.

"Maybe so, but since it's my turn to guess … and it's obviously *not* Snickerdoodle … Hot Dog?"

She literally rolls her eyes. But her lips bend into an amused grin.

"Yesssss!" I turn to her, stopping in my tracks. "I nailed it! Mila Hot Dog Mitchell."

"You're ridiculous." The way her mouth turns up and her eyes crinkle does things to me. Things I should avoid—especially with Mila.

"Hot Dog," I insist, attempting to keep things light so my heart will get the message. "I obviously nailed it and you don't want to admit how clever I am at figuring out middle names. I'm the middle name master. Say it."

I grin down at her.

"You're the middle name master." She glances sideways in my direction, and her playful grin nearly levels me.

Okay, bad idea to ask her to call me that.

We turn onto the street where Sebastian's is three shops up, situated between the bookshop and a place that does a travel and tour business, but also offers photography and dog sitting. Small island life at its finest.

"It's Rose." Mila's face blushes softly again.

"Rose."

I know my voice comes out with a reverent note. It just fits her. *Mila Rose Mitchell.* Why did I even ask?

"Well, I'm going with Hot Dog." I wink over at her.

Then I open the door to Sebastian's so Mila can pass through.

And when her vanilla and cinnamon scent swirls up around me, I nearly confess, *Mila Rose Mitchell, I think you might be the death of me.*

I barely see Mila the whole next week. We've had snorkeling tours, surf lessons, kayak rentals, and a few night rides on the glass-bottom boat along the shoreline to keep us busy. I'm assuming Brad has left Mila alone since his call announcing his plans to buy an entire cove of the island.

Who does that?

Brad. That's who.

Saturday I'm at the shack early, waiting for my next surf lesson with Noah. My sister and Bodhi are due back in town this evening after an international flight from Portugal and the ferry ride back to Marbella. Their two-week trip is coming to a close. I'm happier than I'll let on to have them back. I haven't minded the time alone, but I like my house better when they're in it. And it's been an unusual two weeks. Maybe them being back will help bring things back to some semblance of normalcy.

Shaka's trailing behind me from spot to spot in the shop as I straighten merchandise. Ben's singing, "Me and My Shadow," and chuckling at my misfortune. This dog. I turn and look at him. He sticks his tongue out and pants at me from his seated position just behind where I'm standing.

"What?" I ask the mutt.

"Just love me!" Ben says in a cartoon-dog voice.

"Are you on the clock, or just hanging out here?"

"Both?" Ben laughs.

"Do something besides turning my morning into a live-action Disney movie."

"Awww, but he loves you so much. Just pet him and I'll stop. I'll even tag the new merch. Just pet Shaka." Ben starts chanting, "Pet him! Pet him! Pet him!" with his hands cupped around his mouth.

Jamison walks in with a rightfully confused expression on his face.

"Pet him? What exactly is going on in here? Or should I ask?"

"Nothing." Ben smiles over at Jamison. "I'm just trying to get Kai to give Shaka some love."

"Ahhh." Jamison looks at me. "Are you allergic?"

"I wish," I grumble.

I'm not a grumpy man. Serious? Yes. Sometimes I'm up in my head a bit more than the guys around me. To be fair, I'm surrounded by surfers. It's a chill community and we tend to be an easygoing culture. I tend to be the leader, and I watch out for everyone. That makes me less free flowing than guys like Bodhi and Jamison. And then ... Ben ... Ben is on the other end of the spectrum from me. Nothing gets that guy down. He's like a living, breathing one-man party bus.

Jamison shakes his head and walks to the back of the shack toward the back door. He's got a stand-up paddleboard lesson at the same time as I'm taking Noah out surfing.

Ben crosses his arms over his chest as if he's not budging until I pet the dog. So, I bend down and scratch Shaka behind his ears.

"Good boy," I say in a neutral tone.

The tail starts going anyway, even though I obviously wasn't putting any emotion behind my words.

"There. Was that so hard?" Ben asks.

"Honestly? Yes."

Ben chuckles.

Mila and Noah come bounding into the shack. Well, Mila doesn't bound. She's walking in with her beach bag over her shoulder and a soft smile on her face, and when she aims that smile at me, I go a little weak. It's ridiculous. I'm a man. And we're faking. But she's Mila. What can I say?

"We're here!" Noah shouts as if his entrance weren't already an event.

"Heyyyy! Look who's here!" Ben shouts.

"Mila, looking lovely today," he adds.

Why that makes me want to go put my arm around her is beyond me. She's not mine.

She's not mine.

She's not mine.

Maybe if I repeat it enough, I'll remember.

Mila smiles at Ben and says, "Good morning." Then she looks across the shop toward me and in an unusually shy voice she says, "Hi, Kai."

I smile at her. "Hey."

"Hey, Ben!" Noah shouts. "Are you coming out with us?"

"I wish I could. Someone has to hold down the fort in here while Kai has all the fun. That happens to be me today."

"Awwww," Noah pouts.

He turns to Jamison. "What about you, guy?"

"I'm Jamison. And I've got a paddleboard lesson."

"That's my next thing I'm going to learn too," Noah announces. "Right, Mom?"

"We'll see." Mila smiles.

Shaka trots over to Noah's side and Noah bends to ruffle Shaka's fur.

"Hey, Shaka! You're a good dog," Noah says. "Are you working today?"

Noah laughs at his own joke.

"Would you rather surf with Ben?" I offer, sincerely.

Mila's eyes go wide for the briefest moment. I instantly recognize my error.

"That is, if your mom says yes."

"Uhhhh ..." Noah stammers.

Mila nods at me and Ben to let us know she's alright with a switch.

"Tell you what," I suggest. "You and I will go out as planned so you can buff up your skills, and then I'll cut the lesson short by a little so you still have energy to show your moves to Ben. He can take over at the end and you two can surf together. Sound good?"

"Yeah!" Noah shouts. "Only you don't have to cut it short, Unko. I've got plenty of energy."

"I'll say," Mila says softly with a look of adoration aimed at Noah.

"Okay then, boss man, let's get in the water."

"I'm ready!" Noah looks at Ben. "Kai calls me boss man. He's your boss, right?"

Ben nods. "Yep. He's the man in charge. I do whatever he says."

I mutter, "If only."

"That means I'm the boss of the boss of you!" Noah says, cracking himself up.

"Man. You're awfully young to be so powerful, but I'm not arguing with the boss of the boss of me." Ben smiles at Noah. "I'm at your service."

Ben bows as if he's approaching the king, and Noah's peals of laughter fill the shop.

"I'll see you at the end of my lesson, worker," Noah says to Ben as we walk out to grab his wetsuit from the rental rack.

Ben's laughter follows us out the door.

"Tell him to get busy tagging merchandise," I say to Noah.

Noah repeats my instructions, shouting them in a commanding voice into the shop, and Ben cackles.

"Oh, man! Don't listen to Kai, Noah. He's a bad influence!"

I get Noah suited up and he and I walk toward the waves with Mila strolling alongside us. I already put the boards out on the sand earlier this morning.

We're in the water for about forty minutes, Noah picking up right where he left off. Ben comes paddling out just as we promised, and I take a wave in once I know Ben's got Noah.

When I hit the shore, I shake the water out of my hair and pull my board up onto the sand. Then I join Mila where she's got a blanket spread out just beyond the edge of the shorepound. Shaka's on one side of her, laying on the blanket like he owns the whole beach.

"He did great," I tell her.

"I'm so grateful to you for teaching him. It's his dream, and I wouldn't want anyone else to be the one."

She pats the blanket. "Want to sit?"

"I'm soaked. I'll get your blanket all wet."

"That's what beach blankets are for. Come on. Have a seat."

I nod and settle in beside her. Shaka stands up and comes to my side.

I give him a gentle nudge trying to coax him into going back to Mila's side, but he ignores me and lays down right next to me, half on the blanket, half in the sand.

"That's going to mean a shower for you," I tell him. "Wet dirty dogs don't get in my bed."

"Your bed, huh?"

"Don't ask."

Mila smiles warmly, but to her credit, she doesn't push the subject like Ben does. Then she digs into her bag and pulls out a granola bar and a juice box.

"Here. Have a snack."

I chuckle. How many years has it been since I had a juice box?

"Thanks. I'm not taking Noah's food, am I?"

"I've got plenty."

I open the wrapper and pop the straw in the juice, and we both fix our eyes on the waves where Ben and Noah are taking ride after ride, settling on their boards next to one another between sets. From here, they look like two black wooden bobs in the water, but we can tell it's them. One taller than the other, their faces turned in so they can talk while they wait for the next wave.

The silence between me and Mila is comfortable. She puts me at ease. Always has.

I'm watching Noah get up on a bigger wave than any he's taken so far when a voice behind me asks, "Is that Noah?"

EIGHTEEN

Kai

Most things in life come as a surprise.
~ Lykke Li

I turn to see Bodhi and my sister standing behind me with huge smiles on their faces. They look simultaneously travel-weary and blissfully content.

I jump up.

"Kala! Bodhi! You're home? I didn't expect you until sometime after midnight."

I pull my sister into a hug before I consider that I'm still soaked from my surf session. Shaka's jumping right alongside me, whimpering and wagging his tail as if to say, *Thank goodness you're back, your brother did a horrible job being my babysitter.*

Traitor of a dog.

"Surprise!" Kalaine shouts as I lift her off her feet. "We got an earlier flight, so we made it back to LA before sunrise this morning."

"Man, it's good to see you," I confess.

I lean in toward Bodhi and clap him on the back.

Shaka runs between me, Bodhi, and Kalaine, and then he finally settles in a sitting position near my feet. Kalaine bends to rub his head and babbles all sorts of sweet words at the dog like he's her long lost child. He leans into her hand, but stays next to me for some unknown reason.

"You got them all wet," Mila says from her spot on the blanket, then she stands and walks over to Kalaine.

"Welcome home—or back. Back to Marbella," Mila says, warmly.

"It's home. One of my two homes."

Kala stretches her arms out to Mila. The two of them embrace in what I'd almost call a sisterly hug.

Kalaine works part-time at Mila's Place when she's on the island, just to pick up the slack and to keep herself busy. I guess they've developed a friendship.

Kalaine pulls away, a beaming smile on her face. "And don't worry about Kai dripping on us. We're used to it. Surfers never mind a little residual ocean water." She reaches out and gently squeezes Mila's shoulder. "And you. I'm so happy to hear about you and Kai."

Mila's blush fills her cheeks and she looks up at me as if she needs me to bail her out.

I always will. Anytime Mila needs me, I'll do whatever it takes to relieve some of the weight she carries. That's how we got into this fake dating mess, after all. I couldn't sit back and watch Mila struggle when I knew I could do something to alleviate her stress and anxiety.

Was I crazy? Am I crazy to keep pretending now, even when it means deceiving my sister and my best friend?

I already know my answer.

But right now, I'm at a loss for words.

"Sorry!" Kala says, stepping back into Bodhi, who easily slips his arm around her. "I don't mean to make it weird. I know this thing between you two is new. I just figured with your stance on not dating, if you and my brother are giving this a shot it's not exactly casual."

"Right. Yeah. Well, he's amazing," Mila says, smiling up at me as if she means it.

I think I might be blushing now. Thankfully the tan of my skin will hide it a bit if I am.

Bodhi grins over at me. "Way to go, man. Mila's going to be so good for you."

If we were actually dating, I'd have to plan some serious revenge on my best friend and my sister. They're acting like Mila and I are engaged, not just starting to see one another. Maybe it's the jet lag. Or it could be their pre-marital bliss which seems to know no bounds these days. They're so in love they've lost their minds. That must be it.

Bodhi looks over at Mila, and what he says next makes me want to sink into the sand until I'm no longer visible. I want to morph into a sand crab ... one of those creatures who can live under the surface of the beach ... I'd creep into my grainy refuge where I wouldn't have to witness my best friend humiliating me.

Is it too much to ask?

Bodhi reaches over and pats me on the side of my upper arm in a typical bro-move. Then he looks at Mila.

"I always knew Kai had a thing for you. I mean, he tried to hide it. But it was obvious the way he'd jump at any hour of the day or night to help you."

"I help lots of people," I defend.

But no one seems to hear me.

Bodhi keeps going, like there's a well-oiled tube straight from his brain and his mouth. "You're definitely out of Kai's league."

Mila giggles. Maybe she's amused? Embarrassed? Nervous?

" ... so thanks for slumming it and giving my best friend a chance." Bodhi chuckles in my direction.

"Ex-best friend," I mutter.

All three of them laugh good-naturedly as if I'm joking.

Bodhi wraps up his speech of mortification with, "I'm ninety-nine percent sure Kai will make sure you never regret saying yes to him. I'm assuming he asked you, and not the other way around."

"He did." Mila smiles shyly.

When she glances up at me, our eyes lock and I remember the exact moment I announced, *I'm her boyfriend.*

I slip my arm around her waist without a second thought. This isn't about me.

A thousand thoughts ping through my mind, some of them involve creative ways to pay Bodhi back for roasting me and putting us on the spot. But with Mila's soft body pulled against my side, and my arm looped protectively around her waist, one main thought floats to the surface and stays there:

Is Bodhi right? Did I always have a thing for Mila?

If I did, I never knew it. I've definitely always thought the world of her. I've admired her resilience, the way she mothers Noah with a balance of grace and healthy limits. I respect the effort she puts into managing the inn. She's a skilled business-woman. Anyone would attest to how beautiful she is. Of course, I noticed. I might have even considered more than friendship with her early on, but that was years ago, before she made it clear where she stood with men—all men, and that, by default includes me.

I look around at Bodhi, Kalaine and Mila. All three sets of eyes are trained on me.

"Well, this hasn't been awkward at all," I joke. "Glad you two came back early to shine a spotlight on our new status."

Mila's soft smile turns into a carefree laugh. Maybe it's a nervous laugh, but it comes out sweet like a song and it warms something inside me in the process.

Bodhi smiles like he didn't just lay my heart out in front of my sister and my ... whatever Mila is.

"Hey, payback's a bear," he says, casually. "You didn't exactly make it easy for me and Mavs to make our way back to one another. I'm doing you the solid you never did for me."

"Kala's my baby sister," I say, meaning it with my whole heart.

"I think there's a rule somewhere that I'm supposed to make it hard on you."

Kalaine glances at Mila and leans in close. "Tell him I'm not a baby, will you? Maybe he'll listen to you."

Shaka licks my hand, like he knows I'm being humiliated. It's a move of solidarity, and even though the dog is a menace, I scratch his head to thank him.

"Look at you!" Kala says, with unmerited happiness. "You and Shaka. I knew you'd come around."

"I did not come around."

Shaka leans in and presses his whole sandy body against my leg as if to say, *You came around, admit it.*

I didn't. And I won't.

"Oh, I see how it's going to be now," Kalaine says. "Next thing I know, he'll be in your bed at night."

Mila lowers her voice as if she's confiding in Kalaine. "I think that might already be happening."

Kalaine's eyes go wide. "You and ... Shaka?"

"Bro? Seriously?" Bodhi asks.

"The dog jumped in my bed. I didn't invite him. I had to sleep. He whined when I tried to kick him out."

"Oh my gosh! You let Shaka sleep with you!" Kalaine squeals.

I'm pretty sure the guys on the waves can hear my sister.

"Thanks a lot, Hot Dog," I say to Mila, squeezing her side without a second thought.

She jumps like she's ticklish and giggles while retreating from my hand, which only brings her closer into the rest of me.

Bodhi and Kala watch us with twin expressions of delight. They're grinning like they're seeing me come out of the water after winning a heat in a surfing competition. And I'm too overwhelmed to feel guilty for misleading them. They've pushed this to the next level by practically giving their blessing on our nuptials when I only told them we're dating.

Mila doesn't shrug me off. As a matter of fact, she leans into me. I like the feel of her in my arms more than I should. Our farce has an end date, even if we haven't formally set one. The purpose is to keep Brad at bay, not for me to get my heart all tangled up. Mila's still a woman dead set against dating—for valid reasons. That hasn't changed, even if my feelings have.

Man. *Was Bodhi right?* Talk about an inconvenience.

"You did not just call me Hot Dog." Mila nudges me playfully.

Bodhi wags his eyebrows. "I'm pretty sure there's a story behind that nickname ... one you don't have to share."

My sister looks between me and Mila. "You two are adorable together."

When I glance down at Mila, our eyes connect. One hundred things seem to pass between us, and I can barely decipher a few of them.

Bodhi saves me from having to respond to my sister. "Hey! You never answered me. Is that Noah out there with Ben?"

Mila looks away from me to answer Bodhi. "Yes. He just had a lesson with Kai."

She beams up at me. "But he wanted to surf with Ben too."

Then, she returns her focus to the ocean, stepping away from me to track Noah like the devoted mother she is. My eyes remain on Mila as if she's a brand new puzzle I need to study and solve.

"If my wetsuit weren't packed in our bags and I hadn't just traveled for eighteen hours, I'd be joining them right now," Bodhi says.

The reminder of how long they have traveled seems to cue a yawn from Kalaine.

"Where are your bags anyway?" I ask, my eyes still on Mila as she stares out into the water.

"At the house," Bodhi says. "We dropped them, and then Mavs talked me into coming to the shack to see you right away. I can't say no to her. You know how it is."

I take Mila in, the way her ponytail rests on her back, the

waves of her hair barely tamed. The slope of her shoulders. The apples of her cheeks, pink in the warmth of the sun. I glance back at Bodhi.

"Yeah. I know."

And, the crazy thing is, I do know.

"Look! Noah caught a good one!" Bodhi shouts.

All four of us watch as Noah rides a long right into shore. Ben follows behind on the next wave in.

They drag their boards up onto the sand.

While they're still a decent distance from us, I lower my voice and tell Kala and Bodhi, "We're keeping things quiet for now—from Noah."

Bodhi nods earnestly. "Sure. Sure, man. We get it. Mum's the word."

Then he actually makes that motion, zipping his lip with his pinched fingers.

I shake my head. "Not you too!"

Kalaine and Bodhi slept the whole day and into the night. I heard them rustling around at two in the morning, getting food in the kitchen and talking in low murmurs to one another. But they settled back into their rooms after a while, and they're both still dead to the world right now. Their internal clocks must be so wonky. It's the downside of world travel. A week in Hawaii put them three hours behind us, but then Portugal is eleven hours later than Hawaii. Their days and nights are temporarily flipped.

Speaking of flipped, Shaka is sitting at my heels while I wash my breakfast dishes. He tried jumping into my bed last night, and it took more than a bit of coaxing to remind him he sleeps with Kalaine. Needless to say, she was tickled with the whole *my dog loves you so much* situation. Emphasis on *her* dog. When I woke, he whimpered to come out of her room, so like the spineless man

I apparently am, I let him out, and he's been trailing after me ever since.

I look down at Shaka, "What? What do you want?"

Great. Now I'm talking to a dog.

He looks back at me like he's got those hearts in his eyes like the ones on that emoji Kala uses when she texts me. It's like he's the dog version of a lovesick teen. And I'm the target of his misguided affection.

"Really, man? You've got my sister. She loves you. Go give her your puppy dog heart eyes."

He sticks his tongue out to the side of his mouth for good measure, just to add to the potential cuteness factor—if you were into those kinds of things and thought they were cute, which I am not, and don't. Then, when the whole tongue thing doesn't work on me, he drops to the ground and tilts his head. He's so pathetic, he's the canine reminder of me when I crushed on this girl, Tootie, in ninth grade. Tootie Lynn had just moved to Hawaii from Dallas, Texas. She had long wavy blond hair and had been a cheerleader in her old high school. Tootie's accent alone made me want to drop to the floor with my tongue out and my head tilted.

Call it camaraderie or call it being worn down by some form of mutt-driven waterboarding, but this dog has me bending down and petting his head, and then he rolls just the slightest like the true con artist he is, so he has my hand on his belly rubbing in slow circles and scratching his ribs while he lays there like he owns the place.

And, of course, this is the moment when my sister decides to wake from her Rip van Winkle slumber and amble into the kitchen.

"Oh. My. Gossshhhh." She stretches and says in her scratchy morning voice. "That is the sweeeetest. Kai. I need my phone."

"Take a photo of this and die."

She just laughs as I stand up quickly before she can actually grab her cell. Shaka has the decency to roll over and trot to Kalaine instead of laying belly-up as a testament to my foolishness. So, I don't hate the dog as much as I did. I still don't love him, let's be absolutely clear.

Kala moves through the kitchen, grabbing down a mug and walking toward the coffee pot.

"You are a saint. You already made coffee."

"Not only that," I add. "I get bonus brother points for grinding the beans you brought back."

"Kona coffee! I'm so excited." Kalaine literally bounces on her toes as she pours her cup three-quarters full and then opens the fridge to grab the milk to top it off.

"I slept like the dead."

"You doing okay?"

"Yeah. I'm great." Kalaine holds her mug with both hands and leans into my side. "It's good to be back."

"It's good to have you back. I thought you might want to stay in Oahu this time."

"Nah. Makuahine was so over the top about reception details. I love her enthusiasm, and we needed to finalize things, but it would be a lot to deal with if I were there full time. Besides, this is where Bodhi and I want to be."

"Our mom has waited forever for one of us to get married."

"She has." Kala takes a long sip of her coffee and hums.

"Oh! Speaking of ..." Kalaine looks at me. "Makuahine brought up Aima. At first it was here and there, but by day three, she was mentioning her a lot. She even had her over two days before we left for Portugal while we were deciding on the food for the reception. It's a good thing you called about Mila."

"Why?"

"I think our parents had told her parents to try again at my wedding. She had a boyfriend for about a year, but they broke up nearly a year ago. She's very, very single ... and ready to ... "

I groan—audibly and long. "Hold that thought. Don't even finish your sentence." I run my hand through my hair. "Wait. Aima's coming all the way to California?"

"She is. Of course. She might as well be our cousin. How

could she not come? I want her to be here, Kai. I just don't want our parents pulling their usual tactics on you two."

"I thought she'd be at the Hawaiian reception, not the wedding here on Marbella." I sigh.

Our parents had been planning to play matchmaker along with Aima's parents. Of course, they had. Aima and I grew up like cousins. Our moms have been best friends since childhood. They basically betrothed us in the womb. They deny it, but it can't have been much later than that. They always joked about how sweet it will be when Aima and I finally fall for one another. It's been a set up my whole life. It wasn't a matter of if, but when, in their minds.

I like Aima. She's kind and decent. But I don't love her, not in the way a man loves a woman. We're talking zero sparks. She's literally my ohana—not by blood, but she might as well be a sister.

The expectation of our romance has been looming over me like a contract—one I evaded signing when I went pro and started surfing around the world. And then I moved to California. Visits home always hold the potential for an Aima ambush.

Kala smiles over her mug at me. "When you said you were dating someone? The way your face softened and your eyes got that dreamy tone to them? I don't think Makuahine would have given up her plan to fix you two up unless she saw how you morphed into a man fully devoted to a woman when you talked about Mila."

"Yeah," I say, skirting past my sister to put away the milk carton she left out. "Good thing I have Mila."

Kalaine wasn't the only one cataloging the look on my mother's face when I said I was dating someone—relief, joy, more relief, hope, and most of all, happiness for me. Ugh. I'm a horrible man. Then again, I'm not trying to go around fake dating people. I'd date seriously if the right woman would have me. And, from where I'm standing, there's only one right woman. And she won't have me—not for real.

I allow the cool air of the fridge to rush across my skin. Is there an especially torturous place in the afterlife for guys who stand in the kitchen like it's any other morning, flat-out lying to their sisters in the sweet hours of the early morning? I'm guessing, yes.

"You two are so adorable, Kai. I know Bodhi and I were extra about it. But seriously? You just fit. You're two of the most sincere souls on earth. Both of you have such integrity and you're both always looking out for others. You'll take good care of each other. I really see this working out long term. And you've always lost your cool around her, I should have known. I did have my suspicions. Mila's so smitten with you, too. It's the sweetest."

Mila is smitten? I doubt it. She's just play-acting. That's what we agreed to.

"What are you talking about? I haven't ever lost my cool."

"Um. Okay."

"What? I haven't."

"Does tripping over the step when coming into the inn ring any bells? Stuttering over your words at times? Starting to say something and then acting all befuddled like you did in junior high? Do I need to go on?"

"I don't ..." *Have I regularly lost my cool around Mila?*

"Kai. It's fine. I'll drop it and let you keep your man card. I'm just saying I'm happy for you two. And obviously you have to ask Mila to come to the wedding with you. Makuahine will never back off her attempts to pair you with Aima unless you've got Mila basically attached to your hip. Our mom needs to see you dating someone else with her own eyes."

"I know. You're right."

But what will it mean to bring Mila to my sister and Bodhi's wedding?

And should I even ask that of her—to fake in front of so many people from Marbella?

Maybe we could stage a breakup before then—an amicable parting of ways.

And how would we manage that?

Is there any possible way to appear to end our romance and still maintain a friendship in front of all these gossipy islanders?

Besides, a breakup would leave Mila wide open for Brad to make a move. And the idea of him pursuing her disturbs me infinitely more now than it did the day I met him.

I'm so cooked.

NINETEEN

Mila

If you want a single mom to fall in love with you,
love her child well.
~ Patty H. Scott

"Did someone die, Schmidt?" Chloe asks my bookkeeper.

"It's Johann."

"I know. Johann ... Schmidt. Your last name is Schmidt."

"And you can call me Johann."

"So, was there a death, Schmitty?"

Johann's face is a mask of indifference with only the slightest sneer of his left nostril.

"Not that I know of," he answers my bestie.

Chloe's always poking the bear whenever she and Johann are at the inn on the same day. Thankfully, he only comes in for a few hours a couple times a week.

"Well, tell your face," my bestie says like she's in seventh grade all over again.

"If my face looks like I'm in mourning, I'm only grieving the blessed silence when you are elsewhere. Instead, you insist on being on Mila's payroll while spending your time trying to get a rise out of me. You're wasting her money."

"A rise? Oh. I got a rise. You see that one hair in the middle of your right eyebrow? It flinched. No. It actually wiggled like it was doing the hula. The hula, Schmidt! You have a hula-dancing brow hair. What are you going to do about that?"

"I will pluck it later. Now, get to work."

"I'm sorry, did you just tell me to get to work?"

"I did."

Chloe beams. She's having far too much fun.

"I'll get to work when you flash me a smile, sir."

Johann turns to Chloe and the smile he gives her is thriller-level spooky. He's not a bad man—obviously. I wouldn't have him do my bookkeeping if he were. He's just ... stoic. Reserved. And, okay. Grumpy.

"Chloe, a word?" I tip my chin in the direction of the kitchen.

Chloe ignores me. "That was frightening, Schmidt. Good thing Noah's still at school. He'd have nightmares."

"Noah doesn't bother me."

"How lovely. He doesn't bother you? The world's most precious boy doesn't bother you? Oh, Schmidt. I pity you. What do you do on weekends? You know. For fun?"

"Are you asking me on a date?"

"Of course not! I have a husband. You know that. My man doesn't smile like a clown in a horror movie, either. I'm just curious. So, back to my question. In fact, I might die of curiosity. What do you do? Roast squirrels over an open flame? Collect sand dabs with tweezers and pin them to a cork board to hang on your walls? Dust the doorjambs until they pass the white glove test?"

"Chloe?" I call my bestie again.

"I smiled." Johann grins again, both sets of teeth bared and clenched, his eyes wide. It's very Jack Nicholson as the Joker. "Now shoo."

"It's the squirrels, isn't it?" Chloe says from over her shoulder while she walks toward the kitchen and toward me—finally.

"You're going to run him off," I whisper once she's inside the kitchen.

"And that would be a bad thing because ...?"

"Do you have another bookkeeper who does house calls and also helps me with my taxes hanging around in your back pocket?"

"I know my rear is plenty wide, but it's not that abundant."

I chuckle. "Well then, play nice."

"I do play nice. He's just so fun. Have you ever seen someone so serious?"

"I'm going to be that serious if you mess up my one and only bookkeeping situation."

"Okay. Okay." She holds her hands up, the rag she had been dusting with in one.

"By the way, you look like crud." Chloe eyes me. "What happened to you? Up late with your boyfriend?" She wags her eyebrows suggestively.

"No. And thanks. I was up late researching how to integrate an estranged dad back into a child's life."

"Oh, babe. I'm sorry. What did you find out?"

I sigh. I was up late. Too late. But I had a rush of anxiety once I realized I really wasn't getting around allowing Brad to re-enter Noah's life. The whole situation has me in knots. I can't tell Brad no without some sort of battle or struggle ensuing. He's being friendly now. But I know that would shift if I were to decide he couldn't come around. And besides, Noah deserves to know who his biological father is. I'd never want to be the one to keep him from Brad. Noah could end up resenting me. It's not my place to keep them apart. If Brad were a danger, it would be different.

"I didn't find much. The courts can get involved ..."

"Please, no." Chloe's brows go up toward the center.

"I know. That's the last thing I want." I plop onto one of the barstools. "One blog said I should get Noah into counseling, which could be great, but I'd rather not see someone here on Marbella. And I don't want to ferry over to the mainland weekly. Online isn't viable for kids. Not in my mind, anyway. Plus therapy might freak Noah out. His life is so stable and normal. I don't want anything to change for him. And I don't want to shine a spotlight on meeting Brad. I'd rather ease into it. Several articles suggested that. And a therapist I emailed sent me to a website suggesting the same thing."

"What are you thinking?"

"I think I just have to follow my intuition and take it slowly … as if Brad's a stranger."

"Because he basically is."

"Yeah. He is."

The man I loved and thought I'd spend my forever with is basically a stranger. The only thing we have in common now is Noah, and it's the one thing I don't want to have in common with him.

"Knock, Knock!" Kai's voice comes in through the front door.

I hear him greet Johann on the way in.

"Hey," he says casually as he walks into the kitchen like he lives here.

Kai's wearing a surf T-shirt that's obviously been worn in, it fits him as if it was made for him. His hair is properly tousled and his skin is glowing like he's been out in the sun. The thing that makes my belly tighten and tingle is the way he looks at me, and the broad smile that fills his face. It's like he's been saving that smile all day, letting it simmer and marinate until it was just right and he could serve it up to me. I smile back instantly, and all the worry over Brad and how I'm going to draw boundaries while inching toward revealing his true role to Noah disappears.

Poof. No more anxiety. Just like that.

"Hey there," Chloe says. "Well. I have some cleaning to finish up. So, I'll just leave you two lovebirds to it."

"Chlooooee," I warn, dragging her name out the way her mom did when we were little and she got in trouble.

"What? I'm the third wheel here. So I'm making myself scarce so you two can have your little middle-of-the day rendezvous."

"That's right," Kai plays along, even though he knows Chloe knows. And Chloe knows he knows.

I'm getting a dull headache just thinking of who knows and who doesn't know and all the things we have to keep track of just to keep Brad at bay for the time being.

Kai playfully smirks in Chloe's direction and then he steps up beside me and wraps his arm around my shoulders. "I came here to have a little middle-of-the-day rendezvous with my girl, so skedaddle."

"That's what I'm talking about!" Chloe grins and wags her eyebrows at me.

"Don't encourage her," I warn Kai.

"Like that would make a difference?" His smile fills his face.

"It totally wouldn't," Chloe boasts. "Mkay, lovebirds. Keep it down in here and make it snappy. Noah's due home any minute."

Chloe heads back out into the main room to finish cleaning.

Kai turns to me, shaking his head at the ridiculousness of my best friend.

"Actually, Noah's why I'm here. I have something for him. I wanted to bring it by after he got off school."

"You didn't have to get him anything. Is this for his birthday?"

Noah turns seven this month and it's pretty much all he can talk about.

Kai looks down at his hands and back up at me. Then he takes a seat at the island. I smile shyly at Kai now that we're alone. My body is reacting to him in ways my heart knows better not to. I feel like walking over and collapsing into his arms. I don't, but I really, really want to.

"I wanted to get him something. This thing. And you have to promise not to freak out. I've got plenty of cash and investments and I own my home outright—well, Bodhi and I co-own it, but still. I'm not hurting, Mila. I'm not about to purchase an entire cove of an island, but I'm fine."

"What did you do? This sounds way too extravagant."

"It's not. But I want you to be happy about this and not worry about what it cost me. Okay?"

I'm about to say it's not okay when Noah comes bounding through the house and through the kitchen doorway like a cartoon character with spinning circles under his feet. He drops his backpack on the floor.

"Hi, Unko! You're here. Did you park the golf cart out there?"

"Yep. I did."

"Let's have a snack!" Noah announces.

He goes to the fridge and pulls open his drawer where I keep all sorts of after-school food.

"Let's see. We've got applesauce. Grapes. Cheese Sticks. Hummus. That's gross. You could have it, though. And I think we've got chocolate chip cookies. Right, Mom?"

"We have a few left. But have something healthy with them. Okay?"

Noah comes out of the fridge carrying a bunch of things in his folded arms and then he releases his haul in a heap on the island.

"Plates?" he asks as if that's optional

"Yes." I answer for Kai.

Then I grab two plates, put them on the island and pour a glass of milk for Kai and one for Noah to go with the cookies I place on each of their plates. When I turn from putting the milk back in the fridge, the sight of the two of them at the island slams into me with the force of a fast-pitch softball to the gut.

They're smiling at one another, ripping open their cheese sticks, and Kai's making a mustache with his and talking to Noah in a goofy voice. Noah copies Kai right away and they burst out laughing.

They dig into the menagerie of snack items, talking and eating without any idea how this exchange is traveling straight to my heart, wrapping around it, and squeezing in a way that simultaneously aches and soothes.

"I got you something," Kai says when Noah pauses his stream of endless after-school chatter for a breath and a bite.

"You got me something? Can I guess?"

"Sure. Take a guess."

"Is it a puppy?"

Kai chuckles. "No. Not a puppy. I still want your mom to like me, so a puppy is not happening."

"She likes you," Noah says matter-of-factly.

Kai looks over at me. I hold his gaze, studying the warm caramel of his eyes.

"Is it ... an Xbox?" Noah asks.

Kai looks back at Noah. "Nope. Not an Xbox."

"Thank goodness," I say.

"Mom doesn't like those things. I played one at Forrest's house. He's got Minecraft. Did you ever play Minecraft?"

"I don't really play much. Bodhi does."

"Minecraft?"

"No. Something else."

"You didn't get me clothes, did you?" Noah's face scrunches up.

Kai chuckles.

"Noah." I give him a mom-look.

"What? Clothes are boring."

"He's not wrong," Kai says.

Except that T-shirt Kai's wearing. That's not boring at all.

Agh. What's wrong with me? Probably the lack of sleep. And that shirt. Kai needs a different shirt. Baggier. A bag. That would work. A big burlap bag. I would feel nothing right now if only he'd wear burlap.

"Do you want to keep guessing?" Kai asks Noah. "Or do you want me to show you?"

I can feel the eagerness rolling off Kai in waves. He's got a gift and he's dying to give it. It's adorable. This precious, generous, thoughtful man is as giddy as my son right now.

"Show me!" Noah shouts. "Is it here? Right now? Can we, Mom? Can we?"

"Sure. Clear your plate first."

Noah grabs both plates, dumps what's left of the mostly-eaten snacks into the trash, sets the plates next to the sink and bolts after Kai toward the main room. I trail behind them, loving the sight of the two of them more than I should.

When we're all on the porch, Kai turns to me and Noah. "Close your eyes. Both of you."

He gives me one last look, his one eyebrow raised and his finger pointed at me in a gesture that seems to say, *Settle down, Mila. Let him have this.*

I nod and close my eyes.

"Are your eyes closed, Mom? Are you peeking?"

"They're closed. Are you peeking?"

"No way. Peeking ruins the surprise."

Even with my eyes closed, I can feel Noah's energy buzzing next to me like a hive of bees in springtime.

The door opens behind us.

"I'm done for the ... What's going on out here?" Chloe asks.

"Shhhh, Aunt Chloe. Unko has a gift for me."

"He does, does he?"

"Yep. Close your eyes."

"Okay, sweetie."

"I'm almost seven," Noah says to Chloe. "You have to call me Noah now."

"I can't call you sweetie anymore?"

I feel Chloe's pain. My son is growing up far too fast.

"No, thank you." He pauses, obviously thinking this through. "You could call me dude." Noah pauses again. "Or bruh."

"In that case, I'll stick with Noah."

Kai's heavy footfalls hit the steps. There's a clunk of something heavy being set down.

"Okay," he announces with his smile seeping through his words. "You can peek."

I open my eyes, shut them, and open them again to make sure I'm actually seeing what I'm seeing.

Kai is standing one step down from the porch, and his hand is proudly wrapped around a surfboard that stands taller than he is. It's red with a white stripe down the middle. And Noah is jumping up and down like a frog on a hot tin roof. Which sounds awful. Okay. He's not a frog with his wee little froggy toes getting all blistery and crisp. Let's just say he's got springs in his feet. And he's squealing, "Unko! Unko! Unko! That's for me?"

Kai beams at my son. It's the kind of smile that isn't for me at all. As a matter of fact, I think I could slip into the inn and neither of them would notice. I look over at Chloe. She's clutching her hand over her heart and mouthing, "Put a ring on that."

"What?" I mouth back to her, hoping I misunderstood her.

Maybe she said "Buttering a cat," or "Pooh Bear isn't fat." She can't seriously be telling me ...

"Put. A. Ring. On. That," Chloe mouths again, clear as day.

I shoot her a glance that says, "Put a cork in that." *That*, being her mouth.

During our little exchange, Noah leapt at Kai and now he has his arms wrapped around Kai's waist in a grip that looks like we'll need a crowbar to pry him off.

"Thank you, Unko! Thank you! That's what I always wanted! And you got it! It's my own board!"

Kai's gaze is trained downward at Noah. He's wrapped his free arm around my son. And he has a smile on his lips that leads straight into his thoughts. He's reveling in Noah's reaction, savoring it with a fork, picking up every crumb on the tines until the plate has been cleaned.

I glance at Chloe. She raises her eyes as if to say, *I said what I said.*

"Mom!" Noah releases Kai. "Unko got me a surfboard!"

"I see that."

And then Kai looks over at me, finally. He's got this shy look on his face, the opposite of how Brad would look in a moment like this. Brad always wanted credit for the gifts he gave. He wasn't narcissistic, but he had this part of himself that just wanted to be known as a giver. He'd wait until I was thrilled with whatever he gave me and then he'd say, "I did good, huh?" or something like that. It wasn't ever something that bothered me until now—now that I see what it looks like when a man can give without any thought of himself whatsoever.

And I hate that thoughts of Brad are contaminating this beautiful moment between my son and his Unko.

Kai's face softens and he looks at me so earnestly, I could run to him and wrap my arms around him. I'd secretly hope every single person on this side of the island has misplaced their crowbars.

Instead, I just say, "Thank you."

My words come out soft and possibly a little choked with emotion.

"I wanted him to have his own board. He needs it the way he's surfing. And I wanted to be the one to give it to him."

"I'm glad it was you."

Kai nods softly—just one simple bob of his head that speaks volumes. "Me too."

We're still staring at one another as if no one else on this porch exists. And then it occurs to me what this must look like to Noah. Chloe obviously already picked out napkin colors for a reception that's not happening.

"Well, then." I turn to Noah. "Where are we going to store this board of yours?"

Kai steps in, solving the problem like he so often does. "I thought we could keep it in the locker at the watersports shack with Bodhi's and mine and Ben's. No one will mess with it there."

He looks down at Noah. "You'll be surfing with us for a while anyway, so it makes sense to keep it where we surf, yeah?"

"Makes sense to me," Noah says, sounding like one of the guys, not my son who still needs me to come into his room and sit with him in the dark hours of the night when he has a nightmare.

The line between childhood and the next stage of his life is approaching like a dot on the horizon, becoming clearer and clearer every day. One day, he'll be the man buying some boy a surfboard. And that day is not as far off as I had fooled myself into imagining it would be.

Noah smiles at Kai like he invented surfing and carved this particular surfboard with his own hands. Kai just might have. And if he did, I don't even want to know because then I absolutely will run over and wrap my arms around him ... in front of Noah and Chloe and anyone else who happens to be nearby.

"It's my birthday next week, Unko!"

"I know, boss man."

"I'm gonna be seven. And you should come."

"I'd love it."

"All my friends are going to the beach and we can play in the water and surf and then eat food on the blankets my mom puts out on the sand. And you don't even have to bring a present because you got me my board already."

We all laugh.

"Sounds good," Kai says to Noah, but he looks at me when he says the next sentence.

"I'm looking forward to it."

TWENTY
Mila

"I will be watching you and if I find that you are trying to corrupt
my first born child,
I will bring you down, baby.
I will bring you down to Chinatown."
~ Jack, Meet the Parents

Phyllis is flitting around her dining room, adjusting plates on the table. Yesterday, after Noah insisted on calling each of my aunts and telling them about the surfboard Kai gave him, Phyllis announced that they were having Kai and me over for dinner tonight.

If you don't know Phyllis, let me tell you, when she tells you that you're coming to dinner, you're coming to dinner. She came to my house earlier today to help prepare a meal for my midweek guests. Chloe's there now, with Davis, who is a saint, serving my guests and babysitting Noah so I can get away.

I only have two guests staying with me right now. Spring is approaching and that means my weekends are starting to fill. We have three weeks until Spring Break on the mainland. That always kicks off my busy season. I'm already booked out that whole week. All ten rooms upstairs and the one room on the opposite wing of the downstairs from where Noah and I live are reserved. It won't officially let up until after Labor Day.

"Where should I put this?" I hold the charcuterie board with both hands. "And are you sure Kai and I are the only two guests? There's enough food to feed a crowd in there."

"Never under prepare. You can't ever be sure how much your guests will eat. There's nothing worse than sending someone home hungry."

"I'm relatively sure Kai and I won't eat a pound of lunch meat a piece."

"Set it there." Phyllis points to a side table along the side wall of the dining room. "No. No. On second thought, the coffee table. That way we can nosh before dinner. While we chat."

Chat. Why are images of bare bulbs over metal chairs flashing through my head? This is an interrogation plain and simple.

There's a knock at the door. Phyllis shouts, "Joan? Can you get that?"

Joan answers the door and announces, "It's Alana!"

"Alana?" I look at my aunt. "Alana Graves?"

"Yes. She's my friend."

"I know she's your friend. We're friends too. I guess I just thought it was only going to be the six of us."

My aunt Connie is married and lives a block from here. My other two aunts are single. Phyllis was married, years ago. Joan never married. She's my soul sister. She's the most reserved and quiet of my three guardians. Warm and loving—and eternally single. The main difference between Joan and me is that she has a sister to grow old with.

"Well, I invited Alana. The life of a movie star is incredibly lonely at times. I get worried about her up there in that big house all alone."

Well, when she puts it that way.

"Is she the only guest?"

"You and Kai."

"And? ..."

"Maybe a few other people for dessert."

My aunt's home is large for an island home in this section of town. It's nearly twice the size of the houses on either side of her, but it wouldn't even fill half the square footage of the inn. Yet, she somehow manages to squeeze in a Hollywood-sized crowd at her famous dinner parties.

"I didn't realize this was an official party."

"It's not official."

"But it is a party?"

Phyllis simply smiles at me. My earlier estimation was right. This is a circus and Kai and I are the sideshow. My aunt may as well have sold tickets to the bearded lady and the world's smallest human. At least she plans to wait until dessert to open the flaps to our striped tent. Dinner should be mild in comparison.

Alana walks into the dining room. "With this one, it's always a party." She tips her chin toward my aunt.

"Truer words have never been spoken." I nearly groan.

But I smile at my aunt. She's beyond description with her Meryl Streep looks and her flowing kaftan over her white silk tank and white dress slacks. Her silvering hair flows down her back. She's got gold bangles going up one arm that jingle every time she moves. And she's barefoot, with toes painted a brilliant hot pink. Her lack of footwear is a product of the environment, a secret peek into the contrast between her stint in Hollywood and her upbringing on an island where flip-flops pass as formalwear.

"Thank you, girls. I'll take that as a compliment to my flamboyant personality and charm, along with my intriguing personal history and the fact that I hung with A-listers back in the day."

"All of that," Alana says with a soft laugh. "And more. Honestly, if you ran the local bakery, you'd still be you. You're the draw."

"Flattery will get you everywhere, my dear!"

Phyllis sweeps Alana into a hug and pulls back with her hands on either side of Alana's biceps. She gives her an appraising look.

"Are you eating? Don't let those producers or your agent tell you to starve yourself. Ridiculous, abusive standards, those are."

"It's the job." Alana's face is resigned.

"And your life is worth more than that job. You're not merely a product on a shelf. You're a human being. Don't let them keep you in a corner."

Alana laughs at my aunt's *Dirty Dancing* reference.

"Get some charcuterie in this girl this instant," Phyllis orders me.

I nod, eager to have Kai here for some reason. I shouldn't be. Once he's here, the scrutiny will commence. Alana's an actress. Phyllis was on the big screen in her heyday. Will they be able to tell we're putting on a show? I'm not a trained actress. At least the inconvenient and inappropriate feelings I've been having for Kai will fuel my performance.

As if I conjured him up, there's a knock at the door just as Alana and I step into the living room. Joan opens it, and my breath catches. Kai's eyes find mine and a soft smile pulls at his full lips. We were on the phone for hours last night. We haven't ever really had long conversations by phone before. In person, sure, after he finished a job we'd sometimes sit with lemonade on the porch or in the main room of the inn catching up on life. But this was different. At least, for me it was.

I had called Kai after everyone was in bed and the kitchen was shut down for the night—just to thank him again for the surfboard. We got to talking about Noah, his birthday party, and my plans to let Brad see Noah in a casual way this week. Then we talked about Kalaine and Bodhi returning. I teased him about Shaka ... and the conversation just kept going, neither of us willing to end it.

We're two single adults. Friends. I enjoy Kai's company. He's easy to be with. And recently, there's this hum I can only describe as: *more*. It's a dangerous hum. One I should muffle or mute. But

I can't seem to resist the tug, and it's only growing louder the more we indulge in this charade.

"Hello, everyone." Kai steps over the threshold.

He's wearing a white linen shirt, buttoned up, but he left the top two undone so a triangle of his tanned skin and his clavicle are exposed. Why is a clavicle so sexy right now? And why am I thinking about what's sexy? Am I drooling? I casually lift the tip of my finger to the edge of my mouth to check. Yeah. That's totally normal.

Kai paired his shirt with khaki shorts that look pressed and a pair of upscale leather flip flops. An image of Kai with this same shirt fully unbuttoned, ironing his shorts to put that crease in the front flashes through my brain ... and I am pretty sure I'm losing my mind. I never imagined a man ironing before. *Why is that so sexy?* Why is everything about him so sexy all of a sudden? It's the faking. I'm losing my resolve. And I can't afford to let that slip.

I look at Joan, my spinster aunt, trying to draw some semblance of strength from her years of celibacy and contented singleness. But when I glance at her, she's staring at Kai with stars in her eyes.

"I'm so glad you could make it, Kai. It's so rare that we have handsome young men over to the house."

"Oh my goodness," Alana whispers to me. "Is your aunt hitting on your boyfriend?"

She giggles quietly. And I laugh too. "Looks like it."

I stand, walking over to Kai. He looks down at me and then, as if we're actually a couple, he leans in and places his lips on mine. Yes, he aims to the left. It's a perfect stage kiss. I always wonder about those when I watch actors who are married to someone other than their co-star. But tell my lips this is a stage kiss. They are doing the macarena and a complex cheer maneuver while shouting something like, "Kai kissed us! Kai kissed us!" And then they're like, "More! More! More!"

His jaw rubs against my cheek when he pulls away. And if I didn't know better, I'd say he was blushing. I feel a mirroring heat creep up my neck when he leans in, placing his mouth right next to my ear and whispering, "Sorry. I had to give them no room for doubt."

His warm breath fans across my neck with each word.

I grip his head and whisper into his ear, "It's okay."

It's so not okay. Not okay at all. I might pass out. I definitely feel my heart rate spike into dangerous levels. And my lips are still pulling together like a cheer squad, chanting and wiggling about the joys of Kai's lips on mine. All from a peck—a peck that barely grazed the corner of my mouth. He barely touched me, and I'm lost. Gone. Swooning to the point of nearly fainting.

Kai must sense all this—or maybe he's just pulling off our act at levels that are worthy of a feature film, because he places his hand on my back in such a naturally doting and protective way. When I turn toward the three women gathered in the front room, all eyes are on us with identical looks of adoration and bliss. They're happy for us.

I'm horrible for leading them on. All this for Brad. Though, right now, I can't even be sure why we're doing this, and whether the price tag just soared way above my range. I can't afford to feel anything for Kai or any other man. Noah is about to go through a life quake with his dad reentering the picture. He needs me to be constant. The last thing Noah needs is a surprise from me by way of a new dating life. Besides, Kai is in this because he's trying to protect me. Nothing says he feels what I do. I'd be assuming a lot to think otherwise.

The evening rolls on. We're riddled with questions, including one about how Kai first asked me out. We never prepped the details of our story—which we should have. I've read enough in the fake dating trope to know that's Fake Dating 101: get your story straight.

"I asked her out the day Brad showed up," Kai says smoothly.

We're seated on the sofa, Alana to the left of me and Kai on my right. Connie and her husband, Ethan, arrived shortly after Kai. They're on a loveseat across from us and my other two aunts are in wingback chairs. All of us are centered around the coffee table with a massive charcuterie board taking up nearly a third of the surface.

I'm as eager as everyone else in the room to hear Kai's description of how he asked me out.

"Seeing Brad there on the porch did something to me. It was like a switch flipped."

Kai looks down at me—lovingly. It's the only word I can think of. I smile softly up at him. I'm only half-acting at this point. The part of me that's not all in is the part that wants to slip down between the sofa cushions to avoid this whole production. But the other part of me seems to have joined team Mila's Lips because my knee is screaming, *His hand is on me! He's cupping me! Your knee! His hand! Feel that?* My body is worse than Noah as his birthday approaches.

Kai's eyes are locked on mine as he continues to morph the reality of what happened that day into something so palpable and convincing, even I almost believe him.

"It was like this flash of awareness. I have strong feelings for Mila. Sure, we're friends. And I never want to jeopardize our friendship. But seeing her with Brad made me instantly possessive. And I took my opportunity that day to ask her for more. I wanted her to take a chance on me. I didn't want to let another day go by without asking her."

Two of my aunts audibly sigh. Alana bumps my shoulder. "I love this. It's so perfect."

Oh, yeah. Perfect. Perfectly deceitful. Gah.

"And, Mila?" Connie asks. "What changed your mind? I thought you were committed to singleness."

I nearly blurt, *I am!* But I gather my wits quickly and say, "I was. But I never realized what it could be like when a man who makes me feel genuinely safe came around. I guess I never considered Kai because I was dead set against all men. But when he asked, it just made sense. I'd never consider anyone else."

My answer isn't nearly as romantic as Kai's. But it's eerily accurate. Not that I'm about to *actually* date my handsome, sexy, kind, generous, protective friend. Nope. I'm not. But I'm more tempted than I ever imagined I'd be. And that's a problem.

As the night progresses, I relax a little more. Kai asks my aunts about my childhood. It's pretty common knowledge on the island that my parents died on a trip to Ireland when I was four. They were celebrating their fifth wedding anniversary and they were in a fatal car accident. My aunts always said it was a mercy that neither of them had to outlive the other, their love was just that exceptional.

My three fairy godmothers immediately took me in. At that time they were all living in the inn, a building my grandparents had owned and passed down to them. When Phyllis married, she moved out to this house. When Connie married, she moved to the home she shares with Ethan. And when Phyllis' husband left her, Joan moved in with Phyllis here. They maintained the property, but no one lived there until I turned twenty-one and they surprised me by passing it on to me. I didn't take up residence there right away because I was in college. Brad and I started planning, though. And when we came back to Marbella, we rented an apartment in Descanso, on the south side of the island near the resort, knowing we'd live in the inn as soon as we were ready to turn it into a bed and breakfast.

We had big dreams.

And they all smashed the week I found out I was pregnant.

But my life is better than I could have ever planned it—because I have Noah.

"Mila's dad was our baby brother," Joan's eyes are wistful as if she's traveling back in time to days when they were all young. "He loved Mila's mom with an uncommon devotion. We put that girl through the wringer trying to see if she was good enough for our Bo."

I've heard the story of how my aunts grilled my mother when she and Daddy were dating so many times, but it never gets old.

They carry on, telling how I came to them, and then what it

was like raising me. No embarrassing detail is spared. By the time we're pulling trays of dessert out of the spare refrigerator in the pass-through room that leads to the garage, we're surrounded by over twenty guests who have converged on my aunts' front room. Kai still has his arm around me. He's been touching me all night, and I'd be lying if I weren't leaning into him for support and strength—and, more.

More. It's a dangerous, dangerous word. Especially for me and Kai.

Connie jokingly asks, "So you two, when are you going to tie the knot?"

"Connie!" Joan chides.

"What? They're not in their twenties. Mila has Noah. She swore off men. If they're dating, they're serious. I'm just planning ahead so I make sure Ethan and I are on the island for the wedding."

Bless Kai's heart, he sputter-coughs on his drink. But he regains composure. "We're taking things as they come for now."

I nod, unable to even think of a reasonable response that wouldn't reveal my panic. Kai's answer couldn't be more accurate. Though, for us, taking things as they come feels like we casually stepped into a blow-up rubber boat and found ourselves on a class five whitewater rafting trip. Maybe a little preparation would have been advisable.

After dinner, Kai walks me outside. We simultaneously blow out long gusts of breath as if we've only been partially breathing all night. Then he looks down at me and starts to chuckle. I catch the bug and giggle along with him until we're standing in front of my aunts' house in a fit of uncontrollable laughter.

Alana steps out behind us. "One day ..." she muses.

"What?" I ask, wiping a tear from my eye from all the laughter that just overcame me.

"Nothing. Just ... one day. Maybe after I've had my fill of being on the big screen, I'd love to find this—what you two obviously have. It's lovely."

There's a sadness in her voice. But I can tell she's genuinely happy for us. And, I agree. Kai and I do have something special. Sure, we're faking a romance. But the friendship that caused him to step up in the first place is one of my favorite things on earth.

"Thank you," I say. "It will come. I believe it. You're an amazing woman, and like you told my aunt earlier, it's not your accomplishments that define you. It's just you."

"Thanks." Alana's smile is sweet and sincere. She reaches out and brushes her hand down my arm.

Kai jumps into fix-it mode, as he's prone to do. "I could hook you up ... I know some guys."

"No, thank you." Alana smiles. "I believe in fate or ... something like that. Besides, I don't think the guy I will fall for is here on Marbella. I know nearly everyone, even though I live like a hermit. He's not here."

We all say goodnight, and Kai offers to walk me home. His hand lands on the small of my back almost instinctively, and I wish he had some reason to leave it there, but he realizes at the same time as I do that he doesn't. So, it falls away and we stroll side by side, two magnets, resisting the urge to snap together at every charged point between us.

"Hey," Kai says when we approach my front gate. "I had a question to ask you. A favor, really."

"What is it?"

"It's a lot to ask."

"As if faking a romance so we can throw off my ex isn't a lot? I'm pretty sure I owe you."

"I don't want you to say yes because you owe me, Mila. You don't owe me anything."

"Okay," I say, looking up into his golden-honey eyes and wondering what he'd do if this were an actual date and we were standing right here in this same spot.

Would he kiss me? Of course he would. He'd kiss me fully on the mouth. He'd pour all that quiet intensity into a kiss I'd been waiting for probably longer than I've allowed myself to admit it.

Knowing Kai, he'd be respectful at first, as he always is. Careful. Gentle. Attentive. But then, he'd take charge with that possessive side, the part of him that is all man. He'd hold me up, as he always does, and lean in. And once he got a solid sign that I wanted him, he'd pour all the physicality he uses on the water, all the tenderness he shows when he's looking out for me, and possibly the desire I imagine I see flickering in his eyes on occasion into our kiss. It would be a kiss I'd never forget. One I'd almost risk crossing my carefully drawn lines to experience.

Only I can't.

So I don't.

I blink up at Kai. "What do you want to ask me?"

TWENTY-ONE

$\mathcal{K}ai$

Sorry I annoyed you with my friendship.
~ Andy, The Office

Mila's looking up at me with those soft brown eyes, so willing to do whatever I'd ask of her.

Kiss me, I want to say.

But, instead, I ask what I had planned to ask. "My family is coming from Hawaii for Kalaine and Bodhi's wedding."

"I know. It's going to be beautiful. I can't wait."

"Yeah. Well." I clear my throat. "We have this old family friend. Our parents always sort of planned for us to end up together."

"Oh."

It's dark out, but I could swear I see a flash of disappointment cross Mila's features.

"I see, that's fine, Kai."

"What exactly do you see?" I ask.

"The family friend. She'll be your date? Right? And then ... maybe more?"

Her voice is softer than the night, thin and wispy. I'd love to tell myself it's because she'd miss me—that she wants what we're doing here to turn real as much as I do. But I know her stance on men. She's probably imagining all the ways me dating Aima would open her up to Brad. No way. I'm not leaving Mila in a position where Brad can make a move.

"Mila, no." I put my hand on her shoulder for reassurance.

I've been touching her all night, foolishly indulging in a dream world, pretending we are more than we are. Yes, we needed to pull this off. But did I have to put my hand on her knee, or to wrap my arm around her back at the dinner table? Was it necessary to brush strands of hair away from her face, or to kiss her on the corner of her mouth? Some physical affection between us was probably important to convey the appearance of a new relationship—but I allowed myself to enjoy the sensation of her in my arms. I spent the whole night openly showing Mila how much I care for her and she never perceived one gesture for what it actually was.

Now this simple act of laying my hand on her shoulder rekindles memories of all the little touches we shared tonight. Her soft skin beneath my roughened fingertips. The way she allowed me to be the one she leans on, the one who pulls her into my arms and feels her settle there as if there's nowhere else she'd rather be—as if my embrace is her haven. What would it be like if she let me in for real? If I could be the man she chooses to cross all her carefully drawn lines for?

I gaze down at her, resisting every urge to pull her nearer, just to hold her one more time this evening. I force myself to focus on what I need to ask instead of all the warring desires firing off just beneath the surface.

"Aima isn't going to be my date to the wedding. She is single, though. And our parents were planning to fix us up. Again."

"Oh." Mila looks stunned and confused. "She's not your date?"

A small smile plays across her lips. Relief, I'm sure, knowing our farce can continue and her barrier against her ex will remain firmly in place.

"No. I told you I'm committed to you and our pretense for as long as you need me. I'd never back out. Not even for a date I wanted to go on—not that I want to date anyone. I don't. Not anyone other than you. In our fake dating arrangement." I run my free hand through my hair. "Anyway. Aima is definitely a date I don't want. Not that she's a bad person. She's just not *my* person."

"Ohhhh." Realization dawns on Mila. "You want me to be your date so Aima can't be."

"Well, yes."

"Of course, I will."

"My parents already think you and I are dating, so they'd expect us to go together anyway. But if you weren't by my side, your absence might lead my mom to think we aren't that serious."

"Totally. It's no problem. I'm glad to be your date. I'm going to the wedding anyway."

"You know this will mean acting out our charade in front of a lot more people. You don't have to say yes."

"It's the least I can do. But, Kai, I think we need to figure out a few more things."

"Like what?"

"Well, like tonight. When everyone started peppering us with questions, I had no idea what to say. What if I had been in another room and someone had asked you the story of how you asked me out? I wouldn't have known how to corroborate."

"Good point," I agree. "Maybe we need to set aside an afternoon so we can get to know things a boyfriend and girlfriend would know about one another."

"It's probably wise."

"Okay. It's a date."

The second the words are out of my mouth, a hush falls over the two of us.

A date.

I'd do just about anything for a date with Mila. For now, I'll have to settle for a date for the sake of perpetuating this illusion we're presenting to the world around us.

The next morning the guys are in rare form. Word somehow got back to them about my dinner with Mila's family. And they just watched me stash Noah's board in the employee locker. It's a coveted space: clean, locked, and reserved for employee boards only. Even Jamison only got a spot there last month. And here Noah's board sits among the rest like it belongs there.

"Who's the board for, Kai?" Ben starts in.

"I've got a Benjamin that says it's Noah's board," Bodhi says.

"No betting at work," I say, even though we aren't really officially working right now.

"I *am* Benjamin and I say it's Noah's board," Ben adds, cracking up at his own joke.

"Good one, bro." Jamison fist bumps Ben. "So," he asks me. "Is it Noah's?"

"It's Noah's. I don't want him to have to haul it down here. He's being raised by a single mom. He doesn't have a dad to help him learn to surf the way we all did."

"My dad didn't teach me to surf," Ben declares. "He taught me to slop hogs, though. And waterski at the reservoir."

Ben grew up in the midwest. Surfing's not exactly a part of that culture.

"My point is," I say, trying to get this crowd of clowns to focus. "Noah doesn't have a dad to tote his board to the beach for him. It's just easier for him to keep a board here."

"And he needed his own brand new Channel Islands CI Mid?" Bodhi asks. His brows raise and he stares at me.

I don't answer. Of course Noah could have kept using loaner boards. He didn't *need* this board. I wanted to get it for him. I smile remembering the way Noah threw his arms around me, the look on his face.

"Don't you guys have something you're supposed to be doing?"

"We're doing it," Ben jokes.

"Yeah. Just this," Jamison adds, walking dangerously close to a line he's not qualified to cross quite yet, considering he's low man on the watersports totem pole.

Bodhi grins at me. "You're too easy of a target. It's way too fun to rile you up."

"I'm not riled. I got Noah a board. No biggie."

"The board costs over one K." Bodhi lets out a low whistle. "That's quite a board."

"What did you want me to get him? A used foam learner board?"

"Nah, man. You did good. Does Mila know how much you forked out?"

I shake my head. "I told her I could afford it."

"I was raised by my mom for a few years. After my dad left," Jamison pipes in. "She's remarried now, but I was the son of a single mom."

"I didn't know that."

"Yeah." He looks so serious, almost forlorn, until he says, "Wanna buy me a board, Uncle Kai? I love the orange on orange CI Mid. It's only fourteen hundred."

"He's not dating your mom, dufus," Ben smacks Jamison on the arm.

"Is that what this is about?" Bodhi asks me sincerely.

"No way," I tell him. And I mean it.

This was all about Noah. If I pursue Mila it will be a straight shot, not some side-handed move to get to her through her son. I hope she doesn't think that's what this was.

No. I know she doesn't. Our long phone call the night I gave Noah the board proves it. She knows I did this because I love Noah and I am taking my role as his first surf instructor seriously.

Besides, I'm not pursuing Mila. As much as I would love to see where something between us could lead, I can't. She trusts me to honor her boundaries. And her number one boundary is no men.

"Mila's gonna be showing you some serious gratitude," Jamison says.

"I hope you're not trash-talking about my girlfriend."

Jamison holds his hands up in a show of innocence. "Nah, man. Never."

"Good."

My girlfriend. The words echo in my head, settling in a deep spot inside me like they belong there.

"You should see yourself," Ben smiles. "So very very different than I ever imagined you'd be."

"Yeah, man," Jamison adds. "You're whipped."

They tease me. It's fine. They don't understand what's happened to me. I'd do anything for Mila. And Noah. That board is nothing compared to what I'd do. I'm basically lying to everyone who matters in my life all because of her and how she's come to mean infinitely more to me than any other person in the world.

TWENTY-TWO
Kai

Co-parenting is the bridge we construct with love,
enabling our children to move freely between us.
~ Unknown

Marbella islanders have a few significant events that mark the calendar year, kind of like Easter, Christmas and Thanksgiving. Only, ours are Beach Bash, Shark Attack, and Last Days of Summer.

Beach Bash is sort of our last local hurrah before our island officially fills with the chaos that is Spring Break. From the week after Beach Bash through the beginning of September, Marbella changes from a sweet small town community, mainly inhabited by full-time residents, part-time property owners, and the low hum of winter vacationers to what I call a controlled madhouse.

For the duration of spring and summer, our island is overrun by tourists. They travel from all over the country and the world to descend on us in droves like seagulls to a dropped sandwich.

The heart of our island—the community behind the tourism —continues to beat in the background, but the outsiders run the show and we exist to meet their every whim so they'll keep coming back year after year to indulge themselves in our slice of paradise. This is our economy. They keep the lights on, so we lay out the annual welcome mat.

Beach Bash is a Marbella tradition. It's hosted by locals for locals. And it's the one party where you'll see just about everyone you know out on the sand, in the water, around barbecues and later hanging at the bonfires. We're saying goodbye to our season of keeping the island to ourselves and easing into the melee that is summer on Marbella.

We host the bash on the resort beach, in Descanso, just south of the watersports shack. I'm here, boards lined up on the sand for people to drag out, ride, and return on the honor system. Usually I'm watching that action, but this year, I'm scanning the horizon for Mila and Noah. They should be here any minute and I'm unable to focus on anything in front of me because I'm so preoccupied with the two people who feel like my world these days.

Bodhi sidles up next to me. "Waiting for your woman?"

He has no idea. Then again, he waited for my sister for years.

"Yeah."

I don't meet his eyes. Instead mine are trained on the edge of the beach toward the direction where Mila and Noah will be coming.

"You know, it's been hard for you and me to get any time alone since Mavs and I got back. I never even heard the story of how you got Mila to change from her *no men* status to being willing to give you two a chance. What happened there? One day you're single and I'm off to Hawaii and Portugal for two weeks, and the next, I'm getting a FaceTime that you're dating someone. And when we got back, you two are like an old married couple— inseparable, intertwined, fully devoted to a relationship. I'm not saying it's fast. You've known one another for years. It's just the transition made my head spin." He pauses. "In a good way. A really good way. Just ... it was such a one-eighty."

"It was. I guess ... when you know someone as long as Mila

and I have, the leap from friends to more happens pretty quickly. And, at our age, we've already dated and know what we want and what we don't. There's not a lot of need for the kinds of dates that let you know if you're interested or compatible."

My gut twists. I'm not exactly lying to Bodhi. The invisible leap in my heart from friends to more gave me whiplash too, but it feels so right. Then again, I'm totally lying to him. And I want to come clean. But not here. Not during this event when we're all out in the open and I'm expecting Mila and Noah to show up any minute. Not on the very day she told Brad he could casually show up and she'd introduce him to their son.

"Makes sense," Bodhi says. "So, what did you say to her? How did you get her to change her stance? Tell me your moves, oh, great one!" He laughs and nudges me lightly with his elbow.

I take a deep breath. Like it or not, today may be the day I let the cat out of the bag with Bodhi. Then what? How can I ask him to keep our secret from my sister? It's not that I don't want her to know we're faking. I'd honestly rather if she did know. It's just … the more people I tell the truth to, the more precarious our secret will be. So far, Chloe is the only one who knows, and she's been surprisingly hush-hush.

I'm about to open my mouth to tell Bodhi everything when I see them—Noah and Mila getting out of the golf cart she keeps at the inn and walking across the sand toward me. My eyes lock on hers and I walk away from Bodhi without even saying another word.

"Yeah. Go get your girl!" he shouts after me, chuckling. "Don't mind me. Just walk on. I see how it is!"

"Sorry! We'll talk later!" I shout back to him.

I trot across the sand in a slow run toward Mila and Noah, waves of relief washing over me the closer we get to one another. I'm so far underwater for her I might drown. And for Noah. That's the thing. It's not just Mila. It's that boy. He's always been ohana to me, but since Mila and I have been faking, my feelings for Noah have grown deeper roots too. I want to lead him, to laugh with him, to protect him, to be there for him. I want to watch him grow from a boy into a man—to pour the wisdom into him that my father gave me. I'm not his dad, but I feel something akin to fatherly feelings for Noah. This whole situation is like a vine, tangling and gripping, and growing faster than I can keep up with it.

"Unko!" Noah runs at me. "Can we surf today? Mom said it's up to you."

I look up from where Noah has run at me and wrapped his arms around my waist to Mila who has on a floral sundress and sunglasses, her beach bag over her shoulder and a smile on her face that feels like it's just for me.

Noah releases his grip on me.

I glance out at the waves and back at Noah. "I think the water's going to be pretty crowded today. Let's boogie board instead and I promise we'll go surfing this weekend. As long as your mom says that's alright."

Mila smiles at me. "That's a good plan."

"Can we make a sandcastle instead?" Noah asks.

"Oh, yeah! We can totally do that. And play spikeball and throw the frisbee around. And we'll eat all the barbecue and then roast s'mores ..."

I look over at Mila.

She chuckles. "Your energy is nearly as off the charts as Noah's."

"What can I say, I love Beach Bash."

I do enjoy Beach Bash, but that's not what I love. I love being here with the two of them, seeing Noah's excitement. Just seeing Mila at all, anytime I can.

"Here. Give me that." I reach for her beach bag. "We'll get you a spot near everyone. Kala and Summer and Riley already laid out blankets. I told them to save a spot for you."

"I'm one of the girls, huh?"

"Is that okay?"

"I like it."

Mila hands me her bag and we walk side by side over to the spot near the shoreline where all my friends have their beach stuff staked out under umbrellas in a cluster. The girls all greet Mila. Noah sees a friend and runs off after asking permission. Mila drops down and joins in the conversation that's already going on —like she belongs here, my girlfriend with all my friends.

An ache forms in my sternum, clenching and pulling. I want this. I want her, here with my people, laughing and smiling and being welcomed. I want to be able to touch her and kiss her freely.

I never saw this coming—the dangerous snare I was walking straight into when I volunteered myself as Mila's protector. And now I'm here, my feelings clamping in around me, unable to wriggle free if I wanted to. And I don't want to. I only want what I can't have. Wanting Mila the way I do may be the worst kind of torture I've ever known.

Mila stays with my friends' wives and my sister under the umbrellas. Noah runs up to me, and not only do he and I build a sand castle, we gather a team of the guys from the watersports shack and a few of Noah's friends and their brothers. Noah dubs us the "Sand Masters" and we enter the contest. The winning team gets gift certificates to Tuesday's Tacos, which is a prize totally worth the amount of OCD focus we put into building our mansion of sand. Later in the afternoon, they announce the winners. We end up taking third place and then, as tradition goes, all the kids under ten get to run around kicking down the castles just before the barbecues are fired up at dusk.

And that's when he shows up.

Brad.

I see him before Mila does, and my instincts kick into over-drive. He's not a threat, but tell my reptilian brain that. I'm like a dragon who just saw someone entering his lair. I look for Noah. Check. He's playing volleyball with a bunch of kids his age. Then I search the crowd for Mila. She's standing with my sister and Chloe near the water, the shore pound licking at her feet and ankles and retreating back to the sea in a rhythm older than time.

Brad sees Mila too. I watch his face as he approaches her, remorse and caution etched in his expression. He knows what he lost. My scales flatten and my talons retract just the slightest. If anyone on earth knows what it's like to love that particular woman and not be able to have her, it's me. In this short suspended flicker of time, Brad and I are kindred souls, pining for something far too beautiful and elusive than either of us deserve.

Only, I would never leave her. Never. And he did. She may seem unaffected, but the way she's sworn off men tells me he left scars too deep for the eye to see. Scars still tender to the touch. I'd kiss those wounds if she'd let me. Bandage them and stay with her while they heal. If only.

I make my way to Mila's side just before Brad does.

He eyes me like the competitor I am. If there's a contest for her heart, I'll win it or die trying.

"Hey," he says to Mila, as if they are the only two people on the beach.

He's appropriately sheepish, I'll give him that.

"Oh, hey, Brad."

Mila looks up at me and my arm loops around her waist as if it has a mind of its own.

"Brad, you remember Chloe," Mila says with a sweetness that makes me love her even more.

"Brad." Chloe's demeanor is nearly chilly. A fellow dragon. I'm glad Mila's got her.

"This is Kalaine, Kai's sister." Mila continues the introductions.

"Nice to meet you," Brad says to Kalaine. Then he turns his attention to Mila. "Sorry I'm later than I planned. I hoped to get here sooner. Work things ..." He trails off.

"No problem. This is for you, not me." Mila leans into me just the slightest. I give her side a gentle squeeze of reassurance.

"Well, yeah. So." Brad stuffs his hands in his pockets.

Bless my sister's heart. She has obviously sized up the situation with Brad. Maybe Mila even told her some backstory.

Kalaine cuts through the awkward silence. "So, Brad. Work kept you from getting to the party on time? What is it that you do?"

"I own an exercise equipment resale. I'm expanding onto Marbella. Just purchased Outriggers Cove. I'll be doing a watersports resale there. And a rental."

"Ahhh." My sister smiles over at me, oblivious to how her next words will sound. She looks straight at me with that classic little-sister tease in her eyes. "So, this is the competition, huh?"

In all the craziness of our fake dating, it never occurred to me that the company Brad is bringing here is in direct competition with the watersports shack. But the way Brad's looking at me, he's not thinking business at all. He's thinking of Mila.

"Well," Mila says, as if she's about to say something significant.

But she doesn't.

And we all just stand there staring at one another in the type of awkward silence that doesn't fit such a chill beach setting.

That is, until Noah comes bursting into our circle of discomfort with his usual exuberance.

"Hey, Mom! Spencer is having a sleepover. Can I go?"

"Let me talk to Marie."

"His mom said it's okay if you said it's okay."

"I'll talk to Marie," Mila repeats.

Noah looks about ready to bolt. I glance at Brad. He's studying Noah like he's never seen a child before. And in this case, I guess he hasn't. I wonder what it would be like to be in Brad's shoes—to have a son and never to have known him all these years. I've been at every one of Noah's birthday parties since I met Mila. I've helped with homework. I've fixed broken toys, goofed off, held him when he cried. I taught Noah to ride a bike when it was time to take the training wheels off. And, most recently, I taught him to surf.

"Noah?" Mila says.

At the sound of his name, I realize I've been standing with my arm around Mila's waist—in front of her son, whom we are definitely not trying to confuse. I drop my arm in a way that hopefully isn't distracting to Noah, while still looking natural enough to keep Brad thinking I'm madly in love with his ex-wife. Which, I am.

"Yeah, Mom?"

"I want you to meet a friend of mine."

"Okay."

Noah's tone couldn't be more disinterested, like any typical child on a beach in the middle of a party would be.

"This is my friend, Brad. We went to high school together."

"Hi." Noah gives a small wave.

"Brad bought Outriggers Cove recently," Mila tells Noah.

"Wow. The whole cove?" Noah asks.

"Yes." Brad says his first word ever to his son. I try to wrap my mind around the fact that he's never said a word to him before now. I can't.

"Wow!" Noah looks at Brad for a fraction of a second and then turns to Mila. "Can I go play now?"

"Sure, sweetie," Mila says.

Meanwhile, Brad is staring at Noah in a way that would almost be creepy if I didn't know the reason behind his fixation.

Noah darts away, oblivious to the fact that he just met his biological dad.

"Well, I think that went well. Don't you?" Chloe says.

"Mm hmm," Mila says in a mildly detached tone of voice.

My arm is back around her before the last mmm sound is out of her mouth. Fake or not, she needs my support right now, and that much couldn't be more real.

"Do you mind if I … hang around a bit?" Brad asks Mila.

"I figured you would."

"I'll just …" he steps away a little, tipping his head toward the area where Noah is playing with friends. "I'll keep my distance. I won't talk to him."

"Okay. Thanks."

"Thank you, Mila. Really."

Brad looks at me. Then at the spot where my arm is secure around Mila. Then back at her as if he wishes he didn't have to talk to her in front of an audience. If he asked to speak to her alone, and she wanted to allow for that, I'd back off, but he's not asking and she's leaning on me in that way that says, stay. So, I am.

"You're welcome, Brad." Mila says softly. "Thanks for being sensitive to the need to take this slowly."

"Of course. Of course. And ... it's good to see you." He looks her over, like a man who's still in love with his ex-wife, his eyes traveling just enough to make me feel uncomfortable.

"Okay, then," Chloe chimes in loudly. "Good talk. Good to see you, Brad. We'll be here chatting. You know, so ..."

Mila gives Chloe a mildly scolding look. Knowing her, she's considering Brad's feelings, even though this whole situation is a consequence of his choices. He could be the one with his arm around Mila, with Noah running up to him on this beach every spring during Beach Bash. But he threw that all away. I'm all for second chances. But certain choices have unalterable ramifications. Walking away from your family and leaving your wife to raise your son single-handedly is one of them.

TWENTY-THREE
Kai

You can't play pretend forever.
~ Holly Black

I'm pacing the living room. Literally pacing. Like the way one of those dads waiting for the birth of their child paced the hospital waiting room in old movies. Only, I'm not awaiting a birth.

I'm debating with myself.

Call her.

Don't call her.

Call her.

Don't call her.

"What is going on?" Bodhi comes around the corner from the hallway followed by my sister.

"What?" I look up at them, stopping dead in my tracks when I do.

Shaka stops right behind me.

"Why are the two of you trying to wear a groove in the hard-wood?" Bodhi asks.

"Nothing. I'm just working something out."

"Such as?" Bodhi asks.

"Nothing. Everything."

"You and Mila?" Kalaine asks.

"Sort of."

"Did you two fight?" she asks.

"What? No." I shake my head. "Not at all. We're good."

I look between my sister and Bodhi. Then I drop my head into my hands, rub the heels of my palms into my eyes and look back at them.

"Spill it, bro," Bodhi says, leaning onto the back of the couch and crossing his arms over his chest.

"You can talk to us, Kai," Kala says with a softness to her voice that basically cracks me open.

"You'd better sit," I tell them.

They stare at me with twin expressions of confusion, then at one another. Bodhi rounds the couch with Kala on his heels. Shaka follows and hops up on an empty cushion once they're seated, plopping his head in Kala's lap.

I guess I'm doing this.

"I really didn't want to tell you before your wedding."

"Is Mila pregnant?" Kalaine guesses.

"No! What? Why would you think that?"

"You're obviously freaked out," Bodhi answers for my sister.

"Not over *anything* like *that*. She's not. At all."

Kala giggles.

"What's so funny?" I ask.

"You. You're so intense."

Bodhi gives Kalaine a look that causes her to relax into him. It's an effect only he has on her.

I think of how Mila relaxes into my arms. Only that's not real, and what these two have has been forged by fire. It doesn't get much more real than Bodhi and Kalaine.

"So ... while you were gone?" I start.

They nod.

I talk faster than I've ever spoken in my life. The words come out like one continuous stream. Or, more like confetti from a cannon, a colorful shredded burst that leaves a mess in its wake. Every thought and emotion I've been bottling up, explodes out of me at my sister and my best friend in one strong blast.

"I ... well ... you see ... Brad showed up. I was just checking the pipes. Brad, Mila's ex, you know? The one you met today. So, I was fixing things. And he was there and I just said, 'I'm the boyfriend.' And then Mila said, 'Yes. He is.' Well, she didn't say it but she didn't not say it. So we agreed we'd go through with it. And Brad backed off when he saw me. So I was thinking this was good for Mila. But not Noah. We can't tell Noah. You guys can't tell Noah either. He'd be rattled. And after Brad showed up and wanted Noah back in his life, well, we had to do something. So that's what we did. But we didn't intend for it to get so out of hand. Now the whole island thinks it's real, which complicates everything. And then I started feeling things. I never thought I'd feel like this for anyone. But I do. I'm consumed with these feelings. And thoughts. All the thoughts all the time: Mila, Mila, Mila. She's all I think about. Her and Noah.

"And I don't know if she feels the same way. Sometimes I think she does. And other times I think I'm alone in this. And we had to tell Chloe. But we didn't tell Mila's aunts. So that's why I had to kiss her at the party. And, that kiss. It was nothing as far as kisses go, but then again, it was everything. It's all I think about now. A simple kiss. One I don't even know if I should have given her in front of everyone. And touching her knee. I think of that too. But then we talked most of the night. I've never felt so comfortable on a phone call. Just a phone call. But it was a long call. Hours. And we never ran out of things to say. Neither of us wanted to hang up. That's why I'm so twisted up over her. One minute I think she's right there with me. And another I know it doesn't matter what she feels.

"And now I'm telling you, but you can't tell Brad. Not that you'll see him. And of course you wouldn't tell him. But you also can't tell Ben. Absolutely not Ben. Or anyone, really. Talk about a disaster. I really didn't want to dump any of this on you before the wedding. We should all be thinking about your wedding. And we will be. I promise. I'll set all this aside to focus on you and the wedding."

I point at each of them. "I won't mess up your wedding. It means everything to me to see you two get married."

They nod, their faces look ... stunned. But, apparently, I'm not finished expelling every last thought in my head, because I start in again. I still need to figure out what Mila needs. That's what matters right now, not my feelings or what we're doing to keep Brad at bay.

"So here I am, pacing at ten at night, after a long day on the beach, trying to figure out if I should try to call her or leave her alone. I mean, would she want to hear from me after a day like today? You know? Or does she need space? Today was the first day Brad ever met Noah—his own son. Mila might need me. But then again, she might not want me. What do you think?"

I stare at Bodhi and Kalaine.

They stare back.

I'm waiting for an answer, but they just stare.

And stare.

And stare.

Finally, Bodhi looks at Kalaine. "Did you understand any of that?"

"My brother's in love," she answers him.

"Obviously." Bodhi chuckles lightly. "But he may also need emergency medical attention."

She giggles softly.

"I don't need medical attention."

"Are you sure? Did you bump your head?" Bodhi seems sincere.

"No. I didn't bump my head. I'm just trying to discern whether I should call Mila or give her space. My gut says call. But I always jump headlong. I'm trying not to be overbearing."

"Hallelujah!" my sister shouts, throwing both arms up in the air.

I roll my eyes at her outburst.

"Seriously, though, Kai," Bodhi says. "I missed the gist of what you were saying. Can you repeat it, but a little less Alvin the Chipmunk on an energy drink and a lot more actual facts we can track with?"

So, I do. I slow down, take a breath, and then I tell them everything, even though my mind keeps traveling up the island to the North Shore where Mila is dealing with the aftermath of today's events alone.

I tell them how Brad showed up, how my knee-jerk instinct was to protect Mila, how I blurted out that I was the boyfriend, and how we thought we'd just fake it with him—only him. I fill them in on the way this first lie gave birth to hundreds of others. And then I ask their forgiveness for not being honest with them in the first place.

They easily forgive me. I'm not sure I would if the shoe were on the other foot, but I'm infinitely grateful they aren't mad. I couldn't take it right now. If anything, they're amused, as if seeing me all twisted up over a woman is better than catching a sold-out comedy show at the resort.

When I'm finished, Bodhi and Kalaine stare at me again.

"Fake dating. You two are faking?" Kalaine asks, even though we've just gone over the whole story at length and in detail.

"Yeah."

"You aren't faking," Bodhi clarifies.

"I'm not. Not anymore."

"And I don't think she is either," Kala says. "You should see the way she looks at you. And the way she leans in whenever you put your arm around her. I know Mila. She's not like that with anyone."

"She's dead set on waiting until Noah's out of the house before she even entertains the thought of trying to date or of allowing romance into her life."

"Dead set?" Bodhi asks, and when I nod definitively, he lets out a low whistle.

"Go to her," Kala says.

"Tonight?"

"Yes. Go now. As a friend. She trusts you, Kai. And today was too big for her to have to process alone. Mila does so much on her own. I don't think she should have to face this without the support of someone who cares for her the way you do."

I'm up and out of my chair before Kala even says, *the way you do.*

"Go get your girl ..." Bodhi repeats what he said on the beach and I smile back at him.

I call Mila on my way out the door.

"Hey," I say when she answers. "What are you doing?"

"Honestly?"

"Well, yeah. I was going to ask how you are, but I think I know, so I went with, 'What are you doing?' So ... tell me."

Mila laughs and a tightness I hadn't even acknowledged unfurls in my chest. I climb into the golf cart.

"I'm sitting on the floor of my walk-in pantry with a tupperware of cookies on my lap."

I think she takes a bite because I can hear her chewing.

"Why are you on the floor? Did you fall?"

I depress the gas pedal a little harder, but face it, this is a golf cart. I'm probably pushing fifteen miles an hour tops. I look like Gru's assistant, Doctor Nefario, going mach speeds that resemble a slug on vacation.

"No, Kai. I didn't fall. I'm in a therapy session. Cookie therapy."

"Ahhh." I smile. "Sounds like the right move after the day you introduce your ex-husband to Noah."

"Thanks."

"Do you ever eat ice cream with your cookies?"

"Of course. I'm not a heathen."

I smile again. Man. This woman.

"Well, I happened to have seen a container of Handel's Graham Central Station and another of Tin Lizzie in the backup freezer the other day. What's your poison?"

"Here? At the inn?"

"Yep. And I can come dish some up for you. You don't even need stand up. You can stay sequestered with your cookies. I'll just dish you up a bowl and bring it to you."

"Kai?"

"Hmmm?"

"Are you offering to travel across an entire island to serve me Handel's ice cream?"

"I guess I am. Yeah. That's what friends do on days like this."

"Friends. Yeah. That's what we are, huh?"

"Mila, you'll always be my friend." The word doesn't even begin to encompass what she is, but I know she needs a friend, and I'm determined to be that for her tonight. "I'll always care when you have crap days. You don't have to huddle in your pantry alone."

"You'll huddle in my pantry with me?" She giggles.

"If that's what you want? We can make a blanket fort and hang out like I do with Noah when it rains."

"You're the best."

"So ... that's a yes?"

"Yes. And it's a yes to both flavors. I think I need to do a taste test."

"You definitely do."

"Oh, and Kai?"

"Yeah? What's up, Hot Dog?"

"Stop it with that nickname."

"You love it. You know you secretly love it."

Mila's still for a beat. Then she says, "Be quiet when you come through the front doors. Actually, come around back. I have this guest here from Scotland. He's up all hours as it is. I don't want to alert him to the fact that I'm awake and in the kitchen."

The idea of Mila in a house with a Scotsman after dark puts a fire under me. I'm sure she's safe. She has a lock on the hallway leading to the wing of the house where she and Noah sleep. She has neighbors right next door and across the street, and they all look out for her. Besides, her guests have to submit their personal details and pass a screening from a company she hires online before a reservation is finalized. Most people coming to Marbella are as harmless as the residents of the island.

Still, I don't like her being alone with a man—let alone some guy in a skirt with bagpipes and a brogue. Women love that stuff. All a guy has to do is stand in a field wearing plaid, speaking in a half-intelligible accent and his Instagram account goes viral. Add in a highland coo and the dude's practically a celebrity. "'Ere's me wee coo. Doncha luhv 'er?"

"Kai?" Mila says.

"Yeah?"

"Thanks for faking. I don't know how I would have gotten through today without you by my side."

I'm not faking. I'm falling, and I can't stop myself. I may as well have stepped off a cliff. All my thoughts and emotions point north to Mila's Place, like a compass needle, vibrating in the direction of its home. She's my true north. And I'm a ship at sea recalibrating my course according to the magnetic pull she has on me.

TWENTY-FOUR

Mila

Be careful who you pretend to be.
You might forget who you are.
~ Unknown

The back door opens. My cell rings immediately. I've pulled out a cardboard box full of surplus bags of rice to give me something solid to lean against. I click the screen to answer Kai's call.

"Hey," Kai's resonant voice is low, whisper-quiet. "I just want you to know it's me. I just came in the back door. Are you still in therapy?"

For a minute I don't know what he's talking about, and then I chuckle. "Yeah. I'm in the pantry. I stopped eating cookies. I only had two. I'm saving the rest."

"For ice cream?"

"Obviously."

He laughs. It comes out in a loud burst and then he subdues the noise. "Stay put. I'm grabbing ice cream and coming in."

I feel like a kid, sneaking around with Kai. Knowing he's here settles me. I'm lighter, cocooned in the safety of our friendship—and him. Just him.

Not even a minute later I hear the opening and shutting of kitchen cabinets, the soft tinkling of spoons on ceramic, and then Kai is standing in the pantry doorway, holding two bowls, smiling down at me like the superhero my son claims he is.

"May I join you?"

"I should hope so. I'm frazzled, but not two-bowls-to-myself frazzled."

"That's good. I'm glad you're at one-bowl status. We can work with that."

Kai walks into the pantry. It's larger than most storage closets, but not huge. And somehow, the space seems to shrink in his presence.

He looks around. "Got room for me there?"

I scoot over, making a space for Kai. He sits down. Our sides touch completely. There's no way for us not to be touching in here, not if we're going to share the comfort of the box at our back.

"This is cozy." He smiles over at me.

Then he dips his spoon into his ice cream and takes a bite. And I watch him. I'm mesmerized, and fully staring at his mouth when his tongue peeks out so he can lick a stray swipe of vanilla off his bottom lip.

"That's so good. I haven't had ice cream in ages."

"You what? Why?"

"I don't know. I don't usually eat sweets. Unless I'm here." He takes another bite.

"So you're saying I'm a bad influence on you?"

I take a bite of my ice cream and moan around the spoon. It's so good—just what I needed after a day like today. Cookies were good, but ice cream is the ticket right now.

"You're the worst." Kai winks back at me. "Now hand me a cookie so you can fully corrupt me."

I giggle. Like a schoolgirl. And then I hand him the whole tupperware so he can take as many as he likes. He takes one.

"Thanks," I say.

"For what?"

"You're kidding, right?"

I look over at Kai, and the way he looks down at me only serves to intensify my awareness of every single place our bodies are touching. My shoulder to his upper arm. Our arms. Our hips. Our legs. Our knees. Our calves. Even the sides of our feet are aligned.

"Thanks for this. For coming out in the middle of the night to bring me ice cream. For being there to prop me up today. For checking in on me."

"Anytime. You know that."

I do. I can't even speak. My emotions well up like a rising tide. Images of Brad meeting Noah for the first time, the way he looked —defeated and desperate—flash in my mind. I might not want Brad back, but I can't help but pity him.

And then there are all the unknowns. Will Noah hate me when he finally learns Brad wasn't just a high school friend? Will my son think I was purposely hiding important facts from him? Will it break our trust? This evening, I asked Noah what he'd do if his dad showed up one day—just to prime the pump. I have to start leading my son toward the truth inch by inch. But every inch feels like a step into something completely unknown and over-whelmingly out of my control.

Then there's Kai. He's the best man I know—the best person I know. And he's not faking the way he cares for me right now. He's always showing up like this for me. He came over here to be alongside me because he knew without me telling him that I needed company tonight. He's the type of man a woman could easily spend the rest of her life with, only by the time I'll possibly be ready for romance, he'll probably have someone else.

That thought hits me hard: Kai with another woman.

I swallow a lump forming in my throat.

Kai nudges me gently. "You want to talk about it?"

"Not really. It's just a lot."

"Yeah, it is. And you handled things with grace, kindness, and wisdom today, Mila. I was so proud of you. Does that sound weird?"

"No. It's sweet, actually."

"I watched you muscle through one of the hardest things I can imagine. And you did it with such care for each person involved. I don't know how you do that."

"Do what?"

Call me greedy, but I need to hear Kai's accolades right now.

"Always thinking of others. Always using a gentle touch when most people would be pulling out the big guns or reacting with intense emotion. They'd be justified. But instead of blowing up or losing it, you're steady and gracious. I could see you trying to smooth the way for Brad, even when it scared you to let him have this opportunity."

"You saw all that?"

"I did. And I was in awe."

I turn and look up at Kai and he doesn't look away.

If this thing between us were real, this would be the moment I'd reach up and kiss him. Oh, would I kiss him. Not on the corner of the mouth either.

We sit like that, quietly studying one another. It could be awkward, but it's not. It's comfortable. And reassuring. I turn back to my bowl of ice cream, and then I lean my head on Kai's shoulder and he lets me. We finish our desserts in this cocoon of ours. It's not a blanket fort, but it may as well be. When we're both scraping the bottoms of the bowls, I stand.

"Try not to run ahead of yourself," Kai says as he pulls himself up off the floor.

"What do you mean?"

"Thinking about what's next and next and next with Brad."

"I've already run that mental path a few times just this evening," I confess.

"I figured. But you're doing great. And as long as you take this one step at a time, one encounter at a time, you'll see the road ahead of you clearly. We're never given the five year plan, but somehow we get to see the next right step if we look for it and only it."

"Wise words."

Kai smiles softly at me before he takes my bowl and walks to the sink to wash it. I want to step up behind him, wrap my arms around his waist and lean my head on his back. To have him turn around and face me, to lean in and kiss me for real. Yes. My emotions are high after today, and my head has been swimming ever since Brad showed up. But I'm not confused about the man currently washing my dishes. Not at all.

He said, *Friends. That's what friends do for one another. Mila, I'll always be your friend.* And that's good, considering I'm not planning to complicate my life or Noah's with any men. I'm so very tempted to make an exception right now. So. Very. Tempted.

But Kai's friendship is a safe harbor for me in a very turbulent season. I don't want to risk losing or damaging what we have—not even for a kiss I'm quite certain would be the best of my life.

Kai dries the bowls and sets them back in the cupboard. I didn't even try to tell him to leave them. I know he wouldn't have listened to me. He wanted to take care of me, so I let him.

He's about to leave now. I wish he could stay. There's something in his presence that makes all the complications of my life fall into order like a winning round of Tetris.

"Thank you again," I say when we reach the back door.

"Lock the door to your hallway." His face turns serious when he says this.

"I always do."

"Good. I don't want some bagpipe player sneaking in and talking in a brogue to you in the middle of the night."

I laugh so hard I have to clap a hand over my mouth. When I try to speak I laugh again.

"Kai. The man is in his sixties. If he did have bagpipes with him, I would have seen them. He does have a brogue, but I'm pretty sure he's not trying to sneak in and talk to me overnight."

I laugh again.

"So he's not a brutish man in a kilt?"

"No!" I laugh again. "He wore board shorts today and a T-shirt."

"Plaid board shorts?"

"Plain orange shorts with white piping."

"Does he own a coo?"

"Kai!"

"He's really sixty?"

"He is. Sixty-four to be exact."

"Is he George-Clooney sixty or Marbella-Senior-Center sixty?"

"Kai Kapule. Are you jealous?"

"I'm concerned. I don't like the idea of you being alone here with a Scotsman wearing nothing but a kilt and talking to you about his wee little coo."

I lose it. I can't help it. I can barely breathe, I'm laughing so hard. Kai isn't laughing at all. He's looking at me with a dead-serious expression on his face that only makes me laugh more.

"His ... wee ... his ... wee ... his wee ..." Tears stream down my face. "His wee little ... I can't!" I gulp in a breath between laughs. "His wee ... little ... cooooo! Oh my! I'm dead! Kai!" I'm swiping at tears and catching my breath.

His mouth ticks up into a crooked grin.

"We're fine," I assure him when I finally regain most of my composure. "I promise the Scotsman isn't any threat. Okay?"

"Okay. If you say so. I just don't trust a man in a skirt."

I chuckle. "What about a grass skirt?"

"That's different. It's a tribal thing. Tradition. For hula cere-monies. Besides, you don't see me running around here in one, do you?"

Not that I'd complain, but no. I haven't.

Kai grins at me and I smile back up at him.

"Are you good? Do you need anything else before I go?" He's all serious and protective again.

I hesitate, but then I ask, "Can I have a hug?"

"Of course."

I realize my error too late. I can't hug Kai when I feel this vulnerable and he's been so amazing.

"No. Never mind. It's okay," I backpedal.

He smiles down at me, cocking one eyebrow. "What if I want a hug?"

"Do you?"

"Actually? Yes."

Kai pulls me into his arms and wraps me up in his warm embrace. He's tropics and sunshine, comfort and ease, strength and goodness. And he's holding me like I'm fragile, precious, and ... his.

Maybe I'm imagining that last bit, but I close my eyes anyway, leaning in and letting out a long sigh into his chest.

"It's going to be okay," he murmurs into my hair. "And I'll be here for all of it."

I don't have words to answer him, so I just nod lightly and squeeze my arms just a smidge tighter around him.

He squeezes me back. Then he steps away, releasing me.

"Okay. Well. Goodnight, Hot Dog."

I shake my head, but I don't correct him. He's right. I kinda love the nickname.

TWENTY-FIVE
Mila

*I promise to kiss you like it's the first time
and the last time, every time.*
~ J. K. Louis

This past week, I barely saw Kai. Brad contacted me when the sale on his property finalized. I called Kai immediately after Brad and I hung up.

Not Chloe.

Not Phyllis.

Kai.

He's becoming so integral to my life these days. He's always been a friend, a steady presence in my life—and in Noah's, now that I think of it. But since we've been dating—*fake* dating—it's different.

I place the sourdough loaf in the oven and step back. Baking fresh bread feels grounding to me. It's a long process of cultivating the starter, feeding it, then turning that into dough, kneading it and letting it rise before baking. It feels like what I need right now, something slow and organic in the middle of all the dramatic changes that seem to be propelling my life at warp speed. Brad's relocating to the island temporarily. Kai and I are knee-deep—more like up to our necks—in the charade we've perpetuated. It's overwhelming at times. Most of the time ... every minute I'm not asleep, really.

Another daily text comes in from Kai. I pick my phone up off the counter to read it.

> Kai: Just checking how you're doing. Brad arrives today, right?

> Mila: Yep. Today's his big day. I've been baking.

> Kai: Stress baking? Because I can get behind you stress baking all day long.

> Mila: Maybe stress baking. It's definitely relaxing me.

> Kai: What's in the oven?

> Mila: Is that like when a guy texts, What are you wearing? And, Sourdough.

> Kai: I just laughed so hard. Ben asked me what was so funny. Needless to say, I did not share your text with him. You wearing sourdough sounds intriguing.

> Mila: Ha! Not wearing it. It's in the oven.

> Kai: Will there be enough left to share? Asking for a friend.

> Mila: I'll save a few slices just for you.

> Kai: You're too good to me, fake girlfriend.

> Mila: You're too good to me, fake boyfriend. Thanks for checking in.

Kai: Always. Have a good rest of your day.

I smile, even though a part of me wishes we could both delete the word *fake*.

Kai has called or texted daily to check in with me ever since the night in the pantry. The day after we hunkered down with ice cream and cookies, he called to let me know he had told Bodhi and Kalaine about us. I'm glad they know. The fewer people we have to fake in front of, the better. And I trust them to protect our secret.

Over the next hour, the bread fills the whole house with that warm, grainy smell that settles my nerves. I pull it out of the oven and lock the kitchen so I can make a run to the hardware and garden shop. Years ago, a friend of my aunts' bought three connected properties and left only one of the buildings standing. They turned the cleared lots into a local nursery, which I've been accused of keeping in business on more than one occasion. I have a penchant for flowers. I adore planting them, watching them grow, and seeing guests appreciate their beauty when they come to stay at the inn.

It's a beautiful spring day, and I need to take every opportunity to clear my head, so I decide to drive the golf cart over to pick out some new plants. Noah can help me fill the front beds later this afternoon. He's still at that age where gardening with his mom is one of his favorite things in life.

The shop is humming with customers, a sign the seasons are turning. I'm walking at an intentionally leisurely pace through hostas and foxgloves, calla lilies and salvia. My mind relaxes and my defenses drop. Too far, apparently, because when I turn toward the double-deep row of fruit trees, Brad is standing there, staring at me. He's not shopping. He's just there, watching me without making his presence known until I startle at the sight of him

"Mila," he smiles warmly. "Planting flowers, as always."

It irks me inexplicably that he knows I love to plant. He knows so many things—secrets and dreams, passions and personality quirks. All of them were gifts I freely gave him once, believing he'd keep them safe to cultivate and guard alongside me.

I nod. "Brad."

"Aww. Please don't be cold, Mila. I know I deserve it. Believe me, I know. I'd hate to think I turned you into some hardened version of yourself. You're the kindest person I know. Don't let my immaturity and recklessness from years ago be what turns you into a skeptic."

His face is soft, pleading even, as if he wouldn't be able to bear the fact that he hurt me that deeply. I see it all, because not only did I share all of me with him, but he returned the favor at one time. Once, in another lifetime, I was his confidante, his lover, his best friend. I read him like I've always read him.

I nod again because words feel like an invitation—one I'm not willing to give.

"I ran into Shaw the other day," he says.

Brad shares this as if we're having a casual conversation, as if he is actually just some guy I knew in high school, and, what do you know! We ended up at Nichols' Nursery and Hardware on the same afternoon. What a pleasant surprise!

"How is Shaw? I rarely see him, since he works at the resort and I stay busy on this side of the island."

"He's good. He mentioned you."

"Did he?"

I guess that's normal. Shaw was in our wedding. A groomsman. He would mention me to Brad, I guess. Though, the thought of people bumping into Brad and mentioning me makes this island feel suddenly suffocating.

"He said he sees Kai every week for the managers' meeting. And he never knew you were dating. He didn't know until that morning we had breakfast. Is this thing between you and Kai that new? Or, is Kai not that into you? I know it's not my place, but you deserve someone who will show you your worth and treat you right, not someone casual who can't appreciate you enough to share the fact that he's seeing you with his coworkers."

Is he serious right now? My thoughts swirl from fears that Kai and I will be outed by some locals, to wondering why Brad thinks he gets to poke around in my relationships, to the fact that I'm not dating Kai at all, and yet he feels like an actual boyfriend in too many ways.

"You're right," I finally muster. "It's not your place. Kai and I are together and that's all you need to know. He's the best thing that ever happened to me. He's reliable and thoughtful. He's kind and funny ..."

Brad's face falls slightly and I instantly feel terrible for throwing Kai in his face, even though everything I said about Kai is accurate, and I haven't even begun to brush the surface as to how special he is.

I've never been a catty person. And regardless of whether Brad overstepped when he told me not to turn sour, I agree with him. I don't want to be resentful and petty.

Brad's eyes snap up to something behind me. I turn to see Kai rounding the corner.

"Mila? I thought I heard you," Kai says.

I'm so thrown by bumping into Brad, and now Kai, that I blurt out. "Oh ... hi ... babe."

Kai is at my side before I can say another word, his arm around my waist, a kiss to my temple.

Is he allowing his lips to linger a little longer this time? I think he is.

I don't have any earthly explanation for what I do next. None.

My hand raises of its own volition and cups Kai's jaw. I turn my head and tilt my chin in an obvious invitation. Time stills. My heart probably stops beating. I'm not sure I'm even breathing. All I know is the feel of Kai's warm skin on my palm and the look of something like desire in his eyes. And that look propels me forward. I might lick my lips. I might give his chin a light nudge with the hand cupping his face. I might cry out, "KISS ME, KAI!"

Okay. I'm pretty sure I don't do that last thing, but I can't vouch for whether I do or don't because Kai's lips meet mine in this moment that feels like, "Finally," and "Yes," and "You ... You ... You."

I run my hand to the back of his neck on instinct. My brain says something like, "Wow, I remember how to kiss!" But then I forget everything I ever knew about kissing or gravity or basic words because *I'm kissing Kai!* And *he's kissing me.* Softly, carefully, tenderly, but with a low burning fire under the surface that promises more—so much more. His lips are commanding and possessive. I wonder how I'm bearing my own weight right now, maybe it's because I've become weightless, floating, feathery light.

All too soon, Kai pulls away and looks at me with a dazed expression. My hand is still on his jaw—the only evidence that I didn't just enter a fugue state and imagine kissing my friend, this man who dominates my thoughts, who comes to my rescue, who means more than words could ever capture.

Kai's lips turn up in a smirky grin. His eyes flit between mine and I feel the soft smile inch onto my face as I watch the corners of his eyes crinkle. Slowly, as if waking from the sweetest dream and stretching lazily from a restful nap, the world starts to come into focus.

Kai turns us toward Brad.

Brad.

Brad was here, watching me kiss Kai, witnessing Kai kiss me back.

Kai aligns me next to him so we're a solid wall of unified post-kiss coupledom.

Then he bends his head so he's whispering into the top of my head. "Babe?"

I just grin up at him, obviously still in a stupor from that kiss.

I'm not one prone to P.D.A. I never was. Brad used to tease me, *Lighten up, Mila. No one cares.*

Brad.

He's standing there with a dejected look on his face, and for a split-second, I feel sorry for him. That's until I remember all the reasons I'm here, kissing Kai next to the hydrangeas and bags of peat moss.

Brad did this. He threw away our future. He rejected me and our son. I'm not sure I want to kiss Kai in front of him ever again, but I can't say I regret the kiss we just shared. I'd be lying if I said I did. And I've done enough lying to last me ten lifetimes lately.

"I'll just ..." Brad stammers. "I've got a lumber order I need to check on."

"Good to see you, Brad," Kai says, as if they're old college roommates.

"Yeah. Uh. You too, Kai." Brad looks at me. "Mila."

"Take care, Brad." I mean it. I hope he does take care. I don't want him to burn in a fiery afterlife or have his toes nibbled off by sharks one digit at a time. I just want peace. And I want my life back—not the one he stole from me years ago, but the one I built from those ashes before he came barging back in asking to see Noah.

As soon as Brad is inside the house turned hardware and garden store, Kai drops his hand from around my waist.

"Sorry," he says, calmly.

"You're sorry?" I scoff. "I'm the one who attacked you!"

Mortification overtakes every part of my brain and face that were previously overrun with giddy ecstasy as a result of our kiss. I finally kissed Kai. And it was as good or better than I had imagined. And, yes, I had imagined it. A lot.

"You did attack me, didn't you?" Kai smirks again.

"What? No!"

He chuckles. "It's okay, Mila. We're adults. We're faking a relationship. You kissed me. We'll live."

I cover my face with my hands. Kai gently pries my arms down so I'll peek up at him. Then he pulls me into a hug. Him holding me does the opposite of what it should do. Usually his hugs calm me. Right now every nerve ending is shouting, "Do it again! Kiss him! Kiss him!"

I pull back so I don't accidentally grip his face and actually kiss him for a second embarrassing time in a row.

"Sorry, I panicked ..." I try to make sense of my actions to Kai, but honestly, I can't even make sense of them to myself yet.

"You ... panicked?" Amusement fills Kai's features.

I nod.

"And when you panic, you kiss people in public?"

He's having far too much fun with this. Also, why is he so calm? Shouldn't we both be freaking out? My kiss didn't affect him like his did me. That's the only explanation for him being this serene and subdued after we kissed like *that*. I felt more sparks than the barge on the bay during our Fourth of July celebration, and Kai, apparently, felt nothing.

TWENTY-SIX

Mila

> *Life brings tears, smiles, and memories.*
> *The tears dry, the smiles fade,*
> *but the memories last forever.*
> *~ Malik Faisal*

I t's been a few days since Brad moved onto the island. I haven't seen him since I subjected him to witnessing me attack Kai for that kiss. Every time I think of how that must have felt from Brad's perspective, I cover my face, even if I'm alone.

What was I thinking?

Kai. That's what I was thinking. The allure of my gorgeous friend made me cross all my lines and act totally out of character.

Three new guests checked in earlier today. The infamous sixty-four-year-old Scotsman checked out. Everyone, including Noah, is down for the night. Everyone but me. I'm restless. So I make my way through the house to the upstairs hallway where I pull down the retracting ladder that's built into the ceiling. I climb up slowly and quietly, careful not to rouse anyone.

I make my way over to the familiar chest under the window in the alcove, and pull open the lid. Then I extract a shoebox and an album. Once I'm nestled into the beanbag in the corner, I open the lid and pull out memorabilia one item at a time, touching each one as if they hold some essence of the people who owned them.

Mom's favorite teacup. Her locket. A bundle of love letters she wrote to my dad when he served overseas. Dad's dog tags. His medal. A postcard from somewhere they stayed in Europe. Movie stubs. An invitation to their wedding. My birth announcement. A souvenir pin that says *Quebec* on it. The air is still around me as I move through the box, touching the last vestiges of my parents' lives—proof they were here, that they lived and loved well.

I carefully return the contents to the box and lift the album onto my lap. *What would Mom think of Kai?* I wonder as I study a photo of her bending over me while I blew out the four candles on my birthday cake. *Would Dad approve?* They knew Brad. Of course, they never knew we married, never watched him walk away. But they knew Brad as a little boy. Island schools are small. Brad and I started dating in high school, but our lives overlapped long before then.

My parents never met Kai. And he never met them. I wish they could all meet one another.

I lift my hand to my cheek where the first tear is rolling down like that first drop of rain in a summer storm. As if it was the scout, testing if the coast is clear, more follow close behind.

I know in my right mind that these tears have been building like water against the wall of a dam. They've been in a reservoir since the day Brad showed up. I cry for every moment Kai and I have had to pretend as if we're something we can never be, for each time I had to wonder what will happen between Brad and Noah, for all the lost years between them, all the dreams I hoped for and never lived. A new wave of tears swells as I release the pressure of keeping life in motion while so much is unraveling at the edges.

Everything.

Every little and big thing.

It's all in these tears.

I close the album to protect the photos from the downpour. Like rain, these tears feel cleansing. Long-awaited moisture to my parched, confused, and privately-weary heart. When I feel the deluge lessen to a sob, and then an occasional sniffle, I pull out my cell phone.

"Hello?" Aunt Phyllis answers on the first ring.

"Hi."

"Oh, sweetie, are you okay?"

"Yeah. I am. I really am. I'm up in the attic."

"Hmmm. Okay. Any particular reason?"

Her voice is soft and compassionate. She knows what's up here.

"I'm not sure. I just ... miss them. I wanted to spend some time thinking about them."

"Yes. I know. I miss them too. Every day."

I don't know if I miss them every day. Some days roll by so quickly with guests and Noah and chores and bills. I just motor through. I don't feel quite guilty about that. A part of me understands like a mother understands her child getting busy in the sandbox and losing all track of time. Not missing them daily doesn't make my grief any smaller. It just means I've learned to live forward.

I live around the presence of my mourning like a woman with a stray cat on her porch. Sometimes you have to feed it. Sometimes it scratches at the door. It's often messy and stinky. And it will never, ever abide by your rules. But it's also a soft comfort in your lap when you learn to live according to its demands and realize it's here to stay.

"Thanks for being there," I say to Phyllis after a stretch of silence where we both made room for our aching hearts. "All these years. And back then."

"Oh, sweetie. I wouldn't have had it any other way. Of course, I would. Ideally. But short of that, I'm so grateful I got to step into those impossible-to-fill shoes and to have the joy of raising you."

I'm about to say something else when Aunt Phyllis continues, "You're the child I never had. The daughter of my heart. I always figured God gives us people to fill in the blank spots. I like to think we've done that for one another."

I smile. "Yes. Me too."

"And I like that man an awful lot."

"What man?" I ask.

"Kai." I can nearly hear her smile through the phone. "I don't know what he did to break you out of your adamant insistence on not dating, but whatever it is besides looking good enough to grace a Hollywood billboard, I approve."

"Thank you."

I'm quiet. Everything in me wants to spill all my secrets to my aunt, like I always have. I will. In due time, I will. I only hope she'll understand why we started this mess in the first place.

We hang up after a little more talking. I promise to come by for lunch sometime this week.

I sit in the charcoal-blue light while the moon casts long shadows across the attic floor.

Aunt Phyllis isn't wrong about Kai. He's exceptional.

In the safety and stillness of the attic, I indulge myself in thoughts of Kai. I picture him on the beach after he taught Noah to surf. The way he looked the night I showed up on his porch bearing dessert. Him leaning on the pantry door frame with two bowls of ice cream in his hands. Us at my aunt's party. The way he kissed me back at the nursery.

Kai.

He's a warm hug. Strong arms wrapped securely so the world can't reach in. He's that mellow spot in the day when chores are done and the wind is blowing in off the ocean, gently rocking the porch swing. He's a kind word. A guard dog on my side of the gate, loyal and fierce on my behalf. Kai is steady like a kayak maneuvering over waves in one smooth slice through choppy waters, never at risk of tipping, always buoyant enough to be reliable, moving forward with measured strokes. He's the smell of salt air and tropics, and the feeling of the sun on my skin as my eyes drift closed and there's no place important to be.

I've never met a man like Kai, and I'm certain I never will again.

And I'm also sure, when daylight comes, I'll remember all the reasons I need to bear in mind that this is all a pretense. What seems plausible in the middle of the night will seem impossible by the light of a new day. I'm sure of it.

TWENTY-SEVEN

Kai

What I love most about my home is
who I share it with.
~ Tad Carpenter

I'm in my office, finishing payroll.

That kiss.

It invades my mind *again*.

And here I go, like the manliest version of a teen girl after her date kisses her goodnight on the porch, lifting my fingertips to my lips as if by doing that I could conjure up the feeling of Mila placing her mouth on mine.

What? Don't judge. I'm touching my mouth in a totally manly, manly way. I'm a dude, sitting here running my fingertips across my lips with a dreamy look in my eyes. It's a masculine as heck look of dreaminess. Pondering, really. Thoughtful. Not at all twitterpated.

If Ben walked in right now without knocking, which, yes, he is prone to doing, I would be the recipient of his grade-A level of teasing for years. *YEARS.*

I drop my hand.

Ben and Bodhi's conversation at the front of the shop tells me I'm safe, but still.

What am I doing?

Mila kissed me.

It still blows my mind.

I kissed her back. Of course, I did. But she was the one who initiated the kiss. If I focus, I can nearly feel the touch of her hand on my jaw, the way she turned my head. I see the invitation in her eyes. And then the feel of her lips, soft, pliant, responsive.

It seems like a year, not a week, since I've seen Mila in person. Ever since that kiss, I guess I've been keeping my distance without really planning to. It has been busier around here, but I could have made time to pop by the inn.

I text her every day. And sometimes I call. But there haven't been any handyman emergencies at the inn, no events to attend together, nothing to make us have to see one another. I had gotten into the habit of showing up for no reason. Now I'm staying away for no reason. No reason except that kiss.

I've been trying to sort my thoughts.

Yes. Mila needed to throw Brad off. But that kiss felt like more. So much more. Maybe that's just how she kisses. Can you imagine? If it is, I don't know what I'd do if we really were dating. I'd never get anything done. I'd either be kissing her or thinking about kissing her all day long. I'd start messing up at work. Things would get so bad, I'd lose my job. Without steady income, I wouldn't be able to keep the house. I'd end up homeless. All over that woman's kisses. She'd kiss me right into being a vagrant.

I chuckle to myself.

I'd like to believe our kiss meant something to her. I'm terrified it didn't.

I've already fallen for her. Fallen head over heels, madly, deeply in love.

I never thought it would happen—not like this. I had started to believe I was too much of an over-thinker, too prone to rule-following, too often the protector, always on the lookout for the people I cared about. I had thought I was just too intense and keyed up to experience the kind of overwhelming longing I feel for Mila. My feelings for Mila are so completely out of my control. As a guy who likes predictability and being in charge, I'm not quite sure how to handle something so unruly and consuming as love.

And I'm not just pining away for another kiss, though I definitely want to kiss Mila again. I want her. All of her. I want us curled up on the pantry floor like two kids sneaking dessert after bedtime. I want her laughter, her smiles. I want to hold her when she needs strength, and to be the man she comes to when she celebrates her victories. I want her highs and her lows and everything in between.

I'm like a piece of paper whose corner touched the match and singed. I am certain the next time Mila touches me, I'll go up in flames. And that's why I'm keeping a healthy distance. I miss her. Our daily texts and calls don't do anything to quench my thirst to be near her. I allowed myself to get accustomed to being around Mila and now I'm aware of her absence like I'm missing a limb.

There's a knock on my office door. I'm grateful for the distraction.

"Come in!"

Ben walks into my office and stands next to my desk as if he's in a boardroom, not a puny excuse for an office, taking up two-thirds of the space with his broad stance and golden-retriever energy.

"I'll come out there," I say.

"Okay. I've got something important to ask you, boss."

Whenever Ben calls me "boss," you can be quite sure he's yanking my chain. He's about to taunt me or poke fun at me, or get a laugh at my expense.

"What is it?"

I glance over at Bodhi as if he's going to help me out. The look in his eyes tells me he isn't.

"Well, we haven't seen you taking off for the other side of the island at lunchtime in days. We haven't heard you on the phone with Mila through that flimsy excuse for an office door. You haven't left early to run over to check on her after work. Basically, it's crickets. And I'm worried there's trouble in paradise."

"You're worried, huh?" I shoot Bodhi a look over Ben's shoulder.

He pinches his lips into a thin line.

"She's been getting busier."

That much is true.

"And we've had more lessons with the season picking up."

Also true.

"But you two are new," Ben says, his brow furrowing with concern. "You need time together. You can't neglect her, Kai."

Ben looks at me with an incredibly sincere expression on his face. "You see, Kai. Women are like gardens."

Bodhi huffs out a laugh.

"Hey!" Ben scolds him. "I'm being serious here."

"Okay. Okay!" Bodhi holds up his hands, but you can still see the vestiges of a suppressed laugh in his eyes.

"Anyway, as I was saying." Ben turns his attention back to me. "Women are like gardens. And you need to water the garden. Fertilize the garden. Weed the garden."

Bodhi starts cracking up. His laughter turns into full-blown cackling within seconds. I can't help it. My laugh bubbles up from inside me. I try. I really do. I'm trying not to laugh. But it's just impossible. Then, Bodhi and I make eye contact which only makes us both laugh harder.

"Fertilize! ..." Bodhi shouts out. "Kai! Fertilize the garden!"

I lose it all over again.

Ben crosses his arms like a dejected child who isn't getting his way.

"Sorry," I say between laughs. "Sorry, Ben."

"Fine, you two. See if I give you my relationship advice. Ask Summer. I make her happy. My wife is a movie star and she's happy—with me. I make her happy. I thought I'd give you some trade secrets. But now? Now you're on your own."

"Secrets like, 'Fertilize the garden'?" Bodhi asks, bursting into more laughter.

"It was an analogy, you doof. I was going to expound."

"Water. Weed. Fertilize," Bodhi repeats. "I think we got the gist, man."

I'm wiping tears from beneath my eyes.

"Just come out with us on a four-way date this weekend, Kai. We're getting together with this guy." He waves a hand in Bodhi's direction. "I'm not sure why right now, except your sister finds him attractive. Cam and Riley are coming out too. You and Mila should join us."

"Sounds good," I say, still laughing softly and trying not to let my laughter escalate. "Let me talk to Mila."

"Good."

"Yeah. I'll bring the hoe," Bodhi says.

And we both crack up again while Ben walks out the back door of the shack throwing up a peace sign over his shoulder and saying, "Peace out."

"And the weed whacker!" Bodhi shouts after him. "Plus! Fertilizer! Can't forget the fertilizer!"

We laugh for a solid minute after Ben leaves the room. Trying to regain our composure a few times and failing every time either one of us says, "Fertilize the garden," or when Bodhi attempts to make a dead serious face and says, "Women are like gardens, Kai." We lose it all over again.

"He's not mad," Bodhi assures me, knowing I'll flip to care-taker mode in an instant as soon as my laughter runs out. "He's fine."

"Yeah. I know. The man's a human rubber ball. He always bounces back, almost immediately."

"Right?" Bodhi smiles warmly. "But seriously, bro? Fertilize? Water? Weed? Where did he get this stuff? Mister Miyagi?"

"I'm so calling him that this week."

"Dude. I'm down. Let's make him a name tag."

Bodhi pulls a blank name tag out from the drawer under the register and the silver sharpie we use for just this purpose. It's usually a setup for new employees until their official name tags come in from The Alicante. But this use is just as legit. He scrawls *Mr. Miyagi* on the tag and smiles.

I grab my phone out and text Mila to ask her to see if Chloe or one of her aunts can watch Noah this weekend so we can hang with my crazy group of friends and their wives.

Later that day, Ben's walking around with the Mr. Miyagi tag on and owning it. He's randomly saying things like, "Wax on, Wax off," and calling me and Bodhi, "grasshoppers." He's always been one to roll with the punches when it comes to pranks around here. I've got mad respect for him for that.

It's later that afternoon when Ben shouts back to me, "Hey, Kai?"

I'm tagging sunglasses and he's at the register waiting for a lesson to show. Bodhi's outside rinsing off some snorkels from a group he took out a few hours ago.

"Are Bodhi and Mavs moving out of your place after the wedding?"

"We haven't discussed it, honestly."

As crazy as it sounds, we haven't considered any changes after the wedding. Bodhi and Kalaine will start sharing a room, I guess. Man. We should have talked about this.

"Our situation just works," I say.

Bodhi comes in from out back. "What's up?" he asks.

"Ben just asked what you and Kala are doing after the wedding."

"Honeymoon, Dude. We're going to Bali, where it all start-ed." Bodhi shoots me a look and smiles.

Bali. I haven't thought of those days in ages.

"Nah, bro. I'm talking about whether you and Kalaine are going to stay in the same house with Kai after you're married."

"We've got built-in dog sitting when we're gone. I guess …"

Bodhi's voice trails off as if he just realized the same thing I did. Things are about to change and not one of us thought to discuss how a transition is going to work. In my defense, I've been just a little preoccupied with this whole thing I'm doing for Mila.

Ben doesn't drop it. "Seriously, bro? What are you going to do, share one of the bedrooms while Kai is in the other room? Tell me that's not your plan."

I feel myself blanch.

Ben looks over at me. "You've thought this through, right?"

"'Fraid not," I admit. "I should have."

I glance at Bodhi. "You're welcome to stay on. I mean, we co-own the house."

"We should have been thinking about this, huh?" Bodhi says.

"We've got time," I assure him. "Let's focus on your wedding. We'll figure out housing after your honeymoon."

Ben shakes his head.

"What?" I ask.

"Nothing. Grasshopper. You will learn the ways of the master in time. Watch and learn. Watch and learn."

Ben zips his lip. He actually zips his lip. Then he says, "No talking. Just observe."

After two afternoon surf lessons, I'm ready to head out for the day. I decide to stop by C-Side coffee for a to-go sandwich and an iced tea. I don't feel like cooking and I could use a change of scenery. I call Mila on my way there.

"Hey," Mila answers, sounding really happy to hear from me.

My thoughts smooth out at the mere sound of her voice.

"Hey. How's it going?"

"Good. I've been thinking about you."

"Yeah? I've been thinking about you too. You know, about this weekend. And about getting some time to get our stories straight."

"Yeah. Of course. Yes. We need to do that." She pauses. "So ... how was your day?"

"Good. Ben brought up something this afternoon."

I tell Mila all about Ben's question about what Kala and Bodhi will do for living arrangements after the wedding. She just listens and doesn't try to solve anything for me.

We talk all the way until I get to C-Side. She waits on the phone while I place my order. Then we talk while I walk home. When I get in the door, I set my food on the coffee table, kick off my shoes and put my feet up. We're still talking—not just about Bodhi and Kalaine now, about her day, Noah's birthday party, the tourists we interacted with this week.

Our talk goes on while I eat my dinner. It turns out Noah's at a friend's for the evening, and Mila already set out warmers with all the fixings for tacos for her guests. So, she's sitting at the kitchen island and I'm sitting on my couch while we share a meal together.

It's dark out when Kalaine and Bodhi come back from wherever they went. Shaka's got his head on my lap and I'm rubbing his ears absentmindedly while Mila tells me a story about her and Chloe from years ago. I don't even know how we got on the subject, but I don't want her to stop talking.

"Hey," I say, waving to my sister and Bodhi as they settle in on the couch across from me.

I stand. Shaka jumps up and walks over to them. I head into my room. I don't need four eyes staring me down while I talk to Mila.

"Did you get my text about getting together with the group?" I ask, reclining on my bed and switching the phone to my other ear.

"Yes. It sounds like fun. And I know we need to make time to work on our get-the-story-straight stuff before the wedding. It's just been really busy."

"Here too. I'll text you some dates. Okay?"

"That would be great."

There's a prolonged silence and I think Mila might be about to say goodbye.

Then her voice comes across softer, more hesitant. "Kai?"

"Yeah?"

"Is it weird to say I've missed you this week? That's weird, right?"

"I missed you too." I smile.

She missed me. Even if it's just our friendship, it's nice to be missed—by her, especially.

I almost say, *I love you, Mila.* The words feel like greyhounds at the gate.

What am I thinking?

Apparently, love makes me crazy.

Certifiably crazy.

TWENTY-EIGHT

Mila

The hardest part of parenting is trying to be fake mad
when your kid does something bad but hilarious.
~ Unknown

Finally, Kai and I found a day when we can both get away at the same time. Noah's in the main room waiting for his ride to pick him up. Chloe's sitting with her legs tucked up under her on my bed, and I'm randomly throwing items of clothes out onto the mattress to see if they're what I want to wear.

"Chloe, you should have seen him. He was so ... just so *there* for me."

I'm rehashing the night Kai showed up to serve me ice cream while I melted down over Brad meeting Noah.

I haven't told Chloe about the hardware store kiss for obvious reasons.

"I've been watching, Mila. Kai's *always* there for you. Remind me why you're so dead set on resisting this man."

"I can't talk about that right now. He'll be here in an hour. Let's put a pin in that."

"Okay. Consider it pinned. And consider me the woman you've always known me to be."

"You're not dropping it." I set another blouse on the bed, hold the last one up to me and raise my eyebrows, silently asking Chloe her opinion.

"Too formal. Isn't he just taking you to the beach? And why are you stressing about what to wear if you two are so fake?"

"I'm just ... I don't know. That's part of the pinned conversation too. Okay?"

"Not by a long shot. We're having tea one night after Noah's in bed—soon. And by tea, I mean tea. The tea you'll be spilling. All. The. Tea, Mila."

"Okay. It's a deal. But now can you help me pick out an outfit? I just need to get dressed."

Chloe purses her lips and raises her brows as if I'm transparent—as if there's more to this time I'm about to spend with Kai than us figuring out our stories so we can convince his family we're real during Kalaine and Bodhi's wedding. And also so we can continue to convince Brad we're real. All of those reasons seem misty and vague right now. Meaningless and trite. This fake romance has taken on a life of its own like a runaway horse pulling a carriage across a dirt road full of ruts. I can't get my bearings anymore and I'm being jostled so hard I'm no longer sure if I'll be upended or survive the ride.

"Anyway, as I was saying, Kai needs a fake date for the wedding. So I'm it. His parents already think I'm his girlfriend."

Chloe laughs. "You're so used to this now. It's like pulling the wool over everyone's eyes but mine is no big deal to you anymore. Are you the same girl who tattled on Jeremy Stein for copying one answer on our math test in sixth grade?"

I am that girl.

"I don't know, Chloe. You're right. It's become too easy to pretend—to deceive people. It's so complicated. How did I even get here? And now ..."

"Now you went and caught real feelings," she finishes for me.

"Yes-ish. Sort of. That's under the pin too."

"This pin is getting pretty darn overloaded. Do I need to rent a yurt on the backside of the island and steal you away for a weekend so you can bring me up to speed?"

"Can't. It's the beginning of high season. I barely managed to take this afternoon off, as you know."

I hold up another shirt and Chloe stands, marching over to my closet and thumbing through a few things. "Here," she says, handing me a gauzy blouse that's not too formal, but isn't schleppy either.

"Kai saved me, Chloe. He saved me on more than one occasion. When you think of it, he's been saving me for years in small ways."

"Yep. Bonafide mouth to mouth." Chloe wags her eyebrows suggestively and then cracks up at her own joke.

"Stahhhp." I scold her while my mind unhelpfully recalls the actual mouth to mouth episode from last week. "All I'm saying is he deserves me to be the best fake girlfriend ever at the wedding. And I will be."

"Pin," Chloe says. "So, so much under that pin."

Noah knocks on my door while swinging it open and walking in.

"Buddy, knocking means waiting."

"I did wait."

Chloe chuckles like the childless woman she is. Noah entertains her infinitely—especially when he's doing something he shouldn't.

"Did you hear me say, 'Come in'?"

"You were going to. I saved you the trouble."

Chloe shakes her head. Her face is pinched with suppressed laughter. I quietly glare at her like she's dead if she lets one puff of a laugh out right now.

"What are you doing?" Noah asks.

"Picking out clothes to wear."

"You're already wearing clothes."

"This is for later."

Noah's face contorts in confusion.

Then, as if in slow motion, Noah walks toward my bed. I feel like I'm in one of those scenes where the person lunging for something moves in freeze frames while the background music sounds like it's being played underwater. Everything happens too quickly and slowly at the same time. I can't get to Noah fast enough because I'm the sluggish girl in the meme, saying "noooooo" while diving for the item he now holds up as if it's a class project on show-and-tell day.

My shapewear.

My son has my Spanx in his hand, his fingers like little clothespins so the entirety of them is on display.

"What kind of shorts are these?" His nose scrunches. "They're ugly. Like skin. You should definitely not wear these out to the beach." He pauses. "Or anywhere."

No kidding!

"They're nothing!" I say in a squeaky voice while I snatch my tummy-tucking, modern-day girdle from my son.

"Oooh. You know what, Noah?" Chloe uses her child-charmer voice while her breath comes out in small bursts of laughter she's trying desperately to contain. "Can you make me a snack?"

I stuff the Spanx behind my back, which only makes them seem all the more suspicious. Today just isn't the day I need to edify my son as to what women wear to smooth out the places where we carried our children in our wombs ... and the other spots on my body that bear the evidence that, yes, I do love scones, thank you very much. Not that I'm embarrassed of those places. I'm proud. But when a man like Kai asks you out for a day on the beach to get to know you better ... Well, you panic. Or at least I panicked. And I needed all the reinforcement I could get. Enter: the girdle.

"Sure, Aunt Chloe," Noah thankfully takes my bestie's bait. "We've got brownies. Want one with milk?"

"You know I do." She smiles sweetly, but there's mirth in her eyes. It's a dangerous look. I know I'll be hearing about this for years to come.

Noah turns and practically flies to the kitchen. He loves serving guests. I guess it's a byproduct of living here all these years.

Once he's safely out of earshot, I cover my face and wail while Chloe laughs hysterically from her spot on my bed.

"My Spanx. Really?"

I look at Chloe who is now literally rolling on my bed in laughter. She's rocking from side to side, holding her stomach.

"He's going to need so much therapy. So. Much." I wail again.

"Calm down," she says between laughs. "He probably won't even remember. Why do you have those out anyway?" She pauses to study me and then says, "Ohhhh. For your *date?*"

"Not a date."

I fold the Spanx and put them in my drawer. What was I thinking? This is Kai. He's seen me at all hours, under all circumstances. Besides, it's *not* a date.

"So you were putting on Spanx for your not-a-date?"

"Can we stop saying Spanx before *I* need therapy? Please?"

Kai made me a picnic. He didn't stop to pick up slaw from the market and fried chicken from a restaurant. The man made me a picnic. And then he walked me down to the local North Shore beach and laid out a beach blanket before opening the cooler with all the food in it. And we've spent the past few hours filling in blanks of our knowledge about one another, coordinating the fake details of how we started dating, and sealing any holes in our stories.

We're prepared.

I look around the blanket at the remnants of the meal we shared. Chocolate's smeared on the dessert plate from the tart Kai picked up at the Patisserie inside Alicante. It's the one item he didn't make from scratch, and I'm not mad about it.

I'm a woman who serves people for a living and loves doing it. There aren't really words to explain what it means when someone turns the tables and decides to serve me. Kai did that. He does it all the time. A slow, soft, but surprisingly intense yearning begins to swell somewhere in my chest. It whispers and nudges: *This. Him. Forever.*

What would it be like to spend my life giving back to Kai Kapule? Out-serving him. Showing him how much he matters. Running my hand along his jaw whenever I wanted. Looking into his honey-gold eyes while they crinkle in the corners with amusement. Sharing my heart with him, because he's safe enough to hold it.

Only, is he? Does he feel anything beyond friendship for me? He's reiterated the word friend all along. He's always treated me like this. Nothing has changed for him. He said he missed me, but then went right into how we needed this day just to get our stories straight.

And then there's Noah. He loves Kai, but he's about to find out who his dad is. I've been subtly leading up to the reveal that's going to happen sooner than later. There couldn't be a more inopportune time to start dating another man. What if Kai and I dated and broke up? Noah would lose the one man in his life who's been anything close to a father figure. I can't do that to Noah. I knew it wasn't time to think about romance, but my heart didn't listen.

"Mila?"

"Huh?"

"You drifted off somewhere."

"Sorry."

"Nothing to be sorry about." Kai smiles softly. "We probably need to talk about one more thing."

"So we're prepared?" I ask.

"Yeah. It's kind of important."

Kai's leaning back on his elbows. I'm laying down, my head propped on my hand. When he says it's important, he sits up. I raise myself off the blanket so we're side by side, looking out toward the ocean.

"We need to talk about that kiss."

I cover my face. "Could we not?"

"Mila ..." Kai reaches over and pulls my hands away. His soft expression melts me. "It's okay. I already told you that. I just think we need to consider what we're doing about kissing going forward."

"What we're doing about kissing?"

Do I sound panicked? Because I feel a little panicked.

"Yeah." Kai doesn't take his eyes off mine. "That kiss was ..."

"Awkward?" I ask, fishing for a sign that would tell me he feels anything other than sweet friendship for me.

"No ..." He shakes his head and it almost seems like he's remembering our kiss. Then he chuckles lightly. "A little awkward. You definitely caught me off guard." He smiles at me. I smile back. Then he finally settles on saying, "It was ...unrehearsed."

Unrehearsed? How can he say it was unrehearsed? The best kiss of my life to date felt unrehearsed to him? I don't know if I should feel insulted or curious as to where he's going with this.

"Definitely," he says. "Unrehearsed. It looked like our first kiss ever."

"Which it was."

"Right. Exactly. And, if you think of it, we shouldn't look like we've never kissed. It won't do. We've been dating. Obviously, we've been kissing."

"We have?"

"Well, we would have been."

"We would?" I nearly swallow my tongue the way Kai looks at me after saying we would have been kissing.

"Sure. I'd be stopping by the inn, sometimes bringing you flowers. Then I'd stay for a meal. I'd even bring the meal on nights you were burnt out on cooking. We'd clean up together. And after Noah was asleep, I'd sit with you on the porch swing. We'd talk. It's not all about the kissing for us."

"It's not?"

"Not at all." He smiles at me like he's not painting a picture like the ones you want to step right into once you've seen them hanging on a gallery wall. "We have a friendship as a foundation. A strong one. We care about one another."

"We do," I agree.

"So we'd chat in the evenings on the porch swing. We'd laugh about something funny Noah said. Maybe you'd ask me for input on a situation at the inn. Maybe I'd tell you some crazy story about Ben. But then, we'd fall into a peaceful quiet with one another."

"We would?"

I gulp and hope the sound isn't noticeable. It must not be because Kai keeps spinning the images of us in a committed relationship.

"Yeah. We'd get quiet, and I'd hold you. And we'd sit in that comfortable silence we always share."

"It is comfortable," I agree, even though my stomach feels like it's on a roller coaster with every single word out of Kai's mouth. Dipping, falling, rising, twisting.

"It is. It's one of my favorite times—when we're just quiet together. That kind of thing is underestimated, if you ask me. Anyway, I was saying, we'd sit like that, and you'd put your head on my shoulder, and I'd kiss the top of your head, and then you'd tilt your face up and smile at me the way you do, and ... well, then we'd kiss."

"Every night?"

"If you wanted. Though, some nights I'd take you out to dinner instead of you cooking at the inn. I'd get Chloe or Phyllis to watch Noah and cover the needs of the guests. And then I'd make reservations. And we'd dress up and I'd take you dancing or out to eat. On our way home, I'd kiss you on the beach, or on the porch of the inn at the end of the night."

"You would?"

"If this were real, Mila? Yeah. That's how it would be. So, you see my point."

"Your point?"

I seem to be only capable of two word answers right now. My mouth is too dry for a full sentence.

"My point is, we should appear to have that life—the life where I'm kissing you daily."

"So our kisses should appear more boring. Like you're used to me."

"I would never be used to you. And believe me, our kisses would not be boring."

"In this fantasy of yours."

"Sure. Yes. In my fantasy. But it's our reality right now. The one we're presenting."

"So we need to look more ... practiced?"

"That's what I think. But that's just my take on it. You have to tell me. Maybe we'll never have to kiss in front of anyone ever again. After all, you did attack me at the hardware store." He winks.

I cover my face again. I'll never live down the fact.

"Mila." Kai nudges me. "I'm teasing. That was us. Not you. We kissed one another. And it was a good move. Brad got the message loud and clear. That's what we want. We don't want a yellow light that he thinks he can run. We want it to be very blatantly red."

Yeah. *Brad.* That's what this is all about. We need to show Brad we're a couple.

Somehow, our objective no longer matters. It's irrelevant, because that picture Kai just painted is everything I've ever dreamed of.

And it's just a fantasy.

TWENTY-NINE
Kai

She knew all my secrets except one:
that I'm in love with her.
~ Unknown

The first drop of water feels like nothing. It could be mist or spray off the ocean, but the next droplets come with certainty, and suddenly we're in a squall—an unanticipated storm that blew in without warning. Our empty plates fill with water, the blanket is instantly soaked. The cooler, which had been sitting open, quickly gathers almost an inch of the downpour. We're up and scrambling around. I dump the water and we throw items pell-mell into the Igloo while I hand a towel to Mila to use as a shield against the wind and water assaulting us.

Her shirt is soaked. My clothes are drenched. Our hair is sticking to our faces and necks as we make a mad dash for shelter, yelling to one another over the hiss and splatter of the rain. The only available nearby refuge is a tiny hut. It's been out here as long as I've lived on Marbella, but it looks like it's been around for decades with its rotting wood and peeling paint. The shack backs up to the cliffs that line this section of beach. It's tiny—probably five by five at most. I'm certain I couldn't lay down on the floor unless I went corner to corner, and even that would be cramped.

I usher Mila inside and follow her, shutting the rickety door behind us. The air smells salty and a bit musty. There's sand and bits of driftwood and dried seaweed on the floor. The sound of the storm hitting the wood surrounds us. Mila's shivering, so I pull her in toward me, even though I'm not going to be of much use in warming her with my sopping wet shirt.

Her teeth chatter, but when she looks up at me, she smiles. And then she starts laughing.

"Oh my gosh! That came out of nowhere. I hope my guests are alright."

"I'm sure they're fine. Didn't you say Stevens was taking them on a marine bio cruise?"

"Yes. Two of the couples went. The other couple had massages at the Alicante."

"Well then, they're covered. Stevens has that interior cabin with tables. They're fine."

Leave it to Mila to think of others when she's shivering in a dilapidated hut during a sea squall.

"So ... should we practice ... our kiss?" Mila's voice is shy.

My arms are wrapped securely around her, my hands rubbing her arms and back to warm her up.

"I ..." I don't even get to answer her before she's speaking again.

"Why did I suggest that? I was just thinking ..."

I cut her off. "Just to get more comfortable, it might be a good idea. What do you think?"

"It might be wise." She nods.

I understand her shyness. It's natural. She's suggesting we kiss. We don't kiss. We're friends. That kiss we shared, though. I probably should heed my better judgment and avoid anything too physical with her, but she's right here, looking up at me with her doe eyes, her hair falling in wet waves around her face, her clothes soaked. I'm only so strong.

"Just for the sake of our ruse," I assure her.

It's not that I want to chalk up another intimate moment to this sham we're embroiled in. But I need to remind myself this kiss is like rehearsal for a play, nothing more. My heart has to listen to reason or I'll be in danger of crossing all the lines with her, and that would mean risking everything we have for something Mila never promised—something she already clearly told me I can't have.

"Of course. For the ruse." She nods.

"Of course," I repeat.

It's only awkward for a flicker of a moment and then our eyes lock. The heat I feel between us could set this hut on fire.

The tip of Mila's tongue darts out and she licks her lips. Then she lets out a short puff of breath as if she's girding herself to go in for the kill. Her nervousness rolls off her, making me question the sanity of what we're about to do.

"Hey," I tell her. "It's just me."

"That's the problem," she says softly.

"Friends kissing?"

"Something like that."

"We don't have to ..."

The words don't make it out of my mouth because Mila reaches up, grips the back of my neck and pulls me down toward her. Once we're in motion I don't need any other encouragement. I'm all in. I pull Mila toward me with the hand I already have splayed on her lower back. She moves with my coaxing, melting against me with a soft sound I've never heard from her before. It's too much. Way too much. If this is acting, I'm calling the Academy.

Maybe Mila's not acting. This could be strictly physical on her part. She's a woman who hasn't been kissed by a man in years, with the exception of that kiss we shared at the hardware store. Maybe she's like someone who gave up sugar and finally takes a bite of a cookie. I'm beyond grateful to be the one Mila's breaking her fast with. I'm so happy that I could write poetry, hire a skywriter, and fall to my knees to thank heaven.

Our lips have barely touched and I'm a goner.

And then, Mila's hand starts to tug at my neck, like she can't help but drag me closer. And I smile. She smiles back, like a dream. Or one of those pick-your-ending stories. *This.* I pick this.

I tilt my head, angling my mouth over hers, gently brushing a kiss there. Practice? We don't need practice. We're naturals. If this were the world championships of kissing, we'd get the gold, and we're only just getting started.

I kiss Mila softly, intentionally restraining myself. Her lips brush against mine and linger. The slightest contact from her travels through me like a licking flame. I'm careful not to push past her unspoken limits. But then Mila starts to run her fingernails along the back of my neck, pulling me nearer with the arm she's got looped around my waist, and that's all it takes. I hold her to me. Our mouths dance and we confirm everything I already knew.

Mila's made for me. We fit one another. She's everything I want and need and can't get enough of. She's satiation and hunger, sweetness and spice. Depth and light, tension and relief. I run my hand down her hair, caress her arm, move my palm so her soft cheek is cupped in it.

The rain falls on the roof of the shack. We're secluded, separated from the world, oblivious to anything but how it feels to finally be in one another's arms again. I pour all my longing and feelings into this kiss as if it's our first and last. It may be.

Practice? This isn't practice. I never needed to practice with Mila. I want a lifetime of her kisses, her soft sighs, the way she feels when she mirrors my movements, telling me wordlessly that she feels this too.

I brush my thumb across Mila's cheek when I pull back. I

have to stop. If I don't, this will go farther than we can handle. Maybe it already has.

Mila's breathing harder, her eyes bashful, studying the neckline of my shirt and then collapsing into me so I can't see her face when we part. Our arms are still wrapped around one another. The silence is thick with unspoken words, damp from the storm, heavy with fresh longing despite the fact that we quenched our thirst only moments ago.

Mila's head rests on my chest. I smooth my hand down her back. We don't move. We should. This isn't part of practicing. I'm afraid to breathe, to shift my weight. The slightest motion could push her away and this whole experience will pass as quickly as the squall outside, which I already sense is dissipating as it moves over the island and further out to sea.

"Um ... so," Mila says, her words muffled in my shirt.

"Yeah." I smile down at her, but her face is still buried into me, her breath warm through the soaked cotton.

"That was pretty good practice." She looks up at me now, an expression on her face I've never seen before. It's playful and flirtatious.

"It was. I'd say we might want to take it down a notch in public, though."

"You think?" She giggles.

Her eyes drift shut and pop open again.

"What did I do?" She seems to be asking herself instead of me.

I take her chin in my hand and tilt it up. "Don't. Mila, we kissed. That's what *we* did. And, it will ..."

I can't even finish my thought. *It will serve the charade ... keep Brad away ... show my parents we're real ...*

That kiss wasn't an act. For me it wasn't. I might be able to lie to Brad. I've even brought myself to the point where I'm willing to deceive this whole island and my own parents. But I can't lie to Mila.

Mila smiles softly up at me. "I think the rain is stopping."

"Look," I say. "I know where we stand. You know where we stand. We're friends who kiss really ... really well."

That much is true. It's obvious Mila wants to redraw the lines in her life. Whether this charade calls for it or not, I won't be kissing her again. Not on the lips. I can't. From this point forward, I'm going to keep my feelings on my side of the line. I'm here to do her a favor, plain and simple. If she wanted more from me, she'd give me a sign. Instead, she's been clear. I'm the one who muddied the waters by falling for her. She doesn't need to be burdened with my infatuation. I'll deal with that on my own time. For her, I'll dial it back.

"Yeah. We do." She covers her face with her hands and then peeks out at me. "We kiss ... well."

"A plus, I'd say."

"Top of the class," she jokes back.

"Valedictorians of kissing," I say.

"If they gave out scholarships, we'd both be getting a full ride."

We both laugh as I open the door and hold it for her. The rain has come to an end along with this lapse from reality. Once we step out onto the beach, we're back to being Kai and Mila: two friends who kiss really, really well, but can't afford to go there. No matter what.

It's been a little over a week since my picnic with Mila. Eight days of being around her without kissing. Eight days into the eternity I'll spend wanting her and learning to quell my longings.

We spent an evening with my friends and their wives barbecuing on the beach and then hanging out around a bonfire last weekend. She fit in like she always does. As if she belongs in my world.

Brad showed up on the beach at the end of my surf lesson with Noah Saturday. Mila had told him he could. It felt like an intrusion on something sacred. But I don't get a say in how she allows him to inch his way closer to his own son. There's no easy way to make room for him, and she's being amazing, so I support her choices and stay out of the way.

I don't stay out of the way when he starts looking at her with the look a man gives a woman he wants. Those longing gazes might slip under Mila's radar, but I see every one of them. And I'm by her side each time, kissing her temple, wrapping my arm around her, whispering in her ear—whatever it takes to fend him off and continue to claim Mila as mine.

Even though she isn't.

I wake earlier than usual, but not before Bodhi.

"Hey. Want some coffee?" Bodhi offers when I round the corner into the kitchen.

Shaka looks up at me and walks over to sit at my feet. Then the dog just stares up at me, waiting for me to pet his head, so I do. I've given up resisting the mutt. He's not going anywhere. I may as well make my peace with him. Kalaine and Bodhi still tease me that I'm secretly in love with Shaka. I'm not. I just know when to throw in the towel.

I fill my mug with coffee and join Bodhi at the kitchen table.

"How was Noah's party?"

"Brad showed up on the fringes."

"I wonder what Noah thinks. Here's this random dude who keeps showing up all of a sudden."

"He doesn't seem to think much of it. He's so in the moment."

"The beauty of childhood."

"Right? When Noah saw Brad, he said, 'Hey, Mom! There's that friend of yours from high school. Should we ask him to join us?' That's what comes from being raised by a gracious and inclusive woman. Noah's got hospitality in his DNA. So, Brad joined the party."

"So, how was it with him there?" Bodhi sips his coffee and studies me.

"I did my part to fend him off and keep him convinced Mila's not available."

"Fend him off Noah?"

I shake my head. "He was watching Mila when she didn't notice. I noticed. He's still got a thing for her. Big time."

"You'd think this whole contrived relationship of yours would send him a message."

"He's not crossing lines, but he's like a vulture circling. He's waiting for me to die so he can go in for the kill."

"Technically, vultures don't kill. You know that, right? They're scavengers. They eat the carrion of someone else's kill."

"Okay. So, he's waiting to swoop in when I die."

"To eat your remains?"

"To reclaim his wife."

"The vulture analogy isn't working for me here," Bodhi says, as if it deeply matters.

"Focus, Bodhi. Forget the vulture. Brad wants Mila. He's waiting for things to go south between us so he can make his move. And I can tell he's in it for the long game. He wants his wife back."

"Ex-wife."

"Exactly." I breathe out a sigh of relief. "Still, Mila's oblivious to how he looks at her. And it kills me, if I'm honest. Sometimes I think how unfair it is that he had her—all of her."

"Look who's got her now." Bodhi means for his words to be a consolation, but they're far from it.

"No one, man. No one's got her. I'm her *fake* boyfriend. As weird as it is, I'm in the same boat as Brad. We both want her and neither one of us gets to have her."

"Beg to differ." Bodhi smirks over at me. "I saw her leaning on you when we had our barbecue. Who was there? Me, Mavs, Cam, Riley, Ben, Summer, you. She didn't need to convince any of us. She's into you."

"Maybe. But that doesn't change the fact that she's not ready to do anything about it. If she even is *into me*, she's not pursuing anything with anyone for years."

"Patience grasshopper."

I shoot Bodhi a look.

"Seriously. Be patient. A woman can change her mind."

I look down at my coffee and back up into the face of my best friend.

Bodhi smiles serenely. "Mavs did. If she did, anyone can."

THIRTY

Kai

Is there anything better than
to be longing for something,
when you know it is within reach?
Greta Garbo

Ꮇy sister and Bodhi will be married in two days.
My family arrived a few hours ago on the ferry, along
with Aima and her parents and some other close friends and rela-
tives from Hawaii. They're all staying at Alicante in rooms at the
resort, but right now, they've converged on my place of work like
a litter of puppies crawling over one another, touching things
they shouldn't and yapping incessantly.

"So, this is where you work?" Aima asks, stating the obvious.

"It is. My office is there." I point to the back of the shop. "And
there." I point out the door toward the ocean.

"It's ideal for you. Really, Kai. Do you love it here?"

Aima's a sweet woman. Kind hearted. If we weren't wrong-
fully "betrothed" I'd be way more welcoming right now.

"Honestly? Yes. I really love it here. When I came to Marbella,

I thought it would be temporary. I needed a break from the surf circuit and from everything going on with Kalaine and Bodhi. But now, I love it."

"I'm glad. You look well." She tucks a strand of her full dark hair behind her ear.

Aima has typical Hawaiian hair. It's wild and long and thick, nearly black, but with mahogany or red tones when the light hits it. She's wearing a floral sundress. She's definitely beautiful. Just ... nothing. I feel nothing but brotherly affection for her.

"Do you think you'll come home one day?" she asks.

"No one knows the future, but if I base it on my life now? No. I don't see myself back on the islands to live. Of course, I'll always visit regularly as long as my ohana is there."

"Wow."

"I know. Life's funny that way. Isn't it?"

"It is. You never know where you'll end up—or with whom."

She bats her lashes up at me. It's a subtle movement, nothing too forward, but I see it.

"You want to end up with someone who can't live without you," I say. "Someone you can't live without."

"Totally." She nods.

"I want that for you, Aima."

I do want the best for her. I hope she ends up happy whether she's single or with a man who wants her the way I want Mila.

"I want that too, Kai."

Pretty sure there was a misfire there. The way Aima's looking at me says she still hopes that man is me.

"Ben!" I shout.

"Yeah, boss?" Ben strides toward me, and I've never been so happy to see him approaching in my life.

"Aima here is from Hawaii. We grew up together, like *brother* and *sister*." I emphasize those words as if saying them will solidify our ohana status.

"Nice to meet you, Aima."

"She's never been to Marbella before."

"Oh, well, let me show you around the shack and give you the lowdown on where to eat."

"Um. Okay." Aima glances over at me.

I grin a full smile at her.

I clap Ben on the back and walk over to my parents. "You know I have a girlfriend, right?"

"Yes, son. Where is she, though?"

"She's working. She runs an inn on the North Shore."

"North Shore?"

"We call it North Shore here too."

My father nods. My mother smiles.

"You'll meet her soon," I tell them. "And she's my date to the wedding."

"So, it's serious?" my mother asks.

"Very."

Whaaat?

My mouth. What possesses me to say things like, *I'm her boyfriend*, and *Very serious*? Usually I'm reserved. I think before I speak. Lately, I don't know what's come over me besides a need to protect Mila and to be there for her any way I can.

My parents exchange a look.

"We've known one another for four years."

"But you are only dating now, and it's already serious?"

If they only knew.

"She's a single mom. She's been through a divorce. Her ex left her years ago. We're being respectful of her son. He's only seven."

"Ahh. That's wise." My dad nods his head a few times in approval.

"We haven't even told her son we're dating," I explain.

"But you're serious?" My mother looks confused.

"She's it for me." There. I said it.

My father's face breaks into a smile. My mother looks conflicted. Of course she does. She hasn't met Mila. She loves Aima. She has plans to matchmake me if there's even a chink in my availability. Her dream is for me to come home to Hawaii and marry Aima. Then we'd give her little grandbabies and raise them nearby. It's a lovely dream, but it's not my dream.

My dream is currently on the other side of this island preparing dinner for a full inn of guests. And like any dream, she's elusive.

Eventually, my family and extended family leave the shack. Bodhi escorts them out and Ben and Jamison linger behind to take over. Bodhi and Kalaine are having a co-ed bachelor/bachelorette party tonight. And Mila and I are going as a couple. They invited us and I presented the invitation to her with a big EXIT sign over the top.

"You don't have to come," I told her.

"Of course I do," she said.

So now I don't know if she's coming because she wants to be with me, or if she is just fulfilling a duty. She could be thanking me for being a buffer to Brad, or she might simply be trying to be a good friend. Whatever her motive, she'll be with me tonight, and I'm not mad about that in the least.

The bachelor-ette party includes every relative and close island friend under age thirty-five. We're a crowd of twenty-seven people total. We eat a meal at Kala and Bodhi's favorite restaurant followed by dancing at Club Descanso. Then we're teamed up for a scavenger hunt to search for a list of twenty wedding themed items. We end the night at one of the pools in the back area of the resort. Bodhi reserved a whole section of patio and an entire pool for us.

Mila comes out in a modest one piece. She warned me, *I'm wearing a mom suit. It's the only kind I have anymore. Sorry I won't be your sexy date. I've given birth. I'm a grown woman in my early thirties with a figure that isn't all it used to be. I hope it's enough to make Aima think you're into me.*

She couldn't be more wrong. I'm into her and she could be

wearing a scuba suit for all I care. But she's not. She walks over to a lounger, drops her towel and then strolls to the edge of the pool where she points her toe and swishes it along the surface of the water to test the temperature. I dunk myself underwater and resurface just to cool off and refocus.

I guess I have a thing for a woman in a mom suit. At least that woman in that suit.

Eventually, Mila descends one step at a time. I push off underwater and sluice my way beneath the surface to meet her at the stairs, emerging just as her feet hit the bottom step.

"Oh!" she startles momentarily.

Her eyes dip to my chest and back up to my face. The chemistry between us feels like it did in the shack: physical, electric, intimate. Only for me that's the least of what I'm feeling.

The ache for her never dulls in me. Even when we're together I want more of her. And when we're apart, I'm only half useful because a part of me keeps reaching to the other side of this island we share trying to tether myself to her with an invisible thread— one that's wearing thin the closer we get to our end date.

Mila won't need me to act like her boyfriend forever. Just the other day she mentioned that Brad will only be here for his project part-time. He's got other store locations to constantly oversee. His time here on Marbella will be intensive at first, but then he'll come and go. Mila will be able to string Brad along without needing me present as a prop in her pretend relationship.

But she's here now, staring up into my eyes as if we're alone.

"Chicken fights!" Ben shouts like a frat boy from the other end of the pool. "Partner up!"

"You in?" I ask Mila.

"Of course. Let's show them who's the number one chicken on the island."

"Somehow that doesn't sound very impressive." I chuckle.

She giggles. "It sounded better in my head."

I lower myself into the water, turning so Mila can easily climb onto my shoulders. We walk toward the middle of the pool, my hands on her shins, her hands in my hair.

She runs her fingertips through from front to back and then says, "Sorry! I don't know what I did that for."

"You can just keep doing that," I tease.

"We'll lose if I do."

"Sacrifices. Sacrifices," I joke.

But she surprises me and runs both hands through my hair, dragging her fingernails along my scalp. I close my eyes like Shaka when I'm rubbing his head. The dog? Really? Mila's touching me and I'm thinking of that mutt.

We play chicken with a fierce competitiveness that's tinged with laughter. She feels like she's *mine*, up on my shoulders, an extension of me in the best of ways. We're synchronized and on a mission to win. Couple after couple falls into the water until it comes down to Mila and me against Kalaine and Bodhi.

It's a brutal contest. Kala and Bodhi and I were all pro surfers. They're back at it these days. Competing is in our blood. Mila must pick up on my energy, or maybe this is a side of her I never knew existed. That thought thrills me. She has layers. I don't know all of her. I want to spend the rest of my life uncovering and appreciating all the facets of Mila.

The girls are screaming on our shoulders while Bodhi and I maneuver beneath them in shoulder-high water. They're pushing at one another and pretending to trash talk. At times one of them says something completely over-the-top ridiculous and the other one cracks up, making them temporarily weaken from laughter. The guests in our group are all chanting the names of one or the other couple. My name and Mila's repeat among the raucous shouts.

"Bodhi and Kalaine!" "Go Kai and Mila!" "Knock her down, Mila!" "Bride and Groom!"

The group around us is surprisingly rowdy after such a full night. And the girls and Bodhi and I are feeding off their energy.

Bodhi and I stare one another down, moving around one another like two young bulls.

"You are going down, Charlie Brown! Down into water town! I hope you don't drown!" Mila shouts like she's some rapping Doctor Seuss queen of the game of Chicken.

Kalaine laughs hard. Mila seizes the moment and gives my sister one last shove. Kala topples off Bodhi's shoulders into the water.

Mila squeals and bounces on my shoulders.

"That's right! Uh huh! We won! Winner winner, CHICKEN dinner!" Mila shouts.

I whoop along with her. She holds on tight while her laughter filters down from her spot above me.

When she pumps her fist, I'm laughing so hard I have to grip her shins to make sure I don't drop her.

I never see Mila letting loose like this. She's always bearing the weight of motherhood and running the inn with grace and finesse. But she's constantly on, never able to fully let go because people rely on her. Even when she relaxes, I can feel the weight of her life like a cloud around her. I never realized it until now. The contrast is stark. Mila free and unhindered is one of my new favorite things in the world.

I vow to get her out more—not just for Noah's surf lessons and Noah's parties and events—but for her. Even as a friend, I will do this one thing for her. If we never become what I wish we would, I still want to give her the gift of letting loose.

I release her legs and she slides down my back. When I turn, she's right in front of me.

Ben starts chanting, "Winners kiss! Winners kiss! Win-ners Kiss! Win-ners Kiss!" and pretty soon everyone in the area is chanting along with him. My eyes scan the crowd and fall back on Mila. She shrugs and lifts onto her tiptoes. I bend down and place a soft peck on her lips. It's reminiscent of the kiss I gave her at her aunt's party. Safe. Chaste. Barely noticeable.

"Oh, no!" Ben shouts. "That's not how it's done, Kai! My

wife's co-stars kiss her like that. That's what we call a show biz kiss. That's not a winner's kiss!"

He's laughing, oblivious to my vow to never kiss Mila again—not during our charade. The next time I kiss her I want us both to know it's real. That day may never come. But I can't keep kissing her while my heart is all in and we're not actually committed to anything more than friendship.

Mila looks up at me. "We can do better."

"Oh, I'm well aware," I say in a voice for her ears only.

She looks straight in my eyes and says, "Win-ners kiss, Kai."

So I bend in and give her what she asked for. It's a winner's kiss.

I only hope I can actually win her heart one day.

THIRTY-ONE
Mila

Love is friendship that has caught fire.
~Ann Landers

Noah and I are sitting in the kitchen for breakfast. He's talking about surfing and what Kai told him during their lesson and how Kai is the greatest surfer on earth. It's pretty cute.

Then, out of the blue, Noah says, "I want to see that cove."

His statement catches me off guard. My son isn't one to stick to a single train of thought as a rule, but bringing up Brad ... that was a turn I hadn't anticipated.

Noah's been asking about "my friend" lately here and there. Things like, "How come he never was here before? Now I see him everywhere." I told him Brad lives off Marbella and has for years. "But he's here now because he bought the cove?" Yep. I told him that's why—the cove. Not because Brad wants reunification.

I've been slowly bringing up the idea of Noah's dad in random conversations. Meanwhile, Brad has been edging his way onto the scene. One day my hints and the reality of Brad will overlap into what I hope is a seamless transition. It's the best I can do, considering the impossible situation Noah and I were left in when Brad abandoned ship. Now, my only hope is the least harmful path toward reunification.

Saying Brad's here for the purchase of the cove isn't a bold-faced lie. Brad is here to expand his business. But I'm putting my toes right up to a deceitful line—for Noah's sake. It still makes me feel ill. I've never lied to my son, not even about Santa Claus. When he asked if Santa was real, I said, "He's someone we like to imagine is real."

The real reason Brad is here isn't the business. And one day Noah will know that. I only hope he understands why we waded into the truth from the shallow end instead of leaping off the high dive. I need to ease him into meeting Brad and then we'll work into a story about how a dad who was estranged can come back. And then, we'll talk about how a mom would need to introduce the child slowly. Basically, I'll tell Noah his own story until he figures out he's the boy I'm talking about, and Brad is the dad in this tale.

It's the best plan I've got in a situation with no guidebook and no roadmap. The Google results on parents who abandon their child and want to reunify were paltry at best. And the Reddit threads were so full of hateful suggestions I stopped searching them. I wish I had found those when I was in my brief season of self-indulgent anger at Brad. They would have felt cathartic then. With so little out there to guide me, I'm winging the way I navigate this critical season based solely on mother's intuition and some wisdom I gleaned from a *How to Tell Your Child They Are Adopted* article along with the few initial resources that therapist sent me.

I swallow a bite of Belgian waffle. I make my Mila's Place Waffles from an actual recipe a guest brought me from Europe. They're from yeast-rising batter and have caramel sauce as an option—one I fully indulged in. I may never go to Belgium, but at least I'll have Belgian waffles.

Noah's studying me. "Can we go?"

"You want to see the cove? You've been there before."

"Yeah. But I want to see it now. I want to see what your friend, Mister Brad, is changing."

I was the one who introduced Brad that way.

Funny, Kai is my friend, and all I can think about is wanting more, and how life is unfair because I can't have romance with Kai right now. Brad was everything to me, yet he did things to me a friend would never do—things Kai wouldn't do to a stranger, let alone a girlfriend or wife. Ironically, I have to call Brad a friend for Noah's sake.

"Excuse me?" One of the guests pops her head into the kitchen. "We ran out of syrup."

"Oh! Sorry. Let me get that. Thank you so much for bringing it back here."

"No problem. Jasper and I just want to tell you how much we adore being here. You're the consummate hostess. And the food is delicious. I'm going to have to double up my Jazzercise when we get home!"

I smile, taking the syrup pitcher from my guest and refilling it.

"That's what vacations are for," I say, as we walk back to the dining room. "A little indulgence, a lot of what you never get to do in your day-to-day life."

"I hope you take vacations." She has a motherly look in her eyes.

"We have an off season, but the inn rarely empties out completely. Sometimes it does for a day or two. But I'm grateful. If it's full, the doors stay open."

"Well, I'm just a nosy old lady, so don't mind me if I overstep, but you need time off. We all do."

"I take time. Around the edges."

She drops it, but her nudges resonate somewhere deep inside me. I don't really ever take time off. Being with Kai lately has been the closest thing to a vacation. He always makes me relax, even if it's just by washing a dish for me, or taking me to the beach for an afternoon.

I make my rounds through the dining room checking the buffet of condiments before I return to the kitchen where Noah is standing on the footstool, rinsing his dish from breakfast.

"So, what do you want to do today?" I ask him. "Jasmin is coming in to sit at the reception desk for a few hours."

"Let's go exploring!"

"On the back side?"

We haven't been on the undeveloped side of the island in ages. Wild animals roam freely there, and there are tidepools and walking paths.

"No, silly." Noah shakes his head and rolls his eyes. "At the cove. I want to see the workers and demo."

"Demo, huh? Where did you hear that word?"

"Aunt Phyllis watches the Home Channel."

"Ahhh."

"I love demo day! I think I want to be a demo day guy when I grow up."

"Hmmm." I smile at my son, his life wide open with possibility. "Would you build things too?"

"Like in Minecraft?"

"Yeah. I guess."

"I could build lots of stuff. Maybe I'd build you something too."

He hops off the footstool and wraps his arms around me. I hold him tight until he wriggles free. Noah has always been affectionate, but he's already at the age where he tells me not to hug him in front of school or when I drop him off for a playdate. I savor each one of his hugs, knowing one day he'll spend years withholding them from me down the road.

"Let me check with Brad to see if we can stop by his construction site."

I grab my phone off the counter.

"You have his number?" Noah asks, his brow scrunched in confusion when I grab for my phone.

"Oh. Yeah. I do."

I'm at a loss for a snappy comeback that would explain why Brad's number is in my phone. So I just send a quick text.

"Does Unko know?"

"Know what?"

"That you have Mister Brad's number?"

"I think so. Yes."

"Okay."

Noah turns and walks out of the kitchen, leaving me dazed by our interaction.

Brad texts back that he'd love to see me and Noah.

Great. Yay.

My next text is to Chloe. She texts back that I'm a saint and she'll miss me in heaven when I'm seated on some special throne for people who are unnecessarily kind to their exes. She follows that with a text that says, *I'll be thinking of you while I huddle alone in my little ramshackle shack in heaven while you live in a mansion reserved for people too good for this earth.* I shake my head, but I'm smiling. Then I type back, *I'll have you over to my palace at least once a week.* She types, *See! That's why you're getting the mansion. You'll never forget the little people.*

I'm smiling despite the fact that I'm taking Noah to see Brad in less than an hour. Chloe should get a mansion in heaven for her loyalty alone, not to mention her quick wit and ability to make me smile.

I text Kai next. I don't even question the fact that I feel the need to let Kai know I'm going to see Brad. Somewhere over this past month I've come to lean on Kai more than anyone else. He's the one person who holds me together like no one else can. I need him to know I'm about to spend time with Brad. Knowing he'll be aware settles me a little. I can take Kai with me in my heart and draw strength from him even when he's not actually there. Besides, seeing Brad without telling Kai feels like an odd sort of betrayal. If Kai really were my boyfriend, I'd definitely be giving him a heads up.

An hour later, Noah and I are walking down the trail that leads to the cove.

"Do you think he's got a backhoe? Or a skid steer? Or a crawler crane?" He's been chattering on about construction the whole fifteen minute walk from the inn to the cove.

I think back to the truck book we used to read every single night before bedtime: *Trucks At Work*. Each page was basically a photo, the name of the machine, and a simple sentence of what it did. We read that book like a Puritan reads scripture. Noah started reciting the contents cover to cover with me by the time he was three.

"I don't know what kinds of machines ..." My voice trails off when I look up to see Brad standing with his arms folded defensively over his chest.

And there he is.

Kai.

He's standing next to Brad, asking a question or something. All I know is Kai is calm and cool as a cucumber and Brad is not pleased with Kai being here—at all.

"Hey," Kai walks over to greet us.

"Hi, Unko! Did you come to see the demo?"

Kai chuckles. "I did. And to see you and your mom."

"How did you know we'd be here?" Noah asks.

Kai looks only momentarily stumped and then he says, "Your mom mentioned it."

"Oh." Noah accepts this without further question.

Then he walks over to Brad while Kai and I stand at a distance watching them.

"Mister Brad, I want to see the demo. Also, I know that's a skid steer."

"Wow," Brad says, smiling a wide smile at Noah. "You're right. Do you know what they do with those?"

"A skid steer digs and hauls in small spaces." Noah quotes the book we used to read.

"I think I might hire you," Brad says, pinching his own chin thoughtfully with a thumb and pointer. "A guy like you could come in handy around a job site like this one."

"Really?" Noah beams up at Brad.

"Well, let's see," Brad pretends to size Noah up. "You're smart. I can tell that much. And you know about demo and skid steers. Do you have a degree?"

"What?" Noah's face scrunches up.

"College? High School? Maybe your contractor's license?"

Noah shakes his head. "I don't have those."

Brad's approach is warm and caring. I can see he's out of practice. But that will get better over time. He's trying so hard. It's written all over his face how much this moment means to him, even if he's playing it cool by joking with Noah.

My heart pinches and then it feels like something hard and heavy falls away. Brad's never going to be my husband again. But this? This is good. He's making an effort with Noah. He's following my timeline and asking me what to do at every turn. If reunification had to happen, at least it's happening in a gentle and good way. For Noah's sake, I'm treasuring this day in my heart.

Brad looks at Noah seriously. "I tell you what. If you like, I'll let you sit in the skid steer and move the levers around to make the bucket raise and lower. And then, if you stay in school and get your degree. Well, we'll talk after that."

"Will you still know me then?"

"I hope I will. I plan on being around."

"Okay."

Brad sticks his hand out and Noah looks at it.

"It's not a deal if we don't shake on it," Brad explains.

Noah grabs Brad's hand quickly like he needs to snatch up his future job opportunity before it evaporates. And then they stand there, shaking hands. And my eyes well with tears. This is the first time Brad has touched his own son. And it's the first time Noah has ever touched his father.

Kai places a hand on my lower back as if he knows. He does. He just knows.

"Mom! Can I? Can I go in the skid steer?"

"Sure, honey. You can."

I look up at Kai and he's smiling down at me like I cured cancer, when all I did was make room for Brad in Noah's life.

"I didn't want you to have to face this alone," he whispers.

He offers his support as if it's nothing. But it's everything. He has no idea that he's the first man to ever think of me and to consider how situations might make me feel. He's the first to step in and make sure I'm not alone. I've gotten so used to handling everything independently. I probably shouldn't get too reliant on Kai for support. But his kindness keeps tempting me to relax into him as someone I can truly count on. It's almost becoming impossible not to constantly wish for more between us.

THIRTY-TWO
Kai

I think a part of me will always be waiting for you.
~ Unknown

K alaine and Bodhi are married. They're actually married. My best friend became my brother yesterday. And my sister is now his wife.

They're leaving for their honeymoon in Bali later this morning. Aima came over to hang out with Kala while we all ate breakfast. Now we're just biding time until they leave for the ferry.

Aima and Kalaine are on the couch talking while Bodhi and I finish washing the dishes. Aima's voice seems aimed into the kitchen instead of at a volume matching a conversation between just her and my sister.

"I'd relocate like you did, Kala. If I found the man who loves me like Bodhi loves you."

"It's been good for me here on Marbella," Kalaine says. "I miss Oahu, but at least we're there for contests and events regularly."

"A woman should be with her man though. Don't you

270

think?" Aima says in a voice more appropriate for an unmiked performance in an amphitheater.

"I think a couple works out what works best for both of them," Kalaine says.

"What do you think, Kai?" Aima tilts her head and looks into the kitchen to make eye contact with me.

I turn my head to meet her eyes. "I think you never know when you'll fall for someone. You can have it all planned out, but when it happens, you're not in charge of the details anymore."

I'm obviously thinking of Mila.

"Oooh. I like that. You always have the best answers," Aima says, obviously misconstruing my meaning again.

"Not always," Kala says. "He says things that are off base all the time."

"Yeah. Totally not always," Bodhi echoes. "Kai isn't always the one with the best answers. Not even close."

He nudges me playfully. Usually, I'd fight them on ribbing me, but right now I hope they paint me out to be just a little better than a serial killer if it helps throw Aima off my scent.

Bodhi and I finish washing up and I hang the hand towel on the hook.

"Got a minute?" Bodhi asks me.

"Sure. What's up?"

He tilts his head toward the hallway leading to our bedrooms. I follow him.

When we're about halfway down the hall and out of earshot of Kalaine and Aima, Bodhi says, "Give me a minute to get sappy here. I didn't get to tell you this last night at the wedding."

I nod, giving him the go ahead he's asking for. "I know you weren't always in favor of me pursuing Mavs. But you came around. Your blessing on our marriage means the world to me. *You* mean the world to me. You've always been a brother in my heart. And now we're really brothers. I couldn't have picked a better guy."

"Hey," I joke. "If you wanted me as a brother, you could have just said so. I would have adopted you. You didn't have to go and date my sister to get to me."

Bodhi chuckles. "Seriously, though. You've always been here for me. For Mavs too. For Mila. Come to think of it, you're there for everyone. I want you to know if you ever need anyone there for you, I'm here. And, don't worry. We'll figure out living arrangements after we're back."

"Thanks. Honestly, our living arrangements are the last thing on my mind."

"Kai, listen to me." Bodhi places a hand on my shoulder. "You will win Mila's heart. This whole fake thing will be a fun story to tell at parties one day when you two are actually for real."

I look up to thank Bodhi, but my eyes catch on something else at the end of the hall. Aima is walking toward the bathroom. Her eyes go instantly wide.

"What did you just say?" she asks Bodhi.

Bodhi stills. He looks to me for some clue as to what to say. I've got nothing.

I stare at Aima with a plea in my eyes.

"You and Mila aren't actually dating?" she asks. "Are you serious right now?"

"Aima."

"Kai. Why? Why would you fake having a girlfriend?"

Aima's quiet for a minute and then a slow grin overtakes her face as if some realization is dawning on her.

"Were you trying to make me jealous?" Her smile widens.

Bodhi runs a hand down his jaw as this goes from bad to worse.

"Kai! You didn't need to go to those lengths. I came here ready to see if something could finally happen for us."

"Aima. Stop. Wait. Please." I look at Bodhi. "Could you ...?"

"Yeah. I'll just ..." He hooks a thumb over his shoulder and walks quickly toward the living room.

"Aima. You are like a sister to me. And you know what that means. I love my sister. I'm committed to protect and lead her above everything. I don't take ohana aloha lightly. And I have ohana love for you. But I don't … It's not … I'm in love with Mila. We were faking. But … well, I'm not."

Aima's face falls. I want to step forward and pull her into my arms to comfort her, but that would probably send her mixed messages. I'm clean here. I didn't do this damage. My parents and her parents did it by constantly setting us up and perpetuating the legend of our future. I never led Aima on. And I'm not leading her on now. The one foolish thing I did was fake a relationship with Mila.

"I'm sorry I didn't tell you Mila and I were faking."

"But … why, Kai?"

"It's complicated. Her ex is back. You saw him last night when we were at dinner? Brad?"

"Yeah. The guy who bought out an entire cove here?"

"Yeah. Him."

"So you're trying to make him jealous?"

"No. I'm helping Mila keep him away from her. It's a long story. But that's it in a nutshell."

"Ohhh. Okay. I get it."

"I'm really sorry, Aima. We also thought faking would draw the line clearly for our parents. If they think I'm with Mila, they will stop trying to push us together."

"It's okay, Kai. I know you love me. I … I'm just embarrassed now. So … I'll just …" She points to the restroom.

"Yeah. Sure. I'm sorry. Don't be embarrassed. We'll get past this. It's a small blip in our lifelong friendship. You're still my ohana. If you'll have me."

"Of course I will. I've always wanted you, Kai."

"Thanks. And, could you keep this quiet? I know it's a lot to ask."

"Sure. I'll take care of your secret. It's the least I can do."

I'm not sure what she means by the least she can do. Maybe to make up for coming on so strong? Whatever her motive, I'm grateful we had that talk.

After Aima joins us in the living room, the four of us sit sharing memories we have from our childhood in Hawaii and visits Bodhi's made there since then.

When it's time for them to go, Bodhi loads a golf cart with their bags and surfboards.

"We're going to head over to the dock," he says. "Do you want to drive Aima to the resort and meet us there?"

I agree to drive Aima to Alicante. On our ride, she assures me that she'll guard my secret as if it is her own. She even says, *I only want what's best for you, Kai.*

After seeing Bodhi and my sister off on the ferry, I drive directly to the inn to talk to Mila. We had an amazing time at the wedding last night. I held her hand during the sand ceremony and gave it a squeeze. I don't know if she understood I was trying to tell her I wanted that to be us one day.

After what happened this morning, I have to let Mila know about Aima.

Then I'm going to figure out what I need to do to move things forward between us.

When I pull up, Noah is in the front yard of Mila's Place throwing a ball, then walking over to where the ball lands and throwing it across the yard in the other direction.

"Hey, boss man. What game is that?"

"Catch."

"Doesn't catch usually involve two people?"

"Yeah. But Mom had to take a guest to the resort because she got sick and they have a doctor there. Jasmin's inside in case anyone needs anything while Mom's gone, so I'm playing catch with myself."

"I see. Well, do you mind if I play catch with you for a little while?"

"Nope. It might even be better that way."

I chuckle.

We throw the ball back and forth using our bare hands until I remember there are gloves in the equipment shed. We pull two out and throw the ball back and forth, back and forth. Noah gets better at catching and throwing the longer we play.

"Unko?" he asks me.

"Yeah, boss man?"

"There's a Bring Your Dad Day at my school tomorrow."

"Yeah?"

"Yeah. But I don't want Mom to worry about it."

"Okay."

"I'm okay without a dad that day."

"Are you? Because I bet your mom would come if you asked her."

"I don't want her to come. Every kid there will have a guy for a dad. Not a mom."

Man. I feel my jaw clench. I want to grab Brad by the collar some days. This is one of them. A kid like Noah should not have to worry about who's coming to dad day. Why do they even have dad day? Why not parent day? Or bring an adult you admire day?

"You could come," Noah says so simply.

"Yeah?"

"I want you to. But I don't want Mom to know. She'll just cry or something."

I chuckle. He's not wrong. And Mila has been stressed. What could it hurt? He wants me there. It's his day.

"Sure. I'll come. Do you know what time it is?"

"It's in my backpack." Noah drops his glove, runs up the stairs, inside the inn, and emerges waving a flyer.

I read the details. Then I text Ben telling him I'll be out of the office from ten to noon tomorrow.

"You've got it, boss man," I tell Noah. "I'll come to your class tomorrow."

"And don't worry," he says. "I'll explain that you're my Unko."

"Sounds like a plan."

My phone rings. Stevens.

I hold up a finger to Noah. "Hey, what's up?"

"Hey, I've got a tour going out. Ben's here alone so I don't have a first mate. Want to come out with me?"

"Jamison's not there?"

"He called in sick. Said he has a fever."

I guess something's going around.

"I'll be right over."

I hang up and tell Noah. "Hey, I've gotta run. I'll be at your class tomorrow. Okay?"

"Thanks, Unko."

Noah throws his arms around my waist and I hold him close. I'd do anything for this boy. Brad's an idiot for letting him go and missing out on this amazing human.

Stevens and I take the tour group out for two hours. We drag a net behind his boat and pull in some sea life. The passengers take turns looking at samples of the water to see microorganisms through a microscope Stevens has on board. Then he takes them on the deck where we allow them to touch and pass around the small marine animals we pulled in and are holding in temporary buckets full of sea water until we release them back into the ocean after the cruise.

Stevens has everyone wash their hands and then immerse them in a bucket of sea water so when we touch the animals we're covered in the elements of their environment.

After the tour, I stay onboard to help clean up from the tour.

We're cleaning petri dishes when I look over at my friend. He's more of a loner than most of us, quiet and thoughtful. He lives up in his head, but he's got a big heart. I've never seen him ruffled or agitated in all the years I've lived here.

"Something on your mind?" he asks me.

"What makes you say that?" I ask.

"Either that, or you're one more person who can't stop staring at me."

I chuckle. "Definitely not that." I release a long breath and then I spill everything. "I'm in a bind, man."

"What's up?"

"It's about Mila."

Without any hesitation, I explain how we're faking, how my feelings became evident to me, and what happened with Aima this morning.

I know I promised to keep everything between me and Mila secret. I also know Stevens. He's a bit reclusive and completely trustworthy. Plus, he's a great friend and a good problem solver. I'm pretty sure he has a genius IQ. I'm desperate for some input after that encounter with Aima. Not to mention the way Mila felt in my arms when we danced at the reception last night—it put a fire under me to push things along with her.

Stevens is quiet, a pensive look on his face as I unload everything about the past two months on him.

"It's kind of like the sea star, or starfish, as most people call them," Stevens says after hearing me pour out all the sordid details of Mila's and my relationship.

"Sea stars?"

"Yes. When startled, sea stars will bounce instead of crawling. It's like when we homo sapiens break into a sprint in our fight-flight response to stress. Sea stars have thousands of tiny hydraulic 'feet' that can work together to synchronize their motion. They bounce away when they feel threatened."

"Fascinating," I deadpan. "And, all props to Bill Nye the Science Guy and all. But I need relationship advice here."

Maybe going to Stevens wasn't such a hot idea after all. He is single. And, that could be for obvious reasons, now that I think of it. Sea stars? Is that all he's got?

Stevens chuckles. "Bill's awesome. And, I am giving you relationship advice. Hang with me here."

"Okaaay."

Stevens continues, "If you want to touch a sea star, you have to wet your hands in salt water. Fully submerge your hands in the elements of their environment. You have to hold them gently and be very respectful. You can't keep holding them for long periods of time. You have to return them where you found them."

"Uh huh. Is this the relationship advice part?"

Stevens chuckles again like I'm missing the whole point. He's not wrong. I'm missing it. Completely.

"You've been doing all that with Mila," he says. "You're submerging yourself in her environment at the inn. You've been gentle and respectful. You give her space. She'll open to you, Kai. Just keep showing up like you have been until she can be touched without running. Because eventually, you will feel like a part of her world. And then she'll trust you. Like a sea star."

"I've been doing all that for four years now."

"But things shifted once you started faking. In science we call that altering a variable. And one alteration can lead to a totally different outcome."

He presents his conclusion as if he's pronouncing a diagnosis. And I feel as unsettled as a patient with a terminal illness.

Stevens only confirmed what I've known. I'll never get enough of Mila. She is oxygen and I'm only able to go so long without inhaling her presence. She's breath and life. At the mere thought of her, I'm light-headed. And I have no way forward if I rush her into something. The only answer is to wait for her to open up to the possibility of something more with me. Gently and respectfully, waiting.

"I'm screwed," I confess to Stevens.

"No. You aren't. You're just a man with a clear knowledge of where you stand. Now. What are you going to do about it? Because I think this feeling you have isn't one-sided. My guess is she's falling for you too."

"Guess? Can you guess in science?"

"We call it a hypothesis, as I'm sure you know. And making a hypothesis is usually something we do before we begin running experiments. But with this situation, I can't run any experiments. You've got to be the one to figure Mila out, not me. Science only takes you so far. There comes a point where you have to act on what science reveals. And there's always the element of mystery—something beyond the scope of our capacity to measure. Love may leave signs we can see, but it's not truly quantifiable. You are going to have to take a risk, Kai. That's always what it boils down to. Risk. And the biggest question is this: Is Mila worth the risk?"

I already know the answer. And, as unconventional as Stevens' thinking is, he made me realize one thing.

"I'll wait eleven years for Mila. I'd wait a lifetime if I had to."

"You're serious?"

"Dead serious. She's it. There's only one Mila. I'm not interested in anyone else. I'll wait."

"Wow." Stevens chuckles and shakes his head. "Then, I hope you get your sea star, Kai."

THIRTY-THREE
Mila

They don't know that we know they know we know.
~ Phoebe, in Friends

K ai texted me this morning. He said he was at work and heading to the resort for a special meeting. He said it was important that we talk asap. All he said was, *We need to work through some things. More people know. Can you meet me after my meeting at the Alicante?* I texted back, but I guess he was busy because he gave my text a thumbs up and we haven't talked since.

I called Jasmin for the second time in two days, and thankfully, she was free. I have a few women on this side of the island whose husbands are the sole breadwinners. During the busy season I call on them to sit at the reception desk and field any needs of my guests. And I have Jasmin, my part-timer.

The resort always takes my breath away with its tropical elegance: grand white stucco buildings with terracotta roofs, marble floors, impossibly high ceilings, ferns inside and out, palms, sparkling pools, and everything maintained down to the finest details. The decor is a combination of whites, creams, and ocean blues. It's such a contrast to the quaint feel of the inn with its wood interior and exterior, comfortable restored furnishings, creaky stairs, a blend of old and new, home and beach. My place feels like a well-kept piece of yesteryear—a welcoming home away from home where you can curl up and rest. The resort is pure affluence and glamour.

I walk through the double high entry doors. Kai is standing near the Guest Services desk in the center of the room. People fill the space, coming and going. But Kai's the one I see first, as if we're connected by an invisible strand. Passing the reception counter on my left, I approach the curved desk of Guest Services with a water feature flowing behind it.

"Hi," I walk right up to Kai, anticipating his embrace or a hand placed gently on my back, a kiss to my temple—all the ways he's been greeting me ever since we started this counterfeit veneer over our actual friendship.

I've gotten too used to it all, to him, to his touches and his care.

"Hey," Kai smiles and brings me in for a quick hug.

His usual sea-spray, tropical scent is covered by a cologne that makes me want to crawl up him and nestle in his arms and then kiss the ever-living bejeebers out of him. I obviously don't do *that*. I won't be crawling up anyone for the foreseeable future and even beyond, so I pull back to ensure there aren't any spontaneous man-scaling occurrences here in the lobby of the Alicante this morning.

"Hi," I say, tucking a strand of hair behind my ear like a love-struck teen.

"Let's step over here so we can talk." Kai points to one of several areas in the lobby where couches and chairs are set up around a coffee table.

We walk over in silence, Kai glancing at me nervously along the way.

"I ... oh, there's Shaw," Kai says in a conspiratorial tone. "Look up at me adoringly."

Looking at Kai adoringly has become second nature for me these days. I follow his instructions and gaze at his citrine eyes, studying the darker flecks within the gold. I could get lost in his eyes, spend hours staring at them—at him. Kai seems to calm once our eyes lock. It's the benefit of us actually caring for one another. I hope we don't lose the ease of our friendship as a casualty of this farce.

"Sorry," Kai says.

And then he leans down and kisses me. The kiss is brief, but he cups my jaw when he pulls away and our eyes reconnect. I nearly cry. I'm not sure why. Maybe it's the stress of Brad meeting Noah. It could be residue from attending Bodhi and Kalaine's beautiful wedding. I tossed and turned wrestling with feelings of longing and loss until the early hours of the morning after I got home. The ceremony was beautiful—because of their love for one another. And for once in my life, I was jealous. Kai held me while we danced, squeezed my hand during emotionally significant moments throughout the night, and never let me out of his sight or away from his side. He was as perfect and attentive as always, and all I felt was the fact that this isn't real, and it can't become what I wish it would.

"So, this morning, Aima was at our house ..." Kai glances over my shoulder, across the lobby mid-sentence. "Oh, shoot. Brad's here. And he's coming our way. I can't talk to you in front of him. Not about this."

"What? What do we do?"

"Follow me."

Kai grabs my hand and speed-walks across the lobby toward a little nook that leads to a single locked door. The space is only about as big as the shack on the beach—the one I wonder if I conjured up when I think back on that kiss we shared in the rain.

Once we're sequestered in our little cubby, Kai says, "Anyway, Aima was at the house to see Kala this morning before she and Bodhi took off."

"Mila?" Brad's voice carries from probably thirty feet away.

"Okay. Not here," Kai says, grabbing my hand and nearly dragging me like a ragdoll out of the small hallway toward the back patio.

We weave through a family coming in from a swim and a few other hotel guests, darting left and then right, connected by our hands like fugitives trying to cross a border without getting shot. Brad's calling my name from behind us, but we're ignoring him as we make our mad dash to the next possible private space we can find.

When we reach the patio area with all the pools and potted ferns and palms, Kai's head glances quickly left and right. Then he nods succinctly and we're off, rushing to a spot behind a trellis where a bougainvillea will cloak our visibility.

We're nearly out of breath when Kai turns to me. "Sorry, Mila. I need to get this out, and I won't get to tell you with Brad around."

I giggle despite the obvious seriousness of Kai's expression. Then I school my features and tell him, "It's okay. I think we're safe."

Kai peeks around the trellis, so I lean over and stick my head out under his. Brad is standing on the steps leading out to the area where multiple pools fill the sprawling patio. Each pool has its own deck chairs and potted plants, setting it apart from the others —the kiddie pool, adults only, lap pool, several shamrock shaped shallow pools, and an olympic pool in the very back. Brad's eyes are scanning the crowds of guests, obviously looking for me and Kai.

"Tell me, Kai." I whisper up at him while we both continue to peek around the flowering vine to watch for Brad.

"Okay ... like I was saying, Aima was at the house ..."

The moment Brad recognizes our heads peeking around the trellis, Kai and I both duck backward, bumping into one another and righting ourselves before we tumble and knock the entire vine and screen over. I feel like we're playing hide-and-seek. That same thrill of childhood rushes through me. I don't even know why we're hiding.

It's obvious Kai is in knots over something, and I want him to get the whole story out. *Aima.* Did something happen with Aima? Did Kai realize she's actually the one for him? It seems improbable, but it could happen. They ended up dancing together one dance last night. Maybe they talked after Kai brought me home. My urge to know the whole story escalates from zero to sixty as I imagine Kai telling me he's decided we need to call off our charade so he can pursue the woman his family has planned for him since childhood.

"Let's go!" I say to Kai, taking off before he has a chance to lead the way.

The pools are filled with people this time of mid-morning, and the mom-voice inside me says, *No running around the pool.* So I speed walk like one of the women who pumps her arms and wiggles her hips dramatically on the shoreline every morning. I've always wondered if those duck-like movements added momentum. I think they just might.

Kai is on my heels as we weave and bob through children wrapped in towels, women slinging beach bags over their shoulders, couples in reclining loungers and various plants in large terra cotta planters with Brad on our heels.

Brad shouts after me, "Mila! Mila, wait!"

I stop in my tracks. *Why am I running?* Brad and I can talk. Then Kai and I can go somewhere to finish our conversation. I'm sure talking to Brad first won't be an issue.

As soon as I stop, Brad reaches us. Only he's not listening to his inner mom voice and he steps on a slick spot next to a pool. Unfortunately a child goes zipping past Brad right at this moment with her parent on her heels yelling, "Sarah Ann, come back here!" Brad has to side-step but he's got no traction because he already hit the slick spot on the concrete. He loses his balance. His arms go up in a windmill formation, spinning wildly like a cartoon character. Before anyone can jump to his rescue, Brad falls into the pool with a huge splash, fully-dressed.

"Brad!" I shout, quickly walking back in the direction of the pool where people are now staring and gathering.

Kai is right behind me.

A child yells out, "Mommy, why did that man go swimming with his clothes on?"

Brad emerges from under the water, sopping wet and sputtering. He glances between Kai and me.

When he speaks, his tone is measured, but frustrated. Understandably. Brad's had to chase me down while I evade him with a man he believes to be his replacement, and now he's in a swimming pool, fully clothed.

"Mila, I need to talk to you. *Alone*," Brad says that last word emphatically.

Gone is the humble man begging entrance into his son's life. This is Brad. The one I knew in high school. The one I married. He's not brutal or mean, but he gets what he wants.

The crowd that had gathered at the sound of the splash starts to disperse now that Brad is obviously alright and we're all talking.

"I ... uh. Kai needed to talk to me alone first."

"So you ran through the resort to avoid me?"

I look at Kai. He shrugs. It wasn't really the most premeditated moment of our lives—or of this charade. We've gotten so used to hiding facts and feelings we're not our usual selves. Instead, we're some fake dating version of Bonnie and Clyde. Minus the murders and kidnappings.

Kai extends his hand to Brad to help him out of the water. "Sorry. I need to talk to Mila. It's important. We overreacted."

Brad eyes Kai's outstretched hand and ignores it, hoisting himself out of the pool without assistance, water spilling from his clothing when he joins us poolside. Kai walks over to a stand where the resort keeps their signature beach towels. He grabs one and hands it to Brad, who reluctantly takes it and begins toweling off.

Brad pulls his phone out of his pocket and tests it.

"Waterproof case survived the submersion test," he jokes.

"Are you okay?" I ask.

"Yeah. I am. But we still need to talk."

"You can talk in front of Kai.

"Not this time, Mila. I need you alone."

His voice is adamant, unwavering. And, considering we put him in a position where he just fell into the water fully dressed, I feel like capitulating. Brad would never hurt me. He just wants to talk.

I'm about to ask Kai to hold whatever he was about to say about Aima so I can step aside with my dripping-wet ex when Shaw walks up.

"Brad, I thought I saw you. Are you ... alright?"

"Yeah. Yeah. I dodged a child and hit a wet spot. Slipped into the pool. What can I do for you, Shaw?"

"I have to go over a part of the contract we drew up. My boss wants the changes approved ASAP. I was about to call you when I thought I saw you walk by. Do you have a minute?"

"Um." Brad looks over at me, then briefly at Kai. Then he answers Shaw. "Yeah. Sure."

He turns to me and pointedly says, "I'll talk to you later."

"Okay."

I owe him that much after this fiasco.

Brad walks off with Shaw.

Kai lets out a long breath. "Sorry. I don't know what came over me."

"It was both of us."

I look around and point back to the secluded area behind the bougainvillea.

Kai follows me. He looks defeated and worn. His voice sounds tired when he says, "I think it's this whole farce. I'm preoccupied with what might change for me now that Bodhi and my sister are married. All of that threw me into a tailspin when I saw Brad."

I giggle lightly. "You think?"

Kai chuckles, "What were we doing back there?"

"Running from the law!" I start laughing.

"We'd be doing time by now if we really were criminals. We're not very good at this."

"I'm not sure it's a skillset I want to master."

"Yeah. No. Me either."

We find two chairs in this little secluded portion of the back patios and sit.

Kai takes a breath and picks up where he left off. "So, as I was trying to say, Aima was at the house. She and Kala were talking. Bodhi pulled me aside down the hallway, out of earshot. He was just saying some man-to-man things. Anyway." Kai pauses, obviously sorting through what he wants to say. "He mentioned us faking."

"Why?"

"Just in context of the conversation."

"Okay?"

"And that was the exact instant Aima decided to round the corner of the hallway to use the restroom."

"Oh, no."

"Yeah. I talked to her. She's fine. It was unfortunate and awkward, but she said she'd guard our secret like it's her own."

"That's sweet of her."

"Yeah. She's sweet." Kai smiles. "I just wanted you to hear it from me."

"She loves you, Kai." The words almost pierce as they come out of my mouth. "She never stopped watching you all night."

"I love her too. Like a sister. There's nothing there for me, Mila."

For a moment, I imagine him telling me, *Nothing like the feelings I have for you*.

But, he doesn't.

THIRTY-FOUR
Mila

Nothing makes a woman love a man
more than when she sees how much
he loves her children.
~ Unknown

I found a flyer in Noah's backpack yesterday. He never mentioned it.

Bring Your Dad to School Day was printed across the top. Icons of traditionally manly items like bow ties and golf clubs, watches and ballcaps lined the edge of the paper. The paper was shoved in as if Noah couldn't care less about the special event.

I don't know why schools have days like this. Some dads work off the island. Other kids are in a co-parenting home due to a divorce. And then there's Noah. He's never had a dad in the picture. I'm surprised his teacher didn't call me. She's usually so good about looking out for Noah when it comes to issues around his parental structure. Maybe she forgot.

After some serious thought, I decided I needed to show up for my son. It will either mortify him, or it will reassure him that he's loved. I'm hoping for the latter. And I can't chance him feeling left out or unloved, so I called Jasmin to come cover the desk while I take a few hours to be at Noah's school.

I walk up the hill through our neighborhood and then down streets lined with more beach cottages and larger homes. Our elementary school sits on a property at the top of a hill. There's a grassy yard and a playground on one side of the building. All the classrooms have an ocean view. It's the same school I attended when I was a girl, North Shore Elementary.

Walking down the halls toward Noah's classroom always makes me sentimental. I feel like a giant returning to a land that has shrunk in her absence. I remember games Chloe and I played when we were young. I even remember my aunts coming to school performances.

I stop outside the doorway of Noah's classroom. His voice rings out into the hallway. My son has no volume button. It's either loud or off.

"I don't have a dad," he says, almost proudly.

I peek in to figure out if I can stealthily make my way to the back of the room. What I see floors me.

Kai is standing next to Noah, his hands in his pockets, his eyes trained on my son, a soft, proud smile on his face.

Noah looks at his classmates and then up at Kai.

"Kai is like my friend who's like my dad. I call him Unko because when I was a baby I couldn't say uncle."

Noah's classmates laugh and he does too.

He looks up at Kai again. "Sometimes Unko's a lot like a dad. He taught me to surf. And he tells me to be nice to my mom, like a dad would. You guys probably know Kai works at the water-sports shack. I think that's what I want to do when I grow up. Plus drive a skid steer and do demo. My mom probably wants me to run the inn. But that's too much doing laundry and cooking. I'd rather teach people to surf. So. Yeah. That's it. This is Kai. Any questions?"

My heart is near my throat, and I feel like my legs won't hold me. In one fell swoop, my son just said it all.

I already was falling for Kai. With this seemingly small gesture, he demolished all doubt. I'm hopelessly, completely, madly in love with him.

The urge to run to Chloe's overtakes me. She'll know. One look at me and she'll sort through all the muck and mire in my jumbled thoughts and feelings and she'll get down to the heart of things.

I step away from the doorway and flatten my back on the wall outside the classroom. Closing my eyes, I still see them standing side by side. I place my hand over my racing heart. This is their moment—Kai's and Noah's. When I collect myself enough to be able to carry myself out of the school, I push off the wall.

As I'm walking away, I hear a little girl asking Kai, "I have a question."

In his usual calm, kind, resonant voice, Kai answers her, "Yes?"

The girl, in typical first grader fashion, says, "I had pizza last night. It was pepperoni. Do you like pizza?" She pauses and I think I hear her add, "How tall are you anyway?"

I stifle my giggle and walk away from a sight I'll never forget for as long as I live.

I'm halfway to Chloe's when my cell rings.

It's Kai.

"Hey," I answer, pausing in front of one of the homes along this street.

"Hey."

The breeze from the ocean blows through and lifts strands of my hair, twisting them and releasing them to fall haphazardly around my face and neck. I turn so the wind caresses my cheeks.

If I could record Kai saying, *Hey*, in that deep, confident, calm voice, I'd play that recording on an infinite loop. Just that. *Hey*. It's a word layered with familiarity, as though he's reaching out through the phone to hold me.

Kai clears his throat. "I want you to know something."

"Yeah?"

"I was at Noah's school just now."

"I know."

"You do?"

"Yeah. I went there. I found the flyer and figured I ought to show up. I never expected you to be there."

"Oh. Well, Noah asked me. I didn't want you to find out about my visit from another source. And I don't want you to think I'm keeping secrets from you. I should have asked you. I just didn't want to burden you. I know it's awkward at times like this, having to be both parents. And you do a phenomenal job of it. I didn't want you to have extra stress with all you're already dealing with bringing Brad into the picture now. When Noah asked, I said yes without a thought."

I almost need to sit on the curb as the waves of Kai's words wash over me. He sees me—the effort it takes to be both parents. He doesn't think I'm weak, but he still wants to prop me up, to shoulder half the weight. And, then as if I hadn't heard when Kai first said it, the most poignant fact of all hits me like a dulcet arrow to the heart: Noah asked Kai.

I pull myself together enough to give Kai a coherent response. "I understand why you didn't tell me. And thank you. It means so much—that you'd go, that Noah asked you. All of it."

"Sorry I overstepped. I can get a bit ... zealous ... when someone I care about needs me."

"You think?" I tease.

"Ask Kala."

"I won't. Because she's got sister-lenses when it comes to you. She wants to prove she's capable. Most women won't have that issue with you, Kai. We like when a man steps up. It's a relief."

"Most women?"

"Yeah."

We both know what I'm really saying. But I can't say it. If I do, I'll crack. I'll start begging him to be there for me from now on. I'll cross over lines Noah needs me to keep in place. He may have invited Kai as his Unko, but Noah doesn't want his entire life rocked.

And with Brad here, and a plan moving forward for Noah to realize Brad is his father, I can't be the one to selfishly bring Kai into our lives as my boyfriend. Not during a lifequake so huge as revealing Noah's dad's identity.

This is what moms do. We sacrifice for our children. And sometimes that sacrifice feels like a death. A death of a dream. A death of freedoms we once took for granted before motherhood. A death of loving someone so deeply it almost aches, but choosing to say no to something more. I'm letting Kai go for Noah's sake. It's the right thing to do.

Maybe in eleven years I'll be able to welcome a good man into my life. By then, Kai will belong to someone else. He will. He's too good to remain single all those years, and I'd never dream of asking him to wait, especially since I don't even know for sure whether he feels more than friendship for me. Though, sometimes I suspect he does.

It doesn't matter what he feels or what I feel. All that matters is Noah. Noah deserves to be fully considered. He deserves this sacrifice.

A silence stretches between Kai and me while I ponder the reality of our situation. Maybe he forgot we're on the phone? Got distracted? Hung up? Did he say goodbye and I missed it while I was lamenting my situation?

"Are you still there?" I ask.

"Yeah. I am. Just tell me if I ever overstep, okay?"

"I will."

And, Mila?"

"Yeah."

"I want you to know I'm not trying to replace Noah's dad."

"Okay. I do know that."

"Good. I wanted to be sure you knew. I might not be Brad's number one fan, but I know my place."

I should feel relieved. Kai is setting healthy boundaries. But my heart sinks like a stone in water. He doesn't want to be Noah's dad. Of course he doesn't. He's not. And I've made it clear no man will ever be in that position.

Kai and I hang up after I thank him again for stepping in and caring for my son. He assures me it's his pleasure. Before we end the call, he says, "I love him." He says it so easily. Those words just flow out of his mouth like they're the most natural thing in the world to say.

"He loves you too," I say.

"I'm pretty lovable," Kai jokes.

I want to say, *You are*. But I say, "Okay, well, have a good rest of your day."

"You too, Mila. You've done a great job with Noah. You're quite a mom."

"Thanks."

"K. I'll see you soon."

Kai hangs up and I walk the last block to Chloe's even more stirred up than I was when I left the elementary school.

Chloe's home is a block up a hill that leads straight to a semi-private beach. She has a deck off the side of the second story overlooking the ocean.

When I show up on her front doorstep, she pulls me into a hug and walks me straight through the house to the deck.

"Sit. I'm getting us iced teas and you're talking."

"Okay."

There aren't words to describe the kind of friend who takes one look at you and knows you're at triage level of emotional crisis. I take a seat in one of the stuffed chairs aimed at the view stretching out over rooftops. The ocean spans in all directions and a faint hint of the mainland shoreline can be seen on clear days, like today, far off in the distance.

Chloe returns with two glasses in hand. Then she settles next to me in her own chair.

I spill everything, ending with Kai showing up at the school for Bring Your Dad Day.

"Were you mad?"

"Mad? No. Why would I be?"

"He went to school with your son without telling you. Aren't they only supposed to let preapproved adults into classrooms? I mean, I know we're Marbella, but we get visitors. What if Brad wanted to take off with Noah?"

My heart stills.

"Not that he would. He totally won't. He won't, Mila. He has asked you permission every step of the way. He's surprisingly respectful and keeps to the lines you draw. I'm just saying, any old yay-hoo can walk into our quaint elementary school unscreened?"

I giggle. "Down, girl. Kai is on the approved list, just like you are. Besides, like you say, this is Marbella. I'm sure when he walked in, Marge recognized him, said, 'Hey, Kai,' and went back to answering phones or filing or whatever she does all day."

"True."

"You're so Liam Neeson in *Taken*."

"You have no idea."

"Oh, but I do." I take a sip of my tea. "I think Kai was trying to step in without making it complicated for me."

"Everything about the two of you is complicated."

"Tell me about it." I collapse backward into the soft cushion of my chair.

"So, how are you feeling about him?"

"About Kai?"

"No, about Ryan Reynolds. Yes. Kai."

"I'm ... so in love." I cover my face. Then I let out this groan of frustration. "Chloe, I love him so much it actually hurts." I peek through my fingers at my bestie.

"I know you do."

I just nod at her. Of course she knows. She knows everything about me. We could be twins but with polar opposite personalities.

"What's keeping you from crossing the line? This whole faking thing made sense at one point, but I don't see the rationale anymore. I think it hit its expiration date a while ago and you two have kept it going out of some subconscious desire to have an excuse to touch and kiss without risking sharing your real feelings for one another. But what do I know? I'm just the wife of a pilot. I don't even remember what it was like to fall for Davis. We just sort of rolled into our relationship and never looked back."

"And you're so good for one another."

"We are. Until he has to retire. He'll drive me nuts then. But maybe I'll start my world travels in my sixties, in earnest. We're great together, but we need these breaks. It just works for us."

"You'll manage when he's here all the time. We just have to find him a hobby."

"More like seven hobbies. One for each day of the week. But we aren't here for my life planning. Stop shifting the topic. We're talking about you and the hot Hawaiian."

"Stop it!"

"What, he's incredibly good looking and you know it."

"He is." I groan again. "And he kisses just like you'd hope he would."

Chloe rubs her hands together. "The good stuff. Finally!"

"Nope. That's all I'm saying. Just ... gah. His kisses."

She cracks up. "You know, you never raved about Brad's kisses."

"I never had anything to rave about. They were good. You know. Pretty good kisses. Not horrible. It's not like he slobbered or made weird noises or breathed funny. His breath smelled nice."

"What a Yelp review that is!" Chloe bursts into laughter. "Would possibly kiss again. Not horrible. No slobbering, weird noises or bad breath. Three out of five stars."

I cackle. Chloe laughs at her own joke.

When we stop laughing, I say, "As if. No one is leaving Yelp reviews for kisses, you dork."

"Well, I'm glad to hear you could tolerate your husband's C+ kisses. Davis is an amazing kisser if you want to know."

"I don't."

"K, then. Back to you and the hot Hawaiian."

"Stop calling him that." I smile over at Chloe. She won't stop, especially now that she knows it bugs me.

"Seriously, Mila. What's the real reason you're hesitating to reach out to Kai and share your honest feelings for him? You'd be hard pressed to find someone who cares for you more than that man does. He's going to handle your feelings with such kid gloves. Even if he's not in love with you—which I'd bet this house that he is—he'll be so careful. That man would die if he was ever the source of your pain. You know that right?"

THIRTY-FIVE

Mila

Of all forms of caution,
caution in love is perhaps the most fatal
to true happiness.
~ Bertrand Russell

I stare out at the ocean, considering Chloe's challenge.

What's the real reason I'm hesitating with Kai?

My voice is softer when I finally speak. "I'm afraid."

"Of?" Chloe's gentler too. She's a powerhouse, but she knows when to dial it back.

"Of being hurt again." I sigh. "It sounds so stupid now that I say it out loud. It's just there's this really deep place inside me. I don't think I can even reach it to reason with myself. I'm so broken way down deep in this unreachable and unalterable place inside my heart—from Brad."

I could be crying. But no tears come. Just this overwhelming numbness and resolve.

"And Noah," I add. "He's a big reason too. It's a crazy time for him and he doesn't even know it yet. He's about to find out Brad's his dad. This isn't really the time to bring a new man into his life."

"A new man? Is that what Kai is? The dude your son just secretly invited to Bring Your Dad to School Day?"

"Right." I scoff at myself. "Yeah. You've got a point. But bringing him to school and actually having to adjust to the idea of me getting into a romantic relationship with Kai are two totally different things. Also, we don't know if Kai feels anything beyond friendship for me."

"Beg to differ, but we'll table that last detail."

I nod. Then my thoughts tumble out like belongings jammed into a closet when the door flies open.

"Kai will disappoint me, Chloe. Men do. They all leave. Davis isn't leaving you. He's different. Besides, he sort of leaves for a living. He satisfies his escapism in spurts every time the plane lifts its wheels off the runway."

I look over at Chloe, and it hits me. That was uncalled for. My grief and pain are making me thoughtless.

"Oh my gosh, Chlo. I'm sorry. Davis isn't leaving you. He adores you. He totally misses you when he's gone. I'm so sorry!"

"I know. I know. That was a slightly careless thing to say, especially for you. You're never anything but sweet. But I get why you said it."

Chloe's face is so forgiving, I somehow release the guilt that was starting to swell inside me.

"It's just ..." Chloe reaches over and puts her hand on my knee. "I never knew you felt all this. You've been so stalwart. So back to business. I figured ... I don't know. You seemed so well-adjusted. I never knew. I should have, though. And I'm sorry I didn't see it. No one moves on from a blow like the one Brad dealt you with the kind of finesse you mustered. Not even you."

"You never knew that Brad gutted me? That he took my dreams with him when he left? That any thought of romance died for me the day our divorce was final?"

"Yeah. *That*. I never knew."

Chloe stands and comes over to my chair. She squishes in next to me, and then she pulls me into a side-hug. I curl into her like a girl soaking up comfort from her mother. It occurs to me then, as it often has, how life fills in the blank spots. My mother was ripped from me at a prematurely early age, but I've been given Phyllis and Joan and Connie. And I have Chloe. I lost one mother and gained four women who would do anything for me, and who love me with a devotion I can only call motherly.

Chloe smooths my hair over my shoulder. "And, Mila?"

"Yeah?"

Her voice is soft like a careful whisper. "Your dad didn't leave."

I choke out a sob.

I tap my temple. "I know that here."

Then I lay my hand on my heart. "But I can't seem to get it sorted out here. All I know is that I feel like men leave. They leave *me*."

"Even Noah ..." I can't say another word after those two come out of nowhere, surprising me with their force.

I sob hard. It takes a few beats for me to even be able to speak.

"He's going to grow up and leave me, Chloe. And I'll be ..." I sob again, sniffling from the tears. "I'll be ... alone." I manage to get the word out between cries.

Chloe lifts me slightly away from her so she can look into my eyes.

"Well," she says. "I should hope so. What do you want? Noah to be one of those forty-year-old guys who sits around with a remote in one hand, a beer in the other, and Cheeto dust down his shirt while he mooches off you the rest of his life?"

I laugh, but all this crying has my nose messed up, so I snort. And not a little. The pig-like, snuffling wheek trumpeting through my nostrils sends both of us into a fit of laughter.

When we finally catch our breath, Chloe looks at me with a sincere expression.

"I know it's scary, babe. People die. They disappoint us. They leave. But this time, it's not about people. And it's not about your past. And it's for sure as heck not about Brad.

"This is you and Kai. That's it. It's just that simple. And that man has shown no signs of being a flight risk. He's here every time I turn around. So you need to do both of you a favor and consider him—without letting all the other men in your life weigh in on your decision."

Chloe's right. I know she is.

"Thanks."

"Anytime. Ride or die, girl. I'm yours. You're mine. No givebacks or tradesies."

We finish our tea and I head out to relieve Jasmin at the inn. My heart feels lighter somehow, even though I don't have a clue as to what I'm going to do about Kai.

Phyllis is in the lobby when I enter.

"There you are." She smiles broadly, opening her arms for a welcoming hug. When I step closer, she says, "Oh. Have you been crying?"

My fingertips move up to my face and gently brush under my eyes.

"I was at Chloe's. We had a heart to heart."

"Are you alright?"

"I am. Really. Possibly better than ever."

"Good." Aunt Phyllis smiles. "Let me get us a snack."

"Are you here for anything in particular?" I ask my aunt.

"No, dear. I'm just here for you."

I allow myself to collapse into her comfort when she pulls me into a hug.

I relieve Jasmin while Aunt Phyllis retreats to the kitchen.

The door to the inn opens behind me. When I turn, Brad is standing behind me.

"Is now a good time?" Brad steps into the main room. "You're not going to make me chase you around the inn, are you?"

He smiles warmly, but I still feel a pang of guilt.

"Of course. Now works. I'm so sorry about earlier. It's kind of ... well, there's no excuse. That was a bit over-the-top."

"It's okay, Mila. Knowing what I do now, I understand."

"Knowing what you ...?"

"That you and Kai were never actually dating." He crosses his arms, but not in an angry way.

This is Brad, challenging me to say anything except the truth. And I can't. I have to tell him.

"You faked that whole relationship," he says it matter-of-factly.

"Yeah." I nod.

I can't look at him at first. But then I do.

He strides nearer until only a few feet separate us.

I don't ask how he heard my relationship was fake. I'm guessing Aima leaked the news once she heard. She's got her reasons. If I were her, I wouldn't have told anyone, but she seems far too interested in Kai to walk away without some attempt to sabotage what she thinks is going on between the two of us. Maybe it wasn't her, but the timing and motives seem too uncanny for it to have been anyone else.

Brad's face softens. "Were you that worried about your feelings for me that you had to bring in a buffer?"

How do I answer that? It's slightly presumptuous. But in another lifetime, that would have been a valid question. As it is, I'm torn. If I tell Brad our charade had nothing to do with my feelings for him, I'll insult him. If I tell him I wanted a buffer from *his* feelings, I'm assuming something he could easily deny.

I opt for complete silence.

"I'm not going to push myself on you, Mila. But I'll be honest. I'm interested in you. I never stopped loving you. I know I did a crap job of acting as if I loved you. I'll never forgive myself for leaving you like I did. But I'm not that man anymore. I think you can see that now."

I blink slowly. I can feel the weight of my eyelids shutting and reopening. My ex-husband is standing here telling me he's interested in me—that he still loves me. Oh, there were years I would have given money—even sold the inn—to hear those words from him. But that season is so long gone, it almost feels like a figment of my imagination.

Brad continues speaking into my prolonged silence. "Think of what it would be like. We could have all we dreamed of, Mila. This time, with Noah. And I'm not rushing you. We can take our time—as long as you need. I don't care if it takes the next seven years for you to trust me again—or longer."

I start to speak and Brad gently raises his hand, indicating he's not finished. "Give this some thought. You don't have to answer me today. Noah could have his family back. And we could have all the things we said we wanted together. I know I hurt you, Mila. I didn't falsify my reasons for coming back. I'm here to get to know my son. But I'd be lying if I didn't say I had hoped you might forgive me and give us a second chance."

"That's why," I finally say.

"Why what?"

"That's why Kai and I pretended we were in a relationship."

"He said it, not you, if you'll recall. You just went along. You're too kind and generous to turn down a friend when you believe they have your best interest in heart. But does he really? Or did Kai use fake dating as a way to get closer to you?"

"No, Brad. Kai isn't like that."

"You're not a man, Mila. No offense. Men see through one another. Kai has ulterior motives. And why shouldn't he? You're amazing. One of the best women on earth. He was taking his shot in a roundabout way."

Brad's compliments do nothing for me. Nothing. I'm not mad. I'm not flattered. I'm like a blank manilla folder, empty and void of anything significant.

"Brad," I see the hope rise in his expression when I say his name, and I wish I had a brake pedal to stop him from careening into his dream with me. "I can't make you that promise—that I'll consider a future for us. We had a beautiful marriage—wide open with possibility, shared dreams, genuine love. That was another life for me. I'm not that girl anymore. And I don't know if I would ever want to be her again. I've forgiven you. I really have. But I'm not in love with you anymore."

The words feel like a key, unlocking that deep down place. Something soft and fragile takes wings within me.

Brad's face falls. But, he rallies, proving the man I always knew is still alive and well inside him.

"We could ... give it time? I think you could love me again."

"No, Brad. I'm not going to lead you on. You're welcome to re-enter Noah's life. And, because of him, our lives will always be intertwined. But I don't want you to wait for me. I'm not coming back."

Brad opens his mouth as if he's going to say something.

But then, Aunt Phyllis walks out. I had honestly forgotten she was here.

She steps up next to me, and faces Brad.

"You made your case. A good man knows when to walk away." Phyllis stares at Brad.

"Okay, then." His lips draw into a thin line and then he blows out a breath. "I'll just let myself out."

"Thank you," I say, not quite sure what I'm thanking him for.

I'm just so relieved we got everything out in the open. And I told Brad the truth.

The truth will set you free, they say.

And that's how I feel. *Free.*

Phyllis and I watch Brad walk out the door.

When the door shuts behind him, I turn to my aunt. "I thought you always told me good men stay."

"I changed my mind this time. That one needed to go."

I chuckle. "So you heard all that?"

"I did. You and Kai were faking?"

"We were. I'm so sorry."

My aunt just smiles at me. There's not a shred of condemnation in her expression or tone of voice.

"I wish you had told me."

"We just couldn't. The more people who know, the more chance it would leak. Not that you would have spilled anything. It was just a precaution. But it killed me to hide the truth from you. I'm sorry."

"I understand. I also don't believe you are that good of an actress. Take it from an actual actress, there's only so much the average person can pull off when they aren't feeling something real. Am I right?"

Her eyes flit between mine, drawing out my confession.

"I love him."

"This is Kai we're talking about, right? Not your ex-husband?" Her grin is mischievous and light.

"Obviously."

"Good. Because, not that I get a vote, you know, for raising you and for pouring wisdom into you over all these years, guiding you ... feeding you ... giving you a home ... paying for ballet ... you know." She winks. "But if I did get a vote, it wouldn't be for Brad. If he weren't Noah's dad, you wouldn't even give him a second thought. So don't be confused by his power of persuasion."

"I'm not. He and Kai aren't even in the same league."

"You've got that right. Kai loves you, Mila."

"He hasn't said so." I almost sound pouty, and I kick myself for needing his words when everything about him has shown me so much more than words ever could.

"What do you want?" Phyllis asks. "A man who said he loved you but walked out on you when you needed him most? Or a man who has shown up for you ever since he met you, even though you've never officially been his?"

I'm pondering those words long after my aunt leaves to go home, and long after Noah comes back from his afternoon with Aunt Connie and Uncle Ethan. They echo in my mind as I serve my guests supper and wash the dishes.

I'm tucking Noah in after this day that feels like it lasted a year.

I'm nowhere close to being prepared for the question Noah asks when I'm about to turn off his bedside lamp.

"Mom?"

"Yeah, buddy?"

"Why did Aunt Connie say Mister Brad is my dad?"

THIRTY-SIX

Kai

I love you so much I'd fight a bear for you.
Well not a grizzly bear because they have claws,
and not a panda bear because they know Kung Fu.
But a care bear,
I'd definitely fight a care bear for you.
~ Unknown

Work is different with Bodhi gone. One and a half more weeks. He and my sister will be back in less than two weeks. The house is empty except me and Shaka, who is back in bed with me at night, of course. We had a talk, me and that mutt, and we came to an understanding. He has his side of the bed and I have mine. Of course, he puts his back right up against me. Dogs. I'm telling you.

Ben's puttering around the shop singing some Taylor Swift song off her new album. It's a song about her daddy. Something about how she loves a boy. Every so often, Ben ad-libs a line as if he's rapping Taylor's dad's answers. I'd be lying if I told you it wasn't funny.

"They don't hate you, Tay ta ta Tay," Ben says, making each word hit a beat. "You should love a crazy man. Love him every way you can. That's the best. And I'm a fan ..."

I'm chuckling under my breath as Ben spitfires between the words of the song.

But under all that usual sunshine, something's off.

Ben looks like someone kicked his puppy. Only, he's the puppy.

"What's wrong?" I ask.

"Huh?"

"I said, 'What's wrong?'"

"Oh. Summer got the part in the movie she wanted."

"That's good, right?"

Ben walks over to me and leans his forearms on the counter. "Yeah. It is. It's great. I'm so proud of her. Massively proud."

"But?"

"She'll be gone for months. Filming is partly in Europe. It's just hard. Bodhi and your sister get to travel together. Their unconventional schedules sync. I don't get that with my wife. It's just ... rough."

"I'm sorry."

"It's okay." Ben shrugs. "I'd rather have her part time than not at all."

"I get that." And without warning, the truth just slips right out of me like marbles down a chute. "Mila and I aren't actually dating."

"What? Did you break up? Bro. Man. Sorry to hear that."

"No. We didn't break up. We've been putting up a front. To keep her ex at bay. And Aima."

"Dude. No." Ben shakes his head, studying me to see if I'm joking. Then he makes a mind-blown gesture with both hands. "But you're so into one another. I could've sworn you were real."

"Yeah, well, I am. But she's not mine. Not even part time."

"Bro. I feel terrible, griping about my wife having to travel for work. Here you are in love with a woman you aren't with at all."

"Yeah. It's okay. It stinks that Summer's leaving for that long."

"Thanks." Ben smiles. "Not even dating. Whaddaya know?"

He seems to be thinking and then he says, "Want me to put a good word in with Mila for you? I've been known to be charming."

"Um. No. That would be a hard pass."

"Let me know if that changes. I'm a persuasive guy, boss."

I chuckle. "Keep it between us."

"You've got it."

And, of course, Ben zips his lips.

I spend the evening in the extreme silence of my home—just me and Shaka eating dinner and hanging out on the couch while some documentary I'm not even really watching plays in the background.

I've been meaning to call Mila to talk to her about me telling Ben this afternoon. I keep myself busy instead. After being at school with Noah this morning, I feel all the more certain that I want to be the man in Mila's life—in Noah's life too.

But something beneath the surface feels like it does when a storm's blowing in. It sounds crazy, but I feel as if this phone call would be the last one—like Mila's finished with me. She doesn't need our charade anymore. Maybe it's instinct or intuition.

It could be fear—I've never wanted anything or anyone like I want her. The stakes are so incredibly high. I'm clinching at the crux moment. I'll call her before it gets too late tonight. I just have to get my bearings.

It's well past dinner when there's a knock on my front door. I click off the TV. When I open the door, I must look confused. Mila's aunt, Phyllis, is standing on my porch. I can't describe her expression except to say she means business.

"Phyllis, what brings you all the way over to the Descanso side of the island at this time of night? Is everything okay?"

She steps past me into my living room where Shaka does some form of doggie hula as a greeting. I know grown hula kāne who wish they could swish their hips like my dog. Kala's dog. Whatever.

"You need to make your move," Phyllis says without any other preface or greeting.

"Okay. Are we talking about Mila here?"

"Yes. We're talking about my niece."

"Have a seat." I gesture toward the couches.

"I'm not staying."

"Okay. Well ... I ..."

I try to think of how to ask Phyllis if she knows Mila and I aren't actually dating. Her command pretty much gives me my answer, but I don't want to assume.

"Kai. I know you and Mila have been putting on a show. Show's over. It's time to make your move."

I want to ask her how she found out, but I'm so beyond caring, so tired of pretending, so weary of longing for the woman I love while I have her right in my arms.

"I'm trying to go slowly." I can't believe I say this next sentence, but I do. "I don't want to startle her like a starfish."

"A starfish?"

"Sea star ... starfish ... whichever name you call it. I don't want to startle her and send her bouncing away."

Phyllis stares at me for a count of three. Then she shakes her head as if she'll never understand the sea star analogy. I get it. I had to have an actual marine biologist spell it out for me.

"Do you love Mila?" Phyllis asks. She's never been one to beat around the bush.

There's an urgency in Phyllis' voice that tells me there's a story there. And a part of me wonders if it has to do with Brad. He was so desperate to see Mila, so eager to get her alone. If Phyllis knows we're faking, does Brad? Did he swoop in the first chance he got? Is Mila actually considering giving him a chance?

My heart rate starts to kick up at the thought of losing Mila to Brad.

"Do you love her?" Phyllis repeats.

I thought I had answered, but I guess my brain spiraled instead.

"Yes. I love her. Love doesn't even start to cover what I feel for Mila."

"Then you have to tell her."

Do I love her? What a question. For me, the line between fake and real has been completely obliterated. It's all real to me. I want to run around screaming about how much Mila means to me. To whisper it in her ear every night for the rest of our lives. I want to sing it and have it sky-written, to etch it in the sand and watch the waves wash the words into the sea only to grab a stick and write them again and again and again until the ocean is filled with my feelings for her and even then it couldn't contain them.

I love you, Mila.

I love you, Mila.

I love you, Mila.

But more than all that, I want to hear her say it too—to tell me she feels the same pull between us. To admit she can't wait eleven long and wasted years to finally be together. If only she would say she wants me the way I want her—with everything I am.

"Yes," I answer Phyllis again. "I love her."

"Then you know what you need to do." And with that, she leaves my home.

THIRTY-SEVEN
Mila

It's not flesh and blood,
but the heart which makes us fathers and sons.
~ Johann Friedrich von Schiller

"Why did Aunt Connie say Mister Brad is my dad?"

I stare at my son and swallow hard. This was not how I planned for this critical moment to happen. But if my life has taught me anything it's that the biggest things, those events that matter most, rarely, if ever, go as planned.

"Well, sweetie." I take a seat on the edge of Noah's bed. "Let me tell you a story and then I'll give you your answer, okay?"

Noah nods. But he's studying me closely.

I let out a long breath, and then I tell him what I'd planned to tell him. Only I hoped I would have more lead time before we got here.

"There was this woman who found out she was pregnant. And the man she married was scared. He didn't know if he could be a dad, even though most dads feel a little scared, but they get past the fear and get the hang of it over time. But this man was sure he couldn't learn, so he left because he didn't know how to stay."

I repeat the words Phyllis told me the day Brad left. Words she said over and over so I would never blame myself for Brad's lack of capacity to step up to the plate.

"Good men stay."

"I know, Mom. You always say that thing, good men stay." Noah looks at me earnestly. "Like Unko Kai. He stays."

"He does. You're right." I smile at the simplicity of Noah's perspective.

"Anyway," I continue. "This man never met his son, because he left. And one day he called the woman saying he was very, very sorry and he wanted to meet his son. But the woman didn't want the man to hurt her son. He's not a bad man, but the son didn't know him at all. The woman had raised the boy alone. But with lots of people around."

"Like me with Aunt Phyllis, Auntie Chloe, Aunt Connie and Aunt Joan ... and Unko?"

"Yes. Like that. Anyway, the woman knew the boy should meet his dad. But she was concerned that it might upset the boy. And she would do anything to protect her son from being sad or upset when he didn't do anything wrong. So she told the dad he could come around but just as a friend. And in time she would let her son know that was his dad."

"But I don't want Mister Brad to be my dad!" Noah's brows draw up and his eyes plead with me.

Noah figured it out. I've confirmed it. As messy and inconvenient as this is, Brad is his dad. And Noah isn't any happier about that fact right now than I am.

Maybe Noah figured it out as soon as I started telling the story. He's a bright boy. Either way, the truth has come home to roost. And instead of eggs, this chicken is laying a bag of bricks. My son looks crushed by the reality of his situation. And there's nothing I can do to spare him this pain.

"Oh, Noah," I say.

I can't think of anything else to say. When I reach for him, he pulls back a little like a frightened animal. So, I sit with him, allowing him the dignity to process this huge chunk of life-altering information. It would be absurd to think he'd just swallow it in one bite without any emotional reaction.

I knew this would happen. Nothing could have prepared me for the feeling of helplessness I'm sitting through right now while my seven-year-old handles the aftermath of his father's broken choices.

"Does Mister Brad have to come live with us?"

"Oh! Is that what you thought?" I smooth my hand along Noah's shin, and he lets me. "No. He doesn't have to live with us. He won't be living with us. I'm not married to him. We won't be getting married again. He just wants to be in your life."

Noah's eyes lift toward the ceiling like he's assimilating all of that into the news that Brad is his biological father.

When he looks at me again, he asks, "Like letting me drive the skid steer?"

"Yes. Like that."

"Okay."

"Okay?"

"Yeah. He can be my dad as long as he doesn't live with us."

Within a matter of minutes, I've been swept out in a riptide and plopped back safely on shore. Relief floods me. Noah knows. The secret is out. And he's temporarily okay. There may be more swells down the road. But for tonight, he's accepting that Brad is his dad, and he also knows my lines. Maybe my lines are the key to his acceptance. He doesn't have to let Brad in too far. But he can allow him into his life at some level.

And those lines of mine are solid and firm, a stone breakwall against the impact of the sea. I won't ever be getting back together with Brad, no matter what happens with Kai. Brad and I are finished. For good.

"Mom?" Noah yawns as he says my name.

"Yeah, Noah?"

"Can I tell you a secret?"

"You can tell me anything."

He pauses, his eyes on mine, as if he's weighing whether he can really tell me whatever it is he wants to say.

Then he says, "I wish Unko Kai was my dad. He does things a dad does. And I think he likes you like a dad likes a mom. He always looks at you too much. And you look at him too much too. Maybe one day he could live here instead of Mister Brad."

I try not to let my smile crack across my face, but I can't help it. I keep it to a grin, though.

"Maybe. We'll see. We'd have to be boyfriend and girlfriend first."

"That's gross. But if you have to, I won't look."

"You won't look?"

"When you kiss." Noah makes a sour face and sticks his tongue out to emphasize just how distasteful the idea of me and Kai kissing is to him. It's the very same face he makes when I try to serve him Brussels sprouts.

"Okay. Deal." I stick my hand out and he shakes it, just like he shook Brad's the other day.

"There's not any guarantee that Kai and I will be more than friends, Noah. Just so you know. But I know this. Kai will always be there for you, because he loves you."

"I know. And he'll always be there for you too."

"What makes you say that?"

"Because he loves you too."

THIRTY-EIGHT

Kai

To write a good love letter, you ought to begin
without knowing what you mean to say,
and to finish without knowing
what you have written.
~ Jean-Jacques Rousseau

Dear Mila,
        I want to say

I crumple the paper and throw it in the small trash can full and overflowing with similar unfinished letters. This is such a bad idea. I should just go over there. She's my friend. I can walk up to the door of the inn, knock, and spill everything in my heart.

I lean my head into my hands, rubbing the heels into my eye sockets and sighing loudly.

I want her to have a letter. Call me sentimental, but I want her to be able to hold my words, read them over and over, to save this letter to come back to later, anytime she wants to remember how thoroughly loved she is. And, face it. I want to get this right.

But I don't want to be sitting here wasting time.

Phyllis never did tell me why I needed to act swiftly. And it's already past Noah's bedtime. It's going to be past Mila's if I can't get it together, write my thoughts and feelings on paper and make my way to her soon.

It's official: Love makes a man crazy.

I take a deep breath, exhale, crack my knuckles and start again.

Dear Mila,

This letter is my way of starting from scratch—as if we never faked, as if we were two friends who had grown close, and one day I looked up and saw you—really saw you.

I wouldn't change how we started. I can't remember the exact day I met you. What I do remember is the day you invited me to see the inn. "Mila's Place," you said, "Named after me." And then you blushed just the slightest. And maybe I fell just a little that day. I think I must have. And I've been falling for you ever since. One blush, one smile, one thoughtful act, one burst of laughter, one quiet evening on the porch at a time.

Your friendship has been a lifeline, a sanctuary, and a lighthouse when everything in my life felt choppy. You listened to me when I was spinning out about Kala and Bodhi. And you talked reason to me until you made me see my part in the situation. You always do that. You balance me, softening my hard edges with your kindness and patience.

I wouldn't change how we met or how our friendship

developed. But I wish I would have asked you out earlier. I would have taken my time. I'd give you all the space you need to warm up to the idea of something romantic between us, and then I'd give even more time to help Noah warm up too. I believe he would—he will—if we decide to take a chance on us.

If I could reverse time, I would not have faked anything with you. Because what I feel for you is real. You wanted something real, Mila. That's all I have to give you. The real me loving the real you. And I know it's enough. What we have is the most real thing I've ever experienced.

If you'll let me, I will spend every day of our lives showing you, reminding you, that real love is possible. Because it's you and me. And this is real.

And while I hope to say these words to you in person, I need to say them now.

I love you, Mila.

I want to start our relationship the right way, if you give me the chance.

For real this time. - Kai

I reread the letter twice. It's not everything I have to say to her, but it's the heart of it.

I fold it over in thirds and then fold that in half, carefully placing it into my shirt pocket. And then I climb onto my bike and ride to Mila's Place, because my patience isn't long enough for a golf cart tonight. I pedal faster than a delivery guy in New York City, up hills and down, around curves, past coves and into the neighborhood of the North Shore. The waning moon is nearly full overhead and the light ripples across the waves. The stars smatter the sky like a crowd holding up individual lights at a show, cheering me on.

Tonight, she'll know everything.

And then I'll know everything: what we are, or what we never will be.

I park my bike and open the front gate. My heartbeat sounds in my ears, a rapid thrum.

I step toward the door and am about to knock when her voice calls to me from across the porch.

"Kai?"

"Yeah. Hi."

"What are you doing here?"

"I had to see you."

"Is everything okay?"

I have to think about how to answer her. She holds the answer to that question.

"I think it is. I hope it is."

"Can I get you something to drink? I have cobbler too."

I smile. Mila. Always serving others. Constantly thinking of someone outside herself.

"I'm fine for now. I brought you something."

"You did?"

I walk toward her. The light from the moon and the decorative lamppost in the yard cast a yellow-white glow across her face.

"Yeah. It's a letter."

"A letter?"

"I wrote it."

"You wrote me a letter?"

"I did."

She's quiet, and I don't feel like I can add anything beyond what I already poured out on paper, so I reach into my pocket and hand the letter to her. She takes it, our fingertips brushing, tempting me to grasp on to her, to pull her up off the swing and hold her in my arms.

What if I never get to hold her again?

In a few minutes, my fate will be determined.

I'm not sure I'm breathing. The air feels still—full of unanswered questions.

Her fingers gently unfold the letter and then she lays it in her lap, squinting down at it.

"I can't read it in this light." She smiles up at me.

"Oh! Here." I pull out my cell and turn on the flashlight, holding it overhead to illuminate her lap where my letter sits waiting.

"Have a seat, Kai."

I take the opposite corner of the swing, holding the light over her shoulder so she can read my heart on paper.

I watch her face as she takes in each line. I didn't plan on sitting next to her. I don't know what I thought I'd do. Hand the letter over and leave?

I really wasn't thinking. I just knew I had to get everything out in the open and let her know how much she means to me. Tonight. It had to be tonight.

"You remember that day?" Mila looks over at me, a soft smile on her lips.

"I do. I wish I remembered the day we met."

"I remember it."

"You do?"

"Of course. You were the 'hot new surf instructor' the island was raving about." She puts air quotes around, *hot new surf instructor*. "I had a few guests that summer who wanted to learn to surf, so I drove them over to Alicante and walked into the shack. It was your first week on the job and the guys who had been running things before you had you wearing flippers everywhere you went and approaching all the customers by saying, 'Just keep swimmin'.'"

I run my hand down my jaw. "Can we possibly not share that

particular story as our first meeting? You know, in years to come, or like ever, with anyone?"

"I think I recall you putting a goldfish in Ben's water during his first week of work, so ..."

"We have rites of passage in watersports. What can I say?"

"Just keep swimmin'?"

"Mila ..." I fake a warning tone.

She turns back to the letter.

My chest feels like someone pumped it full of helium. She's one third through and she hasn't kicked me off the porch yet.

She gasps softly and covers her mouth. The letter falls out of her hand and flutters to the ground.

"You okay?" I ask.

"Kai? You've been falling for me?"

"I have. I am. I love you, Mila."

"You ... love me?" Her eyes are wide. Then she shakes her head in disbelief. "Noah was right."

"Noah? He told you I loved you?"

"Tonight. At bedtime."

I smile. *Noah*. He's got my back. And I'll always have his.

"I don't want to overwhelm you. But, yes. I do. I'm madly, completely in love with you, Mila. You're all I think about. When I wake in the morning, I walk through my house wondering what you made for breakfast. I picture you serving your guests and getting Noah ready for school. Throughout the day, I reminisce about things you said, your facial expressions, your laughter ... our kisses."

Mila looks at me with a softness in her doe eyes. Her eyebrows draw up in the middle of her forehead. She's still here, listening, so I grab this chance to tell her she's everything to me—a chance I hope leads to the rest of our lives together.

"I find reasons to come here when there aren't any. I want to check on you, to make sure you're alright. I know you can manage your life, but I don't want you to have to. I look forward to the times you lean on me for something—a repair, a listening ear, even this whole charade. I want to be there for you."

She's still gazing up at me with that expression of either wonder or shock, I can't quite tell.

"I love you, Mila. And I'll wait. I don't want to push you. If you're not ready—if Noah's not ready—I'll wait. I'll be your friend and I'll wait for you to be ready. If you say you want me, I'll wait for years for you. But I hope we don't have to wait because, honestly, it feels like we've already been waiting too long and I don't want to waste another day we could have together being separated and confused about what we are to one another."

When she looks down at her hands, I think I've lost her. I approached the sea star with too much desire and overwhelming emotion and she's about to shut down and retreat.

But then, she looks up at me, her eyes glistening with unshed tears.

"I love you too, Kai."

"I'm sorry, could you repeat that? Did you say ...?"

"I said, I love you. I didn't expect this. I even fought it—not because of you, but because of my past. And because of Noah. But things change. A woman can change her mind, and apparently, her heart."

I am frozen in place, afraid this fragile confession will shatter into a thousand shards if I move toward Mila or even say another word.

She loves me?

She loves me!

As if she knows I need the reassurance, she says it again. "I love you, Kai."

I reach my hand across the space between us and cup her jaw, running my thumb along her cheek. "I want to kiss you, Mila."

"I want you to kiss me. Please, Kai. Kiss me."

She doesn't have to ask me twice.

I lean in and she bends toward me. This kiss isn't to fend off Brad or Aima. It's not to convince someone we're dating. This kiss isn't practice. When our mouths align and her lips brush across mine, everything in me sparks to life. This kiss is Mila and me, finally expressing our love for one another. I kiss her softly, lingering on her lips with mine. She wraps her arms behind my neck and I pull her closer. The swing moves erratically and we pull apart, laughing.

"We need a do-over," Mila says.

"Definitely."

"We can do better."

"I know we can. We definitely can. Come over here."

Mila shifts so that she's right next to me, and then I take a risk and pull her so she's sitting sideways on my lap, her legs extending out onto the swing. And this time when I lean in, she's right there, tilting her head up, her eyes fluttering shut just before our lips meet. She tugs at my neck, pulling me near and I run my hand down her arm slowly, finding her fingers and entwining them with mine and resting our enjoined hands on her thigh.

I kiss her reverently, savoring the feel of her, listening to everything she's telling me without words. And then our kiss roars to life, like a fire that started slowly, but was licked by the wind causing the flames to spread suddenly.

I need her. And she's telling me she needs me too. Wants me. Loves me. It's all here in this kiss. We're mouths and hands and mingled breath. She's vanilla and cinnamon and warmth and home. All I am yearns for all of her. And she's here, giving and taking, opening for me, saying yes to our connection—yes to us.

I place a final gentle kiss to her lips and then to the tip of her nose, brushing her hair away from her face, letting my forehead drop to hers. Our eyes lock in the dim light of nighttime. She's a vision, staring back at me with hope and contentment etched across the shadows of her features.

"Kai," Mila breathes out my name like a precious secret she's been keeping.

"Hmmm?"

"I didn't even finish reading your letter."

Keeping one hand wrapped around her waist, I bend down. I retrieve the letter from the floorboards of the porch and hand it back to her.

"I wrote it so you could read it whenever you want. Again and again if you need to. I didn't know if you would want me, or if telling you how I feel about you would scare you off."

"I want you. So much. I've never wanted anyone this way."

She reaches up and runs her fingers through my hair. I close my eyes, acutely aware of each spot she gently grazes across on my scalp. I hear the low rumble of contentment rise up from within me.

Mila wants me.

It's a heady drug, finally holding a woman you've been pining away for, and I'm in no hurry to let her go—not tonight or ever.

Mila giggles. "You like that, huh?"

"I do. Everything you do, I like. But especially that."

She does it again.

I wrap my arm around her and pull her in so her head is tucked beneath my chin and she's nestled against my chest. And then I place a kiss on the top of her head.

"You have to set the pace here," I tell her. "And we don't have to talk about anything more tonight. Just know, you're calling the shots."

"I am, am I?" That playful side of her comes out—the one I discovered during Bodhi and Kalaine's bachelor-ette party in the pool. "I like the idea of calling the shots with you."

"Are you flirting with me?"

"I'm trying. I'm pretty rusty, though."

"The last word I'd ever use to describe you is rusty."

Mila sits up just the slightest, my arm still looped behind her, and carefully refolds my letter. "I'm going to read the rest of this tonight—later, in my room, alone."

"It's yours to read whenever you want."

"And. Kai?"

"Yes?"

323

"I don't need time to think about what we're doing here."

Mila tilts her head so she's gazing in my eyes. The moonlight reflects off her cheeks and lips when she looks up at me.

"I'm yours, Kai. No more pretending."

"Mine." I lean in and kiss Mila. "For real this time."

And the world melts away until it's just the two of us, on the porch of Mila's Place, beginning the rest of our forever together.

The End

... BUT, WAIT! THERE'S MORE!

Epilogue

MILA

For the two of us, home isn't a place. It is a person.
And we are finally home.
~ Stephanie Perkins, Anna and the French Kiss

"This place is the cutest!" Ben makes his voice into a falsetto while he looks around at Kalaine and Bodhi's new house after he walks through the front door.

He acts like it's the first time he's been here, even though he actually helped with the move and has been here more than a few times over the past months since Kalaine and Bodhi settled in.

"Ben. Seriously?" his wife, Summer, says. "Sorry, guys. I can only do so much over here. But I'm open to suggestions!"

She acts as if she's exasperated, but she's smiling up into Ben's eyes as he leans down and kisses her on the cheek.

"I'm the worst. I know," Ben says to Summer, still holding her close and saying the words into the top of her head.

"The very worst." Summer smiles, and kisses him on the cheek.

I laugh at Ben's silliness.

"Don't laugh. You'll encourage him," Kai tells me.

Kai's also smiling, despite himself. You can't help but smile at

Ben's antics. Then again, whenever Kai looks at me, he smiles. We've been dating for six months. Officially, real, out-in-the-open dating. Kai's been doing everything he said he would that night he imagined what we might be like together.

He comes by the inn several nights a week, sometimes for dinner, other times after. Once a week he arranges for someone to cover the inn so he can take me out dancing, or to dinner, or for a walk on the beach under the stars.

Noah's thrilled. I worried myself sick about rocking his world, shaking the foundation and ruining things if I brought a man into our lives. And our lives probably would have gone through all that and more—if the man I allowed into our lives wasn't Kai.

Bodhi whistles through his fingers and the chatter dies down. "Sorry! We'll let you guys get back to it in a minute. I just wanted to say, Mavs and I are so grateful you could be here at our official housewarming."

Kalaine is standing next to Bodhi. He's got his arm around her back and she's got one hand behind him and another resting softly on her abdomen.

Kalaine and Bodhi came back from their honeymoon and lived with Kai for two months. They put an offer in on this house the day it went up for sale. It's only one block over from Kai's home. The day after they bid, their offer was accepted. Two days later they left on their next surf trip. This time they were gone for a whole month.

Bodhi looks at Kalaine. "You want to tell them what to do next or should I?"

"You," Kalaine says.

Bodhi smiles around at the group of friends gathered in their home. "Around the room, you'll see envelopes sitting in stacks. We'd love it if each one of you would grab one and not open it quite yet. Just hold on to it. When I count down from three, everyone open your envelope at once. Okay?"

The group of about thirty people gathered in the front living room all say, "Okay."

Kai grabs two envelopes and hands me one.

People murmur, trying to guess what's inside.

I look up at Kai. "It's their housewarming, and they're giving us a gift?"

He shrugs.

Once everyone has an envelope in hand, Bodhi looks at Kalaine. "Count down with me, Mavs."

The two of them count down together. "Three ... two ... one ... Open!"

I tug at the seal of the envelope as the sound of ripping paper fills the room, followed by gasps and exclamations of, "Oh my gosh!" and "Congratulations!"

Kai's mouth drops open. He runs over to his sister and Bodhi.

I reread the announcement in my hand.

> *Get ready to welcome the next surfer*
> *to the Merrick family.*
> *We're expecting!*
> *Bodhi & Kalaine*

Kai's hugging Kalaine and then he and Bodhi embrace and clap one another on the backs.

"You're officially an uncle, bro!" Bodhi says.

People crowd around Kalaine and Bodhi, congratulating them and giving them hugs.

Once the excitement dies down, we move the party to the back yard where Kai and Bodhi man the barbecue. People fill their plates with grilled meat and side dishes from the folding tables off to the side of the lawn. Twinkle lights have been strung overhead, and clusters of patio furniture tastefully sit around the firepit and on a few other patios. The property has a long yard that stretches back, so even though the houses next door on both sides are relatively close, there's a lot of room for entertaining.

Throughout the night, Kai's eyes keep finding mine. When

he's finished manning the barbecue, he's at my side, looping his arm around me and kissing the top of my head. And when everyone's finished eating, I'm sitting sideways across his lap as if I'm in my twenties, not a thirty-year-old mom with a seven-and-a-half-year-old son.

"You look beautiful tonight," Kai murmurs into my ear.

I giggle. "In this?"

I'm wearing a white tank top and the orange oversized sweater I brought to ward off the chill of the evening breeze. My hair is up in what was a pulled-together messy bun, but after a night of helping Kalaine with setup for the party and being held by Kai, I'm sure it's putting the *messy* in messy bun.

"You look beautiful in anything and everything."

"Hey, you two!" Ben shouts over at me and Kai. "Want to share with the class?"

Summer playfully smacks Ben on the arm. "Leave them alone. They're adorable."

"Thanks," I say, leaning into Kai when he tugs me closer.

I don't know when this thing between the two of us will start to lose its magic. I have a hunch it may be a while, if ever. I wake up daily, thankful, and sort of in awe that Kai is actually my boyfriend.

I love him so much. If two people could be intertwined and woven together, I'd find the seamstress to do it. I never want to leave his side, to have him far from me again. After spending those few months pretending, it feels like every day together is a gift we didn't ever know we'd actually have.

I want to spend the rest of my life with Kai Kapule. He hasn't officially asked, but we've talked about the future with the assumption that's where we're headed. I'm grateful he's been sensitive to Noah's need to adjust, despite the fact that my son regularly asks us when we're going to get married so Kai can just move in already. His words, exactly.

And, I'm not sure Noah and I will have Kai move into the

inn. Maybe we'll live at Kai's home and hire someone to caretake overnight at Mila's Place. We haven't gotten that far.

But I'm enjoying every single moment along the way: watching Kai tinker around the inn, baking him something that makes him close his eyes and hum with appreciation, sneaking hidden glances at him when he's playing with Noah or they're having one of their famous man-to-man talks, laughing at how he denies loving Shaka, studying him, inching my way beneath his outer layer to his secretly soft center—a place he seems to only let a few people share—and I'm one of the lucky ones.

I can barely believe I'm allowed to hold his hand, kiss him, wrap my arm around him, sit in his lap, or lean on his shoulder while he rocks us on the porch swing anytime I want. I wanted to touch him every day we were faking, and now, sometimes for the briefest moment, I forget I can. And when I remember, I feel nearly giddy with the reality.

Most importantly, I've given Kai access to places in my soul I had kept boarded shut. He earned entrance through his patient, steady devotion to me over the four years of our friendship, and even more so those few months while we pulled off our farce. Since then, he's blown the walls off all my hesitation and fear until all that's left is him and me and a kind of hope I never thought I'd experience again.

I look forward to the time when he'll be drinking coffee next to me in the morning, and holding me as we wrap up our days together, my head on his chest, his steady heartbeat a home for me and me alone. I want to give him all of me. And I want to explore this man for the rest of our days together on earth—even as we age and lose pieces of ourselves we imagined were immortal.

He's the one. Kai's *my* one.

The fire in the firepit starts to burn to embers, and people start saying their goodbyes a few hours after dinner. Kai and I stay to help clean up and wash dishes.

Then we walk to his house where he parked a golf cart to drive me back to the inn.

We're driving along the street that passes in front of the Alicante when Kai pulls over and parks the golf cart.

"What are we doing?" I ask.

"I have something I need to show you at the shack. Then I'll get you home."

"Okaaay?" The word comes out like a question.

What could Kai possibly need to show me at the shack at this hour?

He comes around the golf cart and extends his hand. I place my palm in his and we walk toward the water's edge in a quiet comfort together.

Kai seems to grow a little tense as we near the dock where the shack sits overlooking the ocean.

"Are you okay?" I ask.

It's the first time I considered that what he wants to show me might not be a good surprise. Maybe something happened at work and he'd rather show me than tell me. I prepare myself for anything as we round the pylons that support the dock and approach a spot on the sand where someone has lit tiki torches and placed seashells all over the ground in little formations of hearts with flower petals scattered all over the sand.

"This is beautiful," I tell Kai. "I wonder who did this."

"This is what I wanted to show you."

"Was it here when you left work this evening for the party?"

"No," Kai clasps both my hands and faces me. "It wasn't. I had Ben and Jamison come out here while we cleaned up at Bodhi and Kala's"

"You had the guys do this?"

"I did."

"It's beautiful ..."

Before I can ask him why, Kai looks down at me and slowly, never breaking my gaze, he drops to one knee.

I hold my breath, gazing down at this amazing, thoughtful, gorgeous man who always shows up for me—the man who stole my heart and returned it to me more whole than it's ever been.

"Mila," Kai's voice is scratchy with emotion. "You're everything to me. We had to go through faking a relationship to wake ourselves up to what was evident to everyone who knew us well. And once I realized how much I loved you, it was like a curtain peeled back and I saw all the moments, all the tiny, seemingly insignificant ways I had fallen bit by bit for you over the years we were friends.

"Then I knew. I had never been pretending to love you. What we have is real. And when you find something real, you risk everything for it. You toss out your shoulds, and your rules, and your expectations, and you jump in headlong. Because when it's real, you can leap, knowing someone will always be there to catch you. So I risked, and I wrote you the letter."

"The one I framed and keep on my bedside table," I say with a smile that feels like it comes from all the way inside my heart— from the place that used to feel unreachable and broken.

Kai smiles and his eyes crinkle at the edges.

"I never felt so nervous as I did that night. I filled an entire wastebasket with wadded attempts at getting my words out. It felt like my entire future and our shared happiness hung on my ability to show you my heart in that letter."

"Oh, Kai."

"The truth was, that letter would have only been my first attempt. I realized later, if you hadn't said yes then, I wasn't going to give up. Because I knew. Somewhere deep inside, I knew we'd get to this day somehow. And here we are."

He reaches up and dabs a tear from his eye.

Then he continues. "I asked Noah earlier today if he'd give me permission to ask for your hand in marriage. He gave us his blessing." Kai chuckles. "That's a story for another day."

Kai swipes another tear from his eye with his thumb. And I can't help myself. I drop to my knees in front of him and pull him into my arms.

"I love you, Kai Kapule." I sniff away the tears forming in my eyes.

Kai murmurs a declaration into my hair as we kneel together, embracing on the sand. "I love you, Mila. You're everything to me. My sunrise and sunset, and the sweetest ocean breeze. You're the warmth of home and my place of comfort, laughter, and desire. I love you with an insatiable ache—one only you can quench. I never knew it could be like this."

Kai puts his hands on my upper arms and holds me away from him just far enough so he can look into my eyes. And then he asks me the question I have been dreaming of hearing for months.

"Mila, will you do me the honor of becoming my wife? I want to spend the rest of my life loving you, sharing a home with you, and parenting Noah together."

"Yes! Oh, Kai! I love you so much!"

Kai's smile fills his face, he closes his eyes like he's savoring one of my chocolate tarts, and then he pulls both of us to our feet. He reaches out and cups my face in his hand. When he leans in, the kiss he places on my lips is tender and reverent, full of emotion. I loop my hand behind his neck and hold him to me. He tugs me close and we kiss like we're the only two people on earth, and this small piece of beach with tikis and shells and flower petals is our universe.

Just Me and Kai, alone.

Until there's a shout from above us on the dock—more like a whoop.

"Oh yeah, boss! That's how it's done! Proposing like a boss!"

Kai looks up at Ben, who is leaning over the railing waving his cell phone. "I got it all on video. I'll airdrop it to you so you've got this memory forever!"

"You're fired!" Kai shouts up at Ben.

"Am I fired too?" Jamison's head pops over the railing next to Ben's.

I cover my face in mortification, but I'm laughing.

"You gonna fire me too?" Bodhi joins his friends, looking down at me and Kai and waving.

"Work at watersports, they said," Kai looks at me shaking his head. "It'll be fun, they said."

I laugh. "You love them."

"No," Kai corrects me. "I love you. I barely tolerate these yay-hoos."

"You love us. Admit it boss!" Ben shouts down.

A woman's voice carries down the dock from further up the beach. "Ben Hayes, what are you doing?" *Summer.* Coming to get her husband.

Kai and I look at one another and laugh.

"Summer! Babe! You've got to see this. Kai just proposed to Mila. I've got the whole thing on video!"

Summer leans over the balcony and waves at me and Kai. "Congratulations, you two! I'll just be taking my man-child home now. Carry on!"

"Party pooper," Ben teases Summer, but then he turns and shouts down to us. "In all seriousness, guys, we're so happy for you. You're perfect for one another. And I won't post this on my socials—that's how much I love you."

Kai shakes his head. We wave up at the watersports guys as they turn to actually leave us alone, for real this time.

"Are you sure you want to commit to me?" Kai asks. "I think they may be part of the package."

"I've never been more sure of anything in my life."

"Me either, Hot Dog."

I playfully punch Kai's arm, pretending I don't love the nickname he gave me when we were still finding our way to one another through all the pretense.

And then, in a very uncharacteristic move, my future husband lets out a whoop that puts Ben to shame. He picks me up and spins me around.

I'm giggling with a happiness I don't even recognize.

"My future wife!" Kai shouts as he gently sets me back on the sand.

He studies my face, a look of awe in his eyes. "Just to be clear, you said yes, right?"

"Yes. I said yes." I chuckle. "Yes, Kai. One hundred times yes. You're everything I want—my best friend, someone who watches over me, a man who believes in me ... the way you love Noah. It's more than I allowed myself to believe I could have."

"You're everything to me, Mila. You and Noah. I love you."

"I love you too."

He looks down at me with such joy radiating off him it's contagious. And then he says, "Oh! I nearly forgot!"

Kai digs into his pocket and pulls out a box. When he carefully opens it, my hand flies up to my mouth. It's a ring with a diamond that glistens in the torchlight. He pulls the ring out and slips it onto my finger. And then he pulls something else out of his pocket. It's a soft velvet bag, no bigger than the ring box. He slips the contents into his hand, and when he holds it up, fresh tears threaten to fall from my eyes. It's a gold chain, and on the end of it is a sea star charm.

"Thank you for not bouncing away," he says, holding my gaze as he sweeps the stray hairs off my neck and secures the clasp.

"I'll never. You can hold me forever. You are my safe place, Kai."

He leans in and kisses me, without a balcony of witnesses, and I open to him, returning his kiss and melting into the space between us, the gift we've found in each other. When we separate, Kai weaves my fingers through his, and we walk hand in hand toward the golf cart so he can drive me to our inn—the one we'll be running together for years to come.

Have you read all the Love Trippin' Stories?

You can read Cam & Riley's story in the road trip romcom, *Are We There Yet*.
And watch Ben try to win Summer's heart in *A Fish Out of Water*, an enemies to lovers romcom.
Bodhi and Kalaine find their way back to one another in *Catch a Wave*, a sweet second-chance romcom you will love.

Coming September 2024: Alana and Stevens' Story in *Reel Love,* a hidden identity, celebrity romcom, and the final book in the Love Trippin' series.

If you love laugh-out-loud, small-town, closed-door romcoms, come on over to Bordeaux, Ohio (pronounced Bored-Ox) **The Getting Shipped Series** is Savannah's well-loved stories set in rural Ohio with found family friendships, meddling townspeople, and book boyfriends so hot they could pop a whole row of corn.

You can fall in love with a Frenchman in Savannah's **Sweater Weather** story from the famous multi-author series: *A Not So Fictional Fall*.

And then, if you still need to hear another man call a woman "Cher," pick up *He's So Not My Valentine*, a single mom romcom with heart.

Want to make sure you get updates from Savannah Scott?

Be one of the readers who hears about new releases first, gets to participate in special giveaways, and sees sneak peeks into Savannah's writing ... join her weekly newsletter for all this and more.

Looking for a sweet group of readers who share life and books together? Join Savannah's Sweet Readers Facebook Group.

Or Follow Savannah on Instagram
And follow Savannah on Amazon for automatic notifications of new releases directly in your inbox.

All the Thanks ...

I want to thank **Gila Santos,** my copy editor. For your thorough and thoughtful eye. For speaking truth. For loving story. Our conversations are some of my favorite on earth.

Tricia Anson. Goodness gracious. You are my friend, my proofreader, my personal assistant, the keeper of my sanity, and a gift in my life. I can't imagine what I'd do without you. Here's hoping I never have to find out. (And, yes, I keep the same thank you in each book ... because it says it all ... over and over.)

Jessica Gobble, You prayed me here. You believed when others didn't see where I was heading. You taught me how to see my worth as an author. I love you, my heart-sister.

To my **Awesome "Shippers" and especially the CORE Team and the Chatty IG Girls** who love me and my books so thoroughly, and to the **AMAZING Bookstagram Community**. I am so thankful for the way you support each book I write. I never knew what I gift I'd receive when I started sharing my author life with you. I love you to the moon and back.

Thank you to **Mary Goad** for this cover. I am dying to say a few things here ... and you know what they are ;) ... Thank you for all the revision and the effort and wanting to get it just right. You are so, so very talented. I love you.

Most of all, I want to thank **God** for calling me to be a story-teller and giving me the ability to make others smile and laugh.

.

Made in the USA
Columbia, SC
17 June 2024

36782469R00192